T0186662

Regulating Blockchain

As the distributed architecture underpinning the initial Bitcoin anarcho-capitalist, libertarian project, 'blockchain' entered wider public imagination and vocabulary only very recently. Yet in a short space of time it has become more mainstream and synonymous with a spectacular variety of commercial and civic 'problem'/ 'solution' concepts and ideals. From commodity provenance, to electoral fraud prevention, to a wholesale decentralisation of power and the banishing of the exploitative practices of 'middlemen', blockchain stakeholders are nothing short of evangelical in their belief that it is a force for good. For these reasons and more the technology has captured the attention of entrepreneurs, venture capitalists, global corporations and governments the world over.

Blockchain may indeed offer a unique technical opportunity to change cultures of transparency and trust within cyberspace, and as 'revolutionary' and 'disruptive' has the potential to shift global socioeconomic and political conventions. But as a yet largely unregulated, solutionist-driven phenomenon, blockchain exists squarely within the boundaries of capitalist logic and reason, fast becoming central to the business models of many sources of financial and political power the technology was specifically designed to undo, and increasingly allied to neoliberal strategies with scant regard for collective, political or democratic accountability in the public interest. *Regulating Blockchain* casts a critical eye over the technology, its 'eco-system' of stakeholders, and offers a challenge to the prevailing discourse proclaiming it to be the great techno-social enabler of our times.

Robert Herian is based in the Law School at The Open University. His teaching and research focus on private law, psychoanalysis, social, economic and political philosophy, and cultural theory.

Regulating Blockchain
Critical Perspectives in Law and Technology

Robert Herian

Routledge
Taylor & Francis Group

LONDON AND NEW YORK

First published 2019
by Routledge
2 Park Square, Milton Park, Abingdon, Oxon OX14 4RN

and by Routledge
711 Third Avenue, New York, NY 10017

Routledge is an imprint of the Taylor & Francis Group, an informa business

British Library Cataloguing in Publication Data
A catalogue record for this book is available from the British Library

Library of Congress Cataloging in Publication Data
Names: Herian, Robert, author.
Title: Regulating blockchain : critical perspectives in law and technology / by Robert Herian.
Description: Abingdon, Oxon ; New York, NY : Routledge, 2019. | Includes bibliographical references and index.
Identifiers: LCCN 2018027455 | ISBN 9781138592766 (hbk)
Subjects: LCSH: Blockchains (Databases)--Government policy. | Blockchains (Databases)--Social aspects. | Blockchains (Databases)--Economic aspects. | Internet governance. | Databases--Law and legislation.
Classification: LCC QA76.9.B56 H47 2019 | DDC 005.75--dc23
LC record available at https://lccn.loc.gov/2018027455

ISBN: 978-1-138-59276-6 (hbk)
ISBN: 978-0-429-48981-5 (ebk)

Typeset in Galliard
by Taylor & Francis Books

For my father.

Contents

Introduction

A report on the 2018 World Economic Forum in Davos, Switzerland, by the *Financial Times* carried the simple headline: 'blockchain can no longer be ignored' (Arnold, 2018). Global economic elites at Davos pulling sharper focus on blockchain is a sign arguably of its emergence from the darker recesses of the Web, and corresponding emergence into the light of the mainstream. Yet there is far more to the unfolding story of the 'blockchain ecosystem' and the so-called 'disruption' it heralds than a few nervous bankers contemplating the threats, challenges and opportunities it poses for legacy systems, networks and institutions of power and the control they have over the world's financial resources and services. The 'blockchain ecosystem' at the centre of global activities is a broad if, I argue, somewhat univocal community engaged in developing blockchain concepts and practices. As Melanie Swan argues: 'There is a need for a decentralized ecosystem surrounding the blockchain itself for full-solution operations' (2015, p. 20). To paraphrase Michael Power: blockchain is an idea as much as a concrete technology or technical practice and there is no communal investment in the technology without a commitment to this idea and the social norms and hopes which it embodies (1997, p. 4). Like much of the vocabulary and many of the terms that will be covered by this book, 'ecosystem' ought not to be considered neutral or apolitical. Instead the blockchain ecosystem has emerged from pre-existing sites of techno-solutionist ideology (*à la* Pierre Machery and Louis Althusser) that are programmed at the level of entrepreneurs, corporations and other likeminded stakeholders of innovationism. If the ecosystem has an ethos it is that 'it's all about the blockchain' (Robinson and Leising, 2015; Tapscott and Tapscott, 2016). But what does that really mean?

This book takes blockchain seriously as a boon for private commercial and corporate self-interest and a corresponding threat to public interest, non-competitive forms of co-operation and the potential for expanding community generosity that extends beyond the closed circuits of entrepreneurial ecosystems. With respect to public interest regulation and political oversight, a meaningful counterbalance to prevailing modes of private and commercial self-regulation which engender narrow economic affordances ('blockchain for good' as a euphemism for blockchain being good for business) must find a place in the ongoing development of blockchain. In the present moment self-regulation and 'rule by entrepreneur' are largely determining the blockchain regulatory environment and enterprise (Kewell et al., 2017; Gupta, 2017). To get past this regulatory trend, which may also be characterised as a form of 'bottom-up' regulation (Murray and Scott, 2002, p. 510; Brownsword and Goodwin, 2012, p. 27), requires understanding of what forms of regulation are ultimately possible in the blockchain context, and in particular where the potential 'choke points' are. Further, the extent to which regulatory adaptability rooted in information gathering, that is, adaption either of blockchain to existing regulatory regimes and standards or vice versa, might suffice to maintain political feasibility of and democratic accountability over this nascent technology.

Focus here is not only on blockchain as something *to be* regulated, however. What involves taking blockchain seriously is an examination of its potential role as regulator and use as a regulatory technology ('RegTech'). Approaching this topic does not simply mean considering the regulatory-like features blockchain provides, but must deal equally with prior concerns for regulatory legitimacy and the ability to call regulators to account based on their deployment of technology and any subsequent failures within the regulatory regime the technology either facilitates or does not prevent. Where technologies such as blockchain are integrated into an environment as regulatory instruments requires, as Roger Brownsword and Morag Goodwin maintain, that 'regulators are called to account, not so much for their failure to create the right kind of environment for new technologies, but for their over-reliance on technological tools' (2012, p. 46). Blockchain as a RegTech will be explored in latter chapters of this book in the context of combatting tax evasion and avoidance.

Whatever forms and uses of blockchain emerge in the coming months and years, deeper critical analysis by publicly accountable bodies is required. Individual governments and domestic regulators, as well as in time a community of international governing authorities able to focus on blockchain and how it is interacting with societies, will need to address profound questions concerning the future relationship between the technology and those who either use it intentionally or are subject to it unknowingly. *Ex ante* regulatory assessments of techno-social integrations and implementations and the nature of self-interested, commercial or corporate 'for profit' relations that exploit the public and private spheres alike have arguably failed to prevent opportunistic behaviour by online businesses in the broader context of the Internet. That is, I suggest, still a conservative estimation of the present socioeconomic state of cyberspace. In all but a few instances private commercial rights and interests are trumping public interest, and capitalism has simply been reimagined in cyberspace, rather than cyberspace providing a domain *other to* prevailing trends in offline economic logic and reason. In short, cyberspace is yet another territory in which self-interest has conquered community and generosity.

The titans of global technology have over the course of the past decades shaped a regulatory environment that enables them to push boundaries often unreasonably and unfairly, only ceasing to do so once damage and harm has been done and significant capital banked. Regulation, law and governance over the commercial domination and economic power of online platforms, networks and systems is weak and complaisant, with regulators falling into step with the fetishistic belief of an entrepreneurial class of innovationist and solutionist ideologues who either want to be left alone (self-regulation), or are happy to engage in regulation so long as it is market-complementing, the effect of which drives more competition and thus 'a permanently unhealthy state of affairs […] a state of perpetual fluctuation without ever reaching its goal' (Engels, 1975, p. 433), that destroys co-operation, community, and above all, generosity. The Organisation for Economic Co-operation and Development (OECD) is one major international body fore-grounding competition in the blockchain regulatory enterprise, stating in a 2018 Issues Paper that, 'the adoption of blockchain poses some regulatory challenges for governments' and co-operation is needed to 'develop a consistent regulatory framework that enables businesses to innovate and develop the technology in a competitive environment, subject to rules that preserve fundamental values such as safety and integrity' (OECD, 2018, p. 3). The suggestion here is of particular acquiescence by regulators (including law and government), supported by the likes of the OECD, to the sway of neoliberalism, which in turn encourages specious innovationist and solutionist strategies and ideologies without reasonable acknowledgement or appreciation of the full range of political consequences or effects, including what is lost in pursuit only of self-interest and rarely if ever community generosity (Cohen, 2011, p. 219).

Tony Prosser has argued that

> whilst regulation may be needed, it is portrayed as a second-best choice for social organization; in principle free markets giving us economic freedom and consumer choice should be preferred wherever possible. Regulation is thus an always regrettable means of correcting market failures […] regulation is part of economic management.
>
> (2010, p. 1)

The influence of economic theories of regulation – that is, regulation predicated on 'value for money' and 'efficient' economic outcomes – means clear and incisive engagement is necessary with the difficult and contestable politics presently underpinning the blockchain ecosystem in order to bring about a viable critique of the blockchain ecosystem and the conduct it produces that is able to challenge the *always already* of economic and market-complementing regulations. What is more, unearthing the politics of blockchain from beneath dense compacted layers of economic reason must be proactive rather than reactive in order to acknowledge forms of power and hegemony being inscribed upon the agenda of blockchain futurity (research, development and implementation). Fundamentally this means consideration and analysis of forms of regulation that do not settle on competition, markets, as well as consumer protection as a corollary of the two, as the best or only options available, but 'include a wide range of other types of social control' (Prosser, 2010, p. 2).

'As a general proposition', claim Richard Whish and David Bailey, 'competition law consists of rules that are intended to protect the process of competition in order to maximise consumer welfare' (2012, p. 1). But the reality of consumer welfare, whilst sounding like a positive outcome, only follows on the heels of protection of competition as an *a priori* inalienable right for members of contemporary economised societies to pursue. The welfare of consumers therefore presupposes a need for protection against the inevitability of market failure, with all the fall-out that entails. Protecting competition assumes that monopoly and in many circumstances the high degree of centralisation that accompanies it are evils that only *more* competition can defeat. Fredrick Engels argued that the antithesis between competition and monopoly was 'quite hollow', as every competitor '*cannot but* desire to have the monopoly, be he worker, capitalist or landowner', and that being based in self-interest 'competition passes over into monopoly' (1975, p. 432). What is more, assumptions as to the inherent virtues of competition invariably ignore the broader non-commercial conceptions of monopoly including, for instance, civic and community-led forms, and instead choose to define monopoly only in terms of cause and effect, that is, as a manifestation of competitive failure that naturally requires competition to be restarted by all and any means necessary. This includes interventions by competition law that deem anti-competitive practices and agreements unlawful, thus acting like an adrenalin shot to restore the hitherto lifeless body of commercial competitiveness to full virility. Whish and Bailey, for example, suggest the following theory of competition which reflects precisely these biases:

> The ideological struggle between capitalism and communism was a dominant feature of the twentieth century. Many countries had the greatest suspicion of competitive markets and saw, instead, benefits in state planning and management of the economy. However enormous changes took place as the millennium approached, leading to widespread demonopolisation, liberalisation and privatisation. These phenomena, coupled with rapid technological changes and the opening up of international trade, unleashed unprecedentedly powerful economic forces. These changes impact upon individuals and societies in different ways, and sometimes the effects can be uncomfortable. Underlying them, however, is a growing consensus that, on the whole, markets deliver better outcomes than state planning; and central to the idea of the market is the process of competition.
>
> (2012, p. 4)

Proposals for regulating blockchain that this book will explore begin with the notion that a combination of capitalist class power and neoliberalism and the features it engenders – celebration of competition, risk, 'free markets' and so on – are a threat to the regulatory enterprise, not a central pillar for its development or justification, and that competitive strategies including proliferation of so-called 'free markets' at all levels of the social and political are not, as many critics of neoliberalism maintain (Harvey, 2005; Dean, 2009; Peck, 2012; Mirowski, 2014; Brown, 2015; Davies, 2017; Hall, 2017; Han, 2017), sustainable in terms of *inter alia* long-term community sustainability, the commons, public interest, or political feasibility. In *The German Ideology*, Karl Marx and Frederick Engels were particularly scathing of what they called 'universal competition':

> It destroyed as far as possible ideology, religion, morality, etc. and where it could not do this, made them into a palpable lie. It produced world history for the first time, insofar as it made all civilised nations and every individual member of them dependent for the satisfaction of their wants on the whole world, thus destroying the former natural exclusiveness of separate nations. Generally speaking, big industry created everywhere the same relations between the classes of society, and thus destroyed the peculiar individuality of the various nationalities.
>
> (1970, p. 78)

A key theme for this book in response to blockchain regulatory approaches in line with deregulatory status quo therefore, is to press for regulation that does not kowtow to a combination of capitalist class power and neoliberal logic and reason, but looks seriously at alternatives including those that contrast with essential features of free markets and thus consider options of planned economy, that is, economy conducted 'in the name of the people as a whole', where the state controls all property; 'production is not for profit, but to satisfy the needs of the citizens'; 'distribution is by central allocation, rather than by trade' (Wolff, 1996, p. 159). This might include co-operative socialist principles as a viable means of structuring the blockchain regulatory environment, as well as an alignment to visions of communism that deliberately impose restrictions on 'the freedom of capitalists, exploiters and oppressors', meaning they are not able to 'do as they will but are governed, controlled, and limited by the rest of us' (Dean, 2012, p. 71). Thus whether blockchain applications ought to be controlled and predetermined in accordance with the needs of the commons, co-operatives and with public enterprise, affordances and goods as priorities, rather than with profit, consumer protectionism, *ex post* competition law or market-aligned and complementing regulation as bases from which use-cases are built and subsequently deemed 'good' by prevailing and dominant neoliberal stakeholders. This approach echoes the Community Informatics declaration for an 'Internet for the Common Good', in which it is stated that,

> [m]ore than a technology or a marketplace, the Internet is a social environment, a community space for people to interact with the expectation that principles of equity, fairness and justice will prevail. Internet governance must ensure that this online social space functions effectively for the well-being of all.
>
> (n.a., 2013)

The proposals introduced here may appear as unjust 'sledgehammer regulation' (Brown and Marsden, 2013, pp. 32–33). Moreover, they may appear illegitimate in proclaiming what is at stake politically and thus departing from the idea that effective regulatory regimes must be 'dispassionate' (Brenner, 2007, p. 188) or neutral. To enforce or expect neutrality or dispassion risks, however, alternative regulatory strategies that leave untouched or unquestioned the politico-economic status quo, itself not neutral or dispassionate, and therefore fails to probe techno-logical use-cases sufficiently in the public interest. To view the proposals here as merely rooted in an ethos of *anti* would be a reductionist assessment of the cri-tique that will unfold in the coming pages. It will be argued that moderate, 'after the event' regulatory reactions risk ineffectuality. There are, in other words, cir-cumstances (arguably more than are given credit) in which 'regulation may be a first choice to administer an area of social provision for which markets are con-sidered in principle inappropriate' (Prosser, 2010, p. 3). In such circumstances, of which the context of blockchain is arguably one, it would be wrong to paint notions of regulation other to market-complementing regulation as simply *anti*. Regulators enamoured by the bright lights and fairy dust of techno-solutionist and innovationist ideologies closely bound up with promotion of market forces and the notion of regulation 'as infringement of private autonomy' (Prosser, 2010, p. 4) risk missing the opportunities and material effects the technology might have for society as a whole.

Possessing a critical vocabulary to account for conduct, activities and rhetoric flowing freely from and through the blockchain ecosystem is crucial for meeting the aims expressed above. This is especially important at this juncture in the short history of blockchain where much remains either undetermined or at stake with regard to the future of blockchain. It is important to note that this book is not simply interested in blockchain as a technology, however, but in the ways it is being (re)produced culturally, politically and so on. It is a book rooted, therefore, in meta-analyses of blockchain aimed at exploring, amongst other things, the shaping of blockchain technology *and* narratives by venture capital, entrepreneurs and, increasingly, legacy sources of elite financial power and control for use in *existing* economies, systems and networks. This is, I argue, the reality of blockchain as well as the so-called 'fourth industrial revolution' (Schwab, 2017). Not 'disruption' or significant or deep-rooted novelty, but the simple (re)imagining and (re)construction of capitalism's next stage of evolution, or put more succinctly: (big) business as usual.

It is imperative that law and regulation do not continue to underestimate the pace of change wrought by blockchain or the *desire* of its stakeholders and the ecosystem they constitute. 'The link between capitalism and the psyche provides the key to understanding the appeal of capitalism', argues Todd McGowan (2016, p. 22), and both mediating and within the structures of the relationship between capitalism and subjective desire are a range of technologies and techniques. Capitalism 'is a system that enables us to envision the possibility of a satisfaction that is structurally unattainable for us while, at the same time, it allows the real traumatic source of our satisfaction to remain unconscious. This double decep-tion', McGowan concludes, 'creates a system with an inordinate staying power, a system that appears to be written into our genetic makeup' (2016, p. 22), and yet I suggest that capitalism may not be as successful as it is in this regard but for technologies like blockchain. Under prevailing technological trends, including pervasive Internet use and mobile technologies in particular, it is inevitable that blockchain will dissolve into the white noise of ever evolving digitalised, data societies, and become invisible. Blockchain, I suggest, is aimed at becoming the 'common sense' way of performing digital economy and thus a way in which to sustain faith in capitalist economy more generally, but also, as McGowan suggests, a way in which to sustain faith in a fantasy of the unending desire of *the Other* with whom we transact and exchange online and on-chain (2016, p. 46). One example of this is the emergent blockchain paradigm of extensive and expansive modes of economised conduct that turn on individuals' auto-exploitation of their personal and intimate data in order to realise *value*. One's value, it might be said, will come to be predicated entirely on an ability to generate micropayments in a constant cycle of upload, attribution and exploitation of personal data on blockchain. For those who welcome blockchain as a means of *data sovereignty*, or as the true potential and long-awaited victory of blockchain as 'the economic layer the Web has never had' (Swan, 2015, p.vii), this will not seem problematic, but instead a healthy response to years of data harvesting and exploitation by the likes of Facebook and Google. As I will argue in this book, however, blockchain data sovereignty is not a meaningful tool of individual liberation but a new form of governmentality: *blockchain governmentality*. Blockchain is heralding a shift away from sovereignty and political rationality to compulsion and a 'hypercompetitive society' (Rouvroy and Stiegler, 2016, p. 9), decentralised control at a distance that can be implemented block by block by block.

Any number of sinister alternatives to the rosy picture painted of personal data sovereignty are possible. For instance, children engaging in so-called 'sexting' (sending, receiving, or forwarding sexually explicit messages, photographs or images, primarily between mobile phones, or via a computer or any digital device), intentionally but without consideration of all the consequences or by duress or compulsion (peer pressure), uploading provocative images to the Internet which then find a way onto a public blockchain. Notwithstanding issues concerning potential criminal liability for users of a blockchain found containing explicit sexual images of children, it cannot be ignored that the recording and attribution of just such an image on the blockchain and the potential for the child to receive micropayments whenever it is copied or downloaded could have serious consequences, including encouraging children to exploit themselves in order to make money. The conditions creating this 'unintended content' are not fiction: researchers in Germany have discovered images of this sort, including child pornography on Bitcoin's blockchain, sparking debate over what the correct criminal or legal procedure and sanctions ought to be and whether or not the overall business viability of blockchain systems may be thrown into doubt (Mattzutt et al., 2018; Suberg, 2018).

With potential to dramatically impact any or all areas of social life in the coming years, the present lack of public education, knowledge, understanding and recognition of what blockchain may involve ought to be of concern, especially a lack of *critical* education. Necessary critical work in the short term is required to find ways to cut through the hype of blockchain and not to be dazzled by solutionist and technologist rhetoric therefore, including a close reading of the way those within the blockchain ecosystem are presenting and *telling* blockchain and constructing the received wisdom of the present blockchain moment. As well to analyse the psycho-politics of blockchain underpinned by the erotics – '*not* the physical mating urge', but rather 'the desire for recognition by others and for wholeness' (Schroeder, 2004, p. 86) – and fetishistic enthusiasm of stakeholders and regulators at work in contemporary technologies that is enabling globalised and totalised world views that might be all about the blockchain but are more likely all about the personal advantages and forms of self-interest blockchain is bringing. This book is not anti-technology, but aims to understand where the balance lies between bare technological necessities, especially in the public interest, on one end of the spectrum, and unscrupulous vanity projects that benefit only a handful of opportunists on the other. Somewhere on that line we find blockchain.

References

n.a. 2013. An Internet for the Common Good: Engagement, Empowerment, and Justice for All: A Community Informatics Declaration. *The Journal of Community Informatics*, Vol. 9, No. 4. http://ci-journal.org/index.php/ciej/article/view/1099 (accessed 31 May 2018).

Althusser, Louis. 2008. *On Ideology*. London: Verso.

Arnold, Martin. 2018. Davos: Blockchain Can no Longer be Ignored. *Financial Times*, 24 January. www.ft.com/content/c0794556-ff50-11e7-9650-9c0ad2d7c5b5 (accessed 1 February 2018).

Brenner, Susan W. 2007. *Law in an Era of 'Smart' Technology*. Oxford: Oxford University Press.

Brown, Ian and Marsden, Christopher T. 2013. *Regulating Code: Good Governance and Better Regulation in the Information Age*. Cambridge: The MIT Press.

Brown, Wendy. 2015. *Undoing the Demos: Neoliberalism's Stealth Revolution*. New York: Zone Books.

Brownsword, Roger and Goodwin, Morag. 2012. *Law and Technologies of the Twenty-First Century*. Cambridge: Cambridge University Press.

Cohen, G.A. 2011. *On the Currency of Egalitarian Justice, and Other Essays in Political Philosophy*. Edited by Michael Otsuka. Princeton: Princeton University Press.

Davies, William. 2017. *The Limits of Neoliberalism: Authority, Sovereignty and the Logic of Competition*. London: Sage.

Dean, Jodie. 2009. *Democracy and Other Neoliberal Fantasies: Communicative Capitalism and Left Politics*. Durham: Duke University Press.

Dean, Jodie. 2012. *The Communist Horizon*. London: Verso.

Engels, Frederick. 1975. *Outline of a Critique of Political Economy. Collected Works, Volume 3 Marx and Engels 1843–1844*. London: Lawrence & Wishart, pp. 418–443.

Gupta, Vinay. 2017. European Parliament blockchain presentation May 2017. *YouTube*. www.youtube.com/watch?v=xEFVuccuHI8&t=4s (accessed 1 February 2018).

Hall, Stuart. 2017. *Selected Political Writings: The Great Moving Right Show and Other Essays*. Edited by Sally Davison, David Featherstone, Michael Rustin and Bill Schwartz. Durham: Duke University Press.

Han, Byung-Chul. 2017. *Psycho-Politics: Neoliberalism and New Technologies of Power*. Translated by Erik Butler. London: Verso.

Harvey, David. 2005. *A Brief History of Neoliberalism*. Oxford: Oxford University Press.

Kewell, Beth, Adams, Richard and Parry, Glen. 2017. Blockchain for Good? *Strategic Change*, Vol. 26, No. 5 (September), pp. 429–437.

McGowan, Todd. 2016. *Capitalism and Desire: The Psychic Cost of Free Markets*. New York: Columbia University Press.

Macherey, Pierre. 2006. *A Theory of Literary Production*. Translated by Geoffrey Wall. Abingdon: Routledge.

Marx, Karl and Engels, Frederick. 1970. *The German Ideology*. Edited by C.J. Arthur. London: Lawrence & Wishart.

Mattzutt, Roman, Hiller, Jens, Henze, Martin, Ziegeldorf, Jan Henrik, Müllmann, Dirk, Hohlfeld, Oliver and Wehrle, Klaus. 2018. A Quantitative Analysis of the Impact of Arbitrary Blockchain Content on Bitcoin. https://pdfs.semanticscholar.org/02dd/8348fbdf459c4ca05245ea6498e9f04bd03f.pdf?_ga=2.19385403.246495524.1525093658-307956779.1525093658 (accessed 30 April 2018).

Mirowski, Philip. 2014. *Never Let A Serious Crisis Go to Waste: How Neoliberalism Survived the Financial Meltdown*. London: Verso.

Murray, Andrew and Scott, Colin. 2002. Controlling the New Media: Hybrid Responses to New Forms of Power. *The Modern Law Review*, Vol. 65, No. 4 (July), pp. 491–516.

Organisation for Economic Co-operation and Development (OECD). 2018. *Blockchain Technology and Competition Policy – Issues Paper by the Secretariat*. OECD, 26 April. https://one.oecd.org/document/DAF/COMP/WD(2018)47/en/pdf (accessed 16 May 2018).

Peck, Jamie. 2012. *Constructions of Neoliberal Reason*. Oxford: Oxford University Press.

Power, Michael. 1997. *The Audit Society: Rituals of Verification*. Oxford: Oxford University Press.

Prosser, Tony. 2010. *The Regulatory Enterprise*. Oxford: Oxford University Press.

Robinson, Edward and Leising, Matthew. 2015. Blythe Masters Tells Banks the Blockchain Changes Everything. *Bloomberg*, 1 September. www.bloomberg.com/news/features/2015-09-01/blythe-masters-tells-banks-the-blockchain-changes-everything (accessed 24 March 2018).

Rouvroy, Antoinette and Stiegler, Bernard. 2016. The Digital Regime of Truth: From the Algorithmic Governmentality to a New Rule of Law. *La Deleuziana – Online Journal of Philosophy*, No. 3, pp. 6–29. www.ladeleuziana.org/2016/11/14/3-life-and-number/ (accessed 14 May 2018).

Schroeder, Jeanne Lorraine. 2004. *The Triumph of Venus: The Erotics of the Market*. Berkeley: University of California Press.

Schwab, Klaus. 2017. *The Fourth Industrial Revolution*. New York: Crown.

Suberg, William. 2018. German Researchers: Child Abuse Content Found On Bitcoin Blockchain, Users Must Be Protected. *Coin Telegraph*, 20 March. https://cointelegraph.com/news/german-researchers-child-abuse-content-found-on-bitcoin-blockchain-users-must-be-protected (accessed 26 March 2018).

Swan, Melanie. 2015. *Blockchain: Blueprint for a New Economy*. Sebastopol: O'Reilly.

Tapscott, Don and Tapscott, Alex. 2016. *Blockchain Revolution: How the Technology behind Bitcoin is Changing Money, Business and the World*. London: Portfolio Penguin.

Whish, Richard and Bailey, David. 2012. *Competition Law*, 8th Edition. Oxford: Oxford University Press.

Wolff, Jonathan. 1996. *An Introduction to Political Philosophy*. Oxford: Oxford University Press.

Part I

Regulating blockchain

1 Blockchain

Introduction

> Every technology resembles what surrealists called an 'exquisite cadaver'.
>
> (Latour, 2002, p. 249)

Melanie Swan defines blockchain as follows:

> The blockchain is like another application layer to run on the existing stack of
> Internet protocols, adding an entire new tier to the Internet to enable eco-
> nomic transactions, both immediate digital currency payments (in a universally
> usable cryptocurrency) and longer-term, more complicated financial contracts.
> A blockchain is quite literally like a giant spreadsheet for registering all assets,
> and an accounting system for transacting them on a global scale that can
> include all forms of assets held by all parties worldwide. Thus, the blockchain
> can be used for any form of asset registry, inventory, and exchange, including
> every area of finance, economics, and money; hard assets (physical property);
> and intangible assets (votes, ideas, reputation, intention, health data, etc.) [...]
> The economy that the blockchain enables is not merely the movement of
> money, however; it is the transfer of information and the effective allocation
> of resources that money has enabled in the human- and corporate-scale
> economy.
>
> (Swan, 2015, pp. x–xi)

Swan is without a doubt an acolyte or evangelist of blockchain technologies; she
is, to put it another way, a stakeholder in the techno-social futurity of blockchain.
Of particular note in Swan's definition are ways in which a collapsing of the
human into the economic is envisaged, and the necessary role blockchain will have
in achieving this end. But whilst Swan's definition offers broad technical details, it
is rather more interesting as a symptom of the sustained insistence of neoliberal
economic reason that is presently at work shaping the 'blockchain ecosystem'.
This 'ecosystem' is thus a community of thought and practice centred on a specific
technology or set of technologies called 'blockchain', but one motivated by universal adherence to neoliberal ideals of innovationism and the desires of what

Evgeny Morozov (2014) calls *solutionists*. As such Swan, albeit inadvertently, reveals the political at stake in the present blockchain moment.

David Harvey's general assessment of the relationship between neoliberalism and technology, whilst written before blockchain became known, is nevertheless striking in the accuracy of a description of the present blockchain moment and offers an antithesis to Swan's acritical celebration of blockchain:

> The neoliberal theory of technological change relies upon the coercive powers of competition to drive the search for new products, new production methods, and new organizational forms. This drive becomes so deeply embedded in entrepreneurial common sense, however, that it becomes a fetish belief: that there is a technological fix for each and every problem. To the degree that this takes hold not only within corporations but also within the state apparatus (in the military in particular), it produces powerful independent trends of technological change that can become destabilizing, if not counterproductive. Technological developments can run amok as sectors dedicated solely to technological innovation create new products and new ways of doing things that as yet have no market (new pharmaceutical products are produced, for which new illnesses are then invented). Talented interlopers can, furthermore, mobilize technological innovations to undermine dominant social relations and institutions; they can, through their activities, even reshape common sense to their own pecuniary advantage. There is an inner connection, therefore, between technological dynamism, instability, dissolution of social solidarities, environmental degradation, deindustrialization, rapid shifts in time-space relations, speculative bubbles, and the general tendency towards crisis formation within capitalism.
>
> (Harvey, 2005, pp. 68–69)

New or emerging technologies invite the desire or need to understand where they ultimately come from and why and how they were produced. 'Most of the time, technological objects issued from ICTs [information and communications technologies] are perceived by users as "black boxes", which is to say that ordinary users pay scant attention to the objects inner workings', claims Serge Proulx, '[c]ode activists, in contrast', Proulx continues

> act as a sort of technical handyman; they do not hesitate to look inside codes or devices to take an active role in how informational objects work, particularly through computer programming and the design and dissemination of new technological devices.
>
> (2012, p. 108)

Further to Proulx's distinction can be added those of us who neither consider themselves technical handymen (or women), nor wish to settle easily with a social domain populated by an increasing number of black boxes. Of course, as Frank Pasquale states, '[d]econstructing the black boxes of Big Data isn't easy. Even if they were willing to expose their methods to the public, the modern Internet and banking sectors pose tough challenges to our understanding of those methods' (2015, p. 6). For present purposes the approach lies in fostering critical curiosity about what lies beneath the technologies increasingly put to work within modern capitalist societies, not to demand to know absolutely the inner workings, but at the very least not passively submit to the narratives and ideologies of technologists and entrepreneurs, even or especially when ideologies are veiled in the language of education and the necessity 'to educate the public' about new technologies. This, I argue, is often a euphemism for interpellation, of 'recruiting' or 'hailing', as Louis Althusser (2008, p. 48) would say, the public-as-consumer with the call of new technologies.

By knowing where different technologies ultimately come from and why and how they were produced it is possible to develop theories, models and lay plans for where they will go in the future and thus what that future will ultimately look like with a particular technology or technologies in it. The necessity, in other words, is always to historicise by locating or situating technologies as particular productive forces in space and time. This can take many forms: from the very narrow, by focusing on incremental developments of or within a specific technological frontier, quantum computing for example; to very broad analyses of the evolution of human techniques; and everything in between. Bruno Latour addresses this notion via the hammer, a more basic although arguably no less forceful or brutal technology than blockchain. 'The hammer I find on my workbench is not contemporary to my action today', says Latour, 'it keeps folded heterogeneous temporalities [and] what is true of time holds for space as well, for this humble hammer holds in place quite heterogeneous spaces that nothing, before the technical action, could gather together' (2002, p. 249). Irrespective of the technology or the scale and breadth of its study, however, it is necessary to recognise the political in any and all forms of telling involving technology, and that cultural 'texts', of which blockchain can be counted one, contain vestiges of cultural dominance and forms of ideological coding (Jameson, 2002, p. 75) that might be disguised in and by the telling, but are never entirely erased.

There is no future perfect where the history of blockchain is concerned, despite what some commentators would like to believe or are busy telling the world. Take for example the future perfection of blockchain implementations that Michael Casey and Paul Vigna are committed to but which simply have not happened yet and may never happen:

> [i]n *resolving* longstanding problems of trust and enabling a community to track its transactions without entrusting that record-keeping process to a central intermediary, the blockchain idea promised a way to bypass the various gatekeepers who control society's exchanges of value.
>
> [emphasis added] (2018, p.ix)

Further, the politics of blockchain are yet to be determined; I insist on this claim as central to critique and in spite of the monolithic solutionist characterisation of blockchain bestowed upon the world by the ecosystem: one that enfolds block-chain within normative conceptualisations of the evolution and the onward march of economic reason. Far from being a project of disruption in the arenas it touches (economics, politics, law and so on), blockchain is symptomatic of entrenched neoliberal aims that stakeholders of the blockchain ecosystem are intoxicated by and wish to inscribe upon blockchain in the many and varied uses to which it is put. A primary aim of evaluating blockchain therefore, is to see it as historically materialistic, that is, as a mode of production of political, economic, cultural and legal conduct, to interrogate the blockchain ecosystem as a site of ideological coalescence and consensus around the broader aims of neoliberalism.

The main thrust of this book is not to act as a technical manual nor to write the history of blockchain from the point of view of ICT. It is, first and foremost, to analyse, interrogate and explore blockchain as a socioeconomic and political phe-nomenon, a juridical and regulatory conundrum and cultural product and text. Nonetheless it would be remiss for a book whose subject is a particular technology to side-line or ignore the technical details entirely. To begin this chapter, there-fore, there will be a brief overview of some of the key characteristics of blockchain.

What lies beneath?

'Blockchain' is not a monolithic description or definition, but covers a hetero-geneity of technological features and possibilities. For present purposes there are at least three main types of blockchain or ledger of interest: *permissioned, permis-sionless* and *hybrids.* Permissioned ledgers are not public but operate in closed sys-tems. They provide many of the same features of public (permissionless) ledgers (of which the Bitcoin blockchain is the most obvious example), including trans-parency and peer-to-peer transactions, but are deployed within closed networks like an intranet or back-office system. This ensures the ledger is accessible to those with requisite permissions. A permissionless public ledger on the other hand, can, in theory, be viewed by anyone at any time because it resides on the network and 'not within a single institution charged with auditing transactions and keeping records' (Tapscott and Tapscott, 2016, p. 6). Hybrids combine permissioned and permissionless ledgers, meaning data from a closed network can be shielded by a registry layer and moved or released to permissionless blockchains for the purposes of allowing public scrutiny of prescribed or specified data at a given point in time (see for example: Factom, 2014). The hybrid distinction also includes the option of using ledgers, most likely in permissioned form, as an *access control* medium for other, additional registries or databases in off-chain or offline servers and storage infrastructures.

'The blockchain is the decentralized transaction ledger', says Swan, 'that is part of a larger computing infrastructure that must also include many other functions such as storage, communication, file serving, and archiving' (2015, p. 20). The access control variant therefore fits broader notions of what the blockchain eco-system ought to be doing in order, as Swan argues, to realise 'full-solution operations' (2015, p. 20). This also brings to the fore more clearly issues relating to *interoperability*, not least from a regulatory point of view of the challenges of negotiating tensions in a commercial dynamic that crosses the public and private sectors. '[O]pen interoperability gives enormous practical advantages', argue Brown and Marsden, 'which resulted in the development of the public Internet as it is widely experienced today' (2013, p. 10). The specific reference to 'public' here is, I suggest, noteworthy because it betrays the notion of a private sphere of commercial interests that do not automatically bring 'enormous practical advantages', but rather seek private profits and stakeholder gains in the first instance.

Decentralisation and distribution are two of the major features of blockchain that extend across the different types. Blockchain decentralisation and distribution builds upon the existing Internet infrastructure by adding another layer to the existing 'stack' of protocols. Alexander Galloway describes distributed networks as follows:

> A distributed network differs from other networks such as centralized and decentralized networks in the arrangement of its internal structure. A centralized network consists of a single central power point (a host), from which are attached radial nodes. The central point is connected to all of the satellite nodes, which are themselves connected only to the central host. A decentralized network, on the other hand, has *multiple* central hosts, each with its own set of satellite nodes. A satellite node may have connectivity with one or more hosts, but not with other nodes. Communication generally travels unidirectionally within both centralized and decentralized networks: from the central trucks to the radial leaves [...] The distributed network is an entirely different matter [...] Each point in a distributed network is neither a central hub nor a satellite node – there are neither trunks nor leaves [...] each node in a distributed network may establish direct communication with another node, without having to appeal to a hierarchical intermediary.
>
> (Galloway, 2004, pp. 11–12)

For some enthusiasts, blockchain does more than simply add to the infrastructure already in place. '[B]lockchain technology could become the seamless embedded economic layer the Web has never had', claims Melanie Swan, 'serving as the technological underlay for payments, decentralized exchange, token earning and spending, digital asset invocation and transfer, and smart contract issuance and execution' (2015, p.vii). Swan's description demonstrates the problem that blockchain is believed to have solved or will solve in the near future, namely, perfection of an economic layer. Blockchain, so it is believed, provides the answer to long-standing (pre-blockchain) complaints as described by Ethan Katsh and Orna Rabinovich-Einy:

> It has taken us half a century to turn the original internet into a network for exchanging information and money in a manner that is easy for consumers at a degree of risk they are willing to accept. The network makes possible a kind of supply chain where information can be communicated, items can be

selected, contractual terms agreed to, and money exchanged. Admittedly, in most instances, at least in the developed world, this is a fairly seamless process. The more we use it, rely on it, and build upon it, however, the more complex that process becomes, and the more likely it is that we will encounter a problem. Publicized data breaches are only one element starting to shake up our confidence a bit.

(2017, p. 76)

The blockchain that Swan and others envisage aims to restore the confidence that Katsh and Rabinovich-Einy see ebbing away with growing network complexities. Starting with the Bitcoin blockchain consensus was recognised as the most effective method of verifying data and thus building the chain, and so-called 'proof-of-work' intimately related to the distributed nature of the blockchain insofar as it reflected the collective effort of nodes or numerous central processing units (CPUs) to achieve the necessary consensus. In the case of public blockchains like Bitcoin, each CPU builds individual blocks and ensures the proliferation of the overall blockchain architecture. Proliferation is achieved by what blockchain founder Satoshi Nakamoto called, 'one-CPU-one-vote', which enabled determination that an incentivised yet consensual, majority decision would lead to the longest chains, and thus also those most likely to be legitimate and honest (2008, p. 3). As each block is chained to the next, as well as the one prior to it (Nakamoto never uses the resolved term 'blockchain', but rather 'block chain'), and verified every ten minutes or so – a lag period that so-called 'layer 2' developments such as the 'lightning network' is eradicating (see: https://lightning.network/) – it becomes less likely that a 'greedy attacker' looking to intermeddle with a chain or the data items represented by each block in order to commit a fraud, would be able to undo or change a particular chain without affecting all the blocks associated with it. Incentives, insofar as they dovetail honesty in Nakamoto's initial plans, also play a significant role in this regard, because they add a further layer of security and legitimacy to the overall network. 'The incentive', Nakamoto claims, 'may encourage nodes to stay honest', and thus a 'greedy attacker [...] ought to find it more profitable to play by the rules [...] than to undermine the system and the validity of his own wealth' (2008, p. 4). Alongside proofing mechanisms, of which proof of work is no longer the only variant – 'proof of stake' being an alternative (Harper, 2018) – blockchain constitution reflects evolution in protocological and software fragments. Two key examples of fragments that coalesce in the context of blockchain are cryptography (encryption) and digital timestamping.

Cryptography

Cryptography can broadly be defined as follows:

The study of 'mathematical' systems for solving two kinds of security problems: privacy and authentication. A privacy system prevents the extraction of information by unauthorized parties from messages transmitted over a public channel, thus assuring the sender of a message that it is being read only by the intended recipient. An authentication system prevents the unauthorized injection of messages into a public channel, assuring the receiver of a message of the legitimacy of its sender.

(Diffie and Hellman, 1976, p. 645)

Ensuring the legitimacy and integrity of data and information using cryptography and hash functions is core to explaining the interest shown in blockchain beyond cryptocurrencies, and is helping justify growth across a proliferation of sectors within the mainstream during the last few years. Take for example the following passage from *The Economist* in 2015, where the benefits of blockchain are tied directly to the art of cryptography:

Blockchains are [...] the latest example of the unexpected fruits of crypto-graphy. Mathematical scrambling is used to boil down an original piece of information into a code, known as a hash. Any attempt to tamper with any part of the blockchain is apparent immediately – because the new hash will not match the old ones. In this way science that keeps information secret (vital for encrypting messages and online shopping and banking) is, para-doxically, also a tool for open dealing.

(2015, p. 13)

The emphasis and importance placed on cryptography in contemporary mass communication networks can be traced to a number of sources in the con-temporary information age, including political and national security concerns and the need to develop viability in transacting across global digital trade and eco-nomic networks. Throughout the 1970s and 1980s the ICT academic community increasingly advocated a role for cryptography 'in shaping the character of emer-ging computer networks' and the Internet 'propelled cryptography to the fore-front of the cyberlibertarian movement' (Blanchette, 2012, p. 5), the same place from which blockchain technology first emerged.

As a fundamental site of socio-mathematical intrigue for millennia cryptography cannot be underestimated as a manifestation of the desire to explore and utilise the inner complexities of social epistemologies and ontologies in order to create deliberate webs of privacy and secrecy within human networks and systems. In other words, secrecy and privacy are central to human experience as products and methods of concealment in the form of codes, puzzles and so on. What is more, the concealment of information shadowed by the possibility of exposure is capable of fostering enjoyment and driving desire, as individuals commune over secrets and seek satisfaction in partially shared secrets that mystify and tantalise (Bok, 1982, p. 84). In their landmark and prescient 1976 article 'New Directions in Cryptography', Whitfield Diffie and Martin E. Hellman introduce a socio-technical context that reflects these webs of privacy and secrecy in order to justify, as part of the community Blanchette is referring to in the quote above, a wider application of cryptography for the new information age:

The development of computer controlled communication networks promises effortless and inexpensive contact between people or computers on opposite sides of the world, replacing most mail and many excursions with tele-communications. For many applications these contacts must be made secure against both eavesdropping and the injection of illegitimate messages. At present, however, the solution of security problems lags well behind other areas of communications technology. Contemporary cryptography is unable to meet requirements, in that its use would impose such severe inconveniences on the system users, as to eliminate many of the benefits of teleprocessing.

(Diffie and Hellman, 1976, p. 644)

To understand, at least in part, the potential import of cryptography through blockchain within contemporary society is to understand the power of the continuing desire of individuals, bureaucracies and corporations to keep information secret and, as Sissela Bok claims, 'to block information' or 'evidence of it' from reaching another, 'and to do so *intentionally*: to prevent him from learning it, and thus from possessing it, making use of it, or revealing it' [emphasis added] (1982, p. 6). Bok is not talking about blockchain in her reference to *blocking the flow* of information to another person. Nevertheless the homology is relevant and her description discloses the ultimate expectation of cryptography to achieve conceal-ment, secrecy and privacy, which contrasts with visions of blockchain promoted by stakeholders as fundamentally public, open and transparent. Again this idea tou-ches on the evolving nature of, in particular commercial and enterprise block-chains, from the initial public permissionless blockchain of Bitcoin, to closed network permissioned ledgers that fulfil an intranet-like, back-office function for businesses, where emphasis on privacy shifts from a requirement for encryption that is able to conceal only selective aspects of the information otherwise exposed in a public domain, to all information excluded from immediate public scrutiny. The role encryption continues to play as blockchains develop will be crucial to defining the contexts in which they are used and by whom. This potentially includes whether or not a formal space will be created for their use by regulators, tax authorities for example, or whether blockchain will only ultimately serve the purposes of those seeking, amongst other things, to conceal information from those self-same authorities and regulators.

A proprietorial assemblage of access rights (existing simultaneously both pri-vately and publicly) that blockchain enables peer to peer creates secure, private spaces that nevertheless remain in public view, if called upon to be so. Unlike existing methods for maintaining the privacy of online transactions which shield the entire process from public view and invariably rely upon a third party to achieve and maintain privacy on the client's behalf – a costly and potentially inef-ficient and ineffective process from the point of view of many stakeholders – blockchain allows privacy to be maintained by 'breaking the flow of information in another place: by keeping public keys anonymous' (Nakamoto, 2008, p. 6). Encryption is thus fundamental to blockchain privacy and reflects a means of protection that arguably recreates the physical or conceptual barriers to unintentional dissemination or theft of property, data or information that law has traditionally upheld. The traditional question of 'privacy', as Lawrence Lessig suggests, 'was the limit the law placed upon the ability of others to penetrate your private space' (2006, p. 201), and this desire to maintain limits in both the encryption modalities associated with public blockchains as well as through permissioned access associated with private ledgers is notable. 'In Lessig's theory', claims Blanchette, 'computer programming, especially as it pertains to the design of network architectures, is understood as a normative practice with power to influence behaviour as great as that of social norms, markets, and even law itself' (2012, p. 11).

The type of encryption in the public blockchain space involves so-called 'public-key' cryptography, where two keys, one public and one private, are used to validate transactions. The growth of cryptography from the 1980s onwards relied heavily on public-key cryptography and led to an expansion of the ICT research agenda from its

> historical focus on confidentiality to the design of technologies that could replicate for networked information systems the protocols, procedures, and artifacts that ensure the integrity of information necessary to a functioning democracy – signatures, voting, electronic cash, copyright protection, certified mail, and the like.
>
> (Blanchette, 2012, p. 5)

Indeed, public-key cryptography underpins the majority of blockchain concepts and use-cases, something that Blanchette categorically missed (despite writing at a time when blockchain was in existence) when he claimed that the 'expected market for public-key infrastructures (PKI), the computing infrastructure necessary for the deployment of cryptographic technologies, utterly failed to materialize', and that the 'prophesied cryptographic revolution did not come to be' (2012, p. 5). Instead the market for blockchain-based cryptography in both public and private forums is huge, and this has occurred in many instances long before many business models utilising the technology have advanced beyond concept stages, something that is attributable, arguably, to the tantalising certainty and above all bankable prospects that advanced mathematical solutions in the form of cryptographic technologies offer to the incongruous world of economics.

While many failures can be chalked-up against blockchain projects as contemporary sites of the significance of cryptography in modern global economic affairs therefore, there is no doubt that Blanchette is simply wrong in his estimation that markets in public-key cryptography have failed to materialise. Online news service TechCrunch summarise some significant points in the growth of the blockchain ecosystem during 2017 and 2018:

> 2017's funding totals were boosted by a number of sizable venture rounds, including: Coinbase's \$108.1 million Series D, \$43.45 million invested in Chinese ASIC chip manufacturer Canaan Creative and a \$42.5 million Series

B raised by multisignature bitcoin wallet provider BitGo. 2018 is off to a strong start with a $75 million Series B closed by secure hardware wallet-maker Ledger, $18 million invested in the seed round of Russian blockchain-for-cargo-tracking platform QUASA and $10 million invested in SF-based Harbor Platform, among other large rounds.

(Rowley, 2018)

Blanchette may have missed a critical development in contemporary cryptography, but stakeholders presently driving forward markets rooted in public-key cryptography, as the *sine qua non* of blockchain projects, clearly manifest what Blanchette calls the 'cryptographic imagination' (2012, pp. 159–185). Including reliance on hash functions – the matching of bit-strings between an original artefact, object or document and its digital counterpart – to enable blockchains globally, and, more importantly, allow for scale and a rendering viable of an array of business models reliant on the need to record and verify data for the purposes of fostering trust and developing transparent networks on a global economic stage. That is, in short, the desire of a majority of blockchain business models. Furthermore, the type of cryptographic imagination Blanchette advocates, 'not an inevitable ascension to mathematics, but rather ingenuity, playfulness, and pragmatism in its devotion to achieving (and defeating) counterintuitive communication goals' (2012, p. 183), adheres to the types of entrepreneurial practices otherwise referred to here as *innovationism* and *solutionism*. It is thus unsurprising perhaps that the blockchain is proving the entrepreneurial project *par excellence*.

Timestamping

Central to blockchain's perceived success as a peer-to-peer network and 'the economic layer the Web has never had' (Swan, 2015, p.vii), is what the Tapscotts have called a 'Digital Reckoning' (2016, p. 7). Akin to double-entry bookkeeping, a blockchain ledger should provide clear, indisputable evidence that 'enables a reconciliation of digital records regarding just about everything in real time' (Tapscott and Tapscott, 2016, p. 7). What lies beneath the Tapscotts' definition is, first and foremost, computational verification and auditability of information and data that is rooted in digital timestamping protocols. Timestamping itself builds on what Stuart Haber and W. Scott Stornetta called a 'naïve solution', namely, a 'digital safety-deposit box' (1991, p. 101) that could be made secure and thus viable for use across global networks by employing *inter alia* hash functions and cryptographic digital signatures – as mentioned above. What the combination of verification and auditability also provide in conjunction with blockchain's relationship to the larger off-chain data storage infrastructure is the ability to archive data in ways arguably more secure than existing online databases. Later chapters will explore how auditability in particular fits into the evolving political economy of blockchain and the questions this raises, and as a precursor it is important to understand the ways in which blockchain is able to create the initial conditions in which data can be verified, audited and securely archived, thereby providing evidence and constituting forms of memory concerning any-thing, from property ownership to the occurrence of an event at a specific time and in a specific place.

A system analogous to the blockchain was first described as a method for securely timestamping digital documents, which accurately recorded the order in which those documents were created, and thus 'announced' an entire history of documents that were fixed and capable of public scrutiny (Haber and Stornetta, 1991; Nakamoto, 2008). The accuracy of the recordkeeping facilitated by time-stamping ought to make a network or system a highly reliable witness for parti-cular data. Yet timestamping still exists within digital arenas defined by the risk of document falsification and tampering, meaning that, at least for some bureau-cracies, individuals and businesses, material artefacts in the form of hard-copy and offline paper records remain more favourable to digital copies. Indeed, Blanchette maintains, 'paper records (and paper work) form the material foundation on which the legitimacy and the day-to-day operation of the nation-state rests' (2012, p. 4). This bureaucratic reliance on materialities is particularly so in the creation of incorporated entities in off- and onshore 'tax havens', and a significant problem for regulators and tax authorities wanting to ascertain *inter alia* accurate lists of asset ownership and tax liabilities (Knobel, 2017).

A notable disjuncture between the belief in verifiability of digital and paper documentation continues, although it could be argued that the timestamping protocol described by Haber and Stornetta is now something actively *avoided* by those who wish to undermine verification, rather than always enable better and more secure forms of it. In other words, stakeholders who deliberately remain offline (or off-chain) in order to preserve a level of privacy that is seen as put at risk by online (or on-chain) bureaucracies. '[T]he integration of computing, ima-ging, and printing technologies makes it easier than ever to scan, copy, alter, dis-tribute, print, and store high-quality documents', argues Blanchette, and therefore if the 'moral authority of paper records has correspondingly diminished, the elec-tronic documents replacing them appear to us even more malleable' (2012, p. 4). In their early justification for digital timestamping Haber and Stornetta were keen to demonstrate that the opportunities that existed for scrutiny of documents in hard copy, which was seen as preferable at their time of writing, could be at the very least replicated digitally, and then, it was hoped, improved upon in order to provide an efficient and highly secure digital document network. As Blanchette describes, however, the documentary transition between offline materialism and online ethereality has not been achieved without a number of corresponding and problematic shifts in both realms.

In order to understand timestamping with blockchain more clearly, as well as why some industries are keen to avoid the type of verifiability that contemporary digital timestamping in the form of blockchain allows, it is worth looking more closely at Haber and Stornetta's initial reasoning behind digital timestamping:

> Businesses incorporate more elaborate procedures into their regular order of business to enhance the credibility of their internal documents, should they be

challenged at a later date. For example, these methods may ensure that the records are handled by more than one person, so that any tampering with a document by one person will be detected by another. But all these methods rest on two assumptions. First, the records can be examined for telltale signs of tampering. Second, there is another party that views the document whose integrity or impartiality is seen as vouchsafing the claim. *We believe these assumptions are called into serious question for the case of documents created and preserved exclusively in digital form.* This is because electronic digital documents are so easy to tamper with, and the change need not leave any telltale sign on the physical medium.

[emphasis added] (1991, p. 100)

Haber and Stornetta were writing at the beginning of the 1990s during the advent of mass online communications. A time when document tamper protection via the sorts of encrypted methods available today were either yet to come, or had not been integrated into mass user systems in the relatively seamless way they now are. There is perhaps, therefore, too stark a contrast to make between on- and offline documents in the contemporary information age. And yet the ascendency of blockchain is predicated in part on the perceived need of stakeholders to provide the as-yet-unrealised solution to precisely the problem Haber and Stornetta focused on. Namely, how the integrity of digital information exchanged over vast networks can be preserved and thus trust promoted between individuals and businesses who are operating at distance, with an 'absence in time and space' (Giddens, 1990, p. 33), and without any additional social and interrelational frameworks or structures in place, including domestic laws and regulations.

Timestamping must aim to achieve two key properties in Haber and Stornetta's proposal (1991, p. 100), both of which are equally relevant in the case of blockchain. First, timestamping data needs to be achieved 'without any reliance on the characteristics of the medium on which the data appears, so that it is impossible to change even one bit of the document without the change being apparent' (Haber and Stornetta, 1991, p. 100). This notion has obvious resonance with the *chained* basis of blockchain, where the aim is to protect the integrity of each block in relation to those before and after it and thus also the integrity of the whole. Blockchain advances this first part of Haber and Stornetta's proposal, as well as their own considerations of 'distributed trust' (1991, pp. 105–106), as a means of preventing collusion between clients including a possible centralised timestamping service (1991, p. 101), by distributing simultaneously updated versions of the same information or data (or document) across a number of individual computers or nodes that do not know each other, in order to provide 'a constantly updated, commonly agreed upon record of truth with no centralized master copy' (Casey and Vigna, 2018, p. 65).

To refer to the information in this context as a 'record of truth', as Casey and Vigna do, is interesting, however, because it clearly separates the notion of truth from that of fact. Timestamping, similar to constantly updated records or documents on blockchain, only ever reflects a one-dimensional view of data – that is, when it was added to a system or network, not whether the information is fact or objectively verifiable truth. This is the problem of *rubbish in/rubbish out*, and timestamping does not solve the issue, it only identifies when the information was added for the purposes of later verification. '[I]t only takes to run the algorithms on massive quantities of data to produce almost with magic some hypotheses about the world', argues Antoinette Rouvroy,

> these will not necessarily be verified but they will be operational and we have the impression to have reached the holy grail. We feel that we have reach [*sic*] the idea of a 'truth' but which, in order to establish itself, does not need to go through any ordeal, any investigation, or any exam and which to come about no longer depends on any event.
>
> (in Rouvroy and Stiegler, 2016, p. 10)

Blockchain, similarly, exacerbates the specious nature and quality of certain 'truths' because it does not easily allow data to be corrected or erased. This is the append-only or *immutable* function of blockchain whereby an entire history of entries or transactions remains on the network or in some other form of storage, and even when data is said to be deleted it never actually is. Accordingly, whilst narratives or other correctional mechanisms may be built around a specious 'truth' residing on a blockchain in order to attempt to nullify its effects, a record of its existence remains intact, something which may be of benefit in some instances but could quite as easily cause harm. We will return to the append-only or *immutable* function of blockchain architecture when considering the notion of the 'document' and blockchain's relationship. Briefly, however, it is worth noting that within the tradition of documentation is, like the rubbish in/rubbish out problem faced by blockchain applications, a failure to achieve a purpose in spite of immutability. Documents, like blockchain data, 'cannot know in advance how any conclusions they draw will be read', and this is a problem rooted in data 'ambiguity and uncertainty', for instance whether the data is comprehensive, accurate or current (Fenster, 2017, p. 113).

Where Haber and Stornetta attempt to remedy the issue of virtual truths, at least to some extent, lies in the second part of their proposal, namely, that 'it should be impossible to stamp a document with a time and data different from the actual one' (1991, p. 100). The informational symmetry between digital and hard-copy documents is important in their proposal because it pushes back against digitisation as an unreserved production of parallel (virtual) truths in cyberspace. This is a fascinating point given contemporary issues surrounding social media and online forums presently engaged in creating and disseminating so-called 'fake news'. As such, Haber and Stornetta's idea seems rather antiquated, an opportunity to keep on- and offline worlds in harmony that has clearly fallen by the wayside or perhaps been deliberately ousted in the urgency to develop greater and more pervasive digital ontologies.

The telling of blockchain

It is clear from the examples in *inter alia* Nakamoto's 'White Paper' and Swan's descriptions that a particular interplay of language and jargon flowing from the blockchain ecosystem is necessary to understand in order to 'get' blockchain. The nature of the language and jargon surrounding technology, whether new or old, including how clear or confusing it is, is vital to the quality the reception of that technology will have either by early adopters or later consumers. Like learning any new language or system of language, education plays a significant role in affecting overall reception and there have been no shortage of calls for the need to educate private and public sector actors alike about blockchain. For example, the UK government have highlighted education as a short- to medium-term need alongside the development of blockchain, something I have experienced as a contributor to the All Party Parliamentary Group on blockchain which first convened on 30 January 2018 – a group that itself used the report by the chief scientific advisor, in which it was stated that blockchain (distributed ledgers) requires 'a lot of education for recipients' (Government Office for Science, 2016, p. 67), as a launch pad. Nonetheless there are a number of other factors to take into consideration, not least what the language or jargon conceals or does not say. This is a similar, indeed interrelated, problem faced by designers of different layers of the Internet stack, whether at the user or infrastructure levels. 'Whenever something online appears to be simple, indeed whenever anything at all is done online', claim Katsh and Rabinovich-Einy,

> there is a great deal of complexity hiding somewhere in the background [...] the magic of software *hides* complexity, thus providing the users of well-deigned software with the illusion of simplicity. The interface may be simple to use but the infrastructure is anything but.
>
> (2017, p. 76)

Swan makes a similar point: 'new technology applications pass into public use without much further consideration of the technical details as long as appropriate, usable, trustable, frontend applications are developed' (2015, p.xiii). Terms such as 'spreadsheet' or 'ledger' conceal the fact that a blockchain is, to paraphrase Galloway, 'a decentralized network composed of many different data fragments' (2004, p. 64).

The telling of blockchain through definitions, descriptions, narratives and private and public discourse often presents the technology in convenient and recognisable material analogues, notably a ledger. As a ledger blockchain not only makes sense to a wider population by providing an accessible comparison for the layperson, but also situates blockchain within the *longue durée* of double-entry bookkeeping and thus technologies central to the normative performance of capitalism. The plain language of the ledger deliberately invokes tenets of auditability, accountancy and calculability therefore, in order to normalise and justify wider adoption of a technology primed to further render porous the line between consumer and citizen, capital and government, and so on. What is more, they consistently defer and disguise the opaqueness of computational know-how (*technê*), or that which is required to *know* blockchain. The language and vocabulary constituting blockchain narratives are as important as, if not more so than, the hard computation the technology performs. To echo Stuart Hall, the language of blockchain is the primary symbolic system used to give the social reality of the technology an intelligible form (2016, p. 59), and the necessity to account for the language of blockchain extends to thinking about regulation as well. Hence in a RAND Europe and British Standards Association 2017 report it was proposed that there was a need to focus on terminology and vocabulary as a short-term goal in determining the prospective role of standards to support the development of the technology (Deshpande et al., 2017, p.xiii).

Being central to the regulatory and legislative enterprise (something that would apply regardless of whether programming language, code, were used rather than natural languages), language is clearly an important factor in defining and thus determining blockchain ontologies as the technology continues to evolve. Angela Walch has identified this issue closely with the matter of blockchain hype and the need to overcome or cut through it, as well as the linked issue of how language (terminology and vocabulary) is crucial as regulators begin to contemplate assuming some control over the blockchain ecosystem. 'As blockchain technology has gained attention from the financial sector and others', claims Walch, 'its vocabulary has rapidly grown and changed. Copious jargon is used in the field, often imprecisely' (Walch, 2017, p. 10). She continues: 'Language in general is always on the move, but is particularly fluid around a fast-moving innovation such as blockchain technology. As the technology is tweaked, new terms are created to distinguish the new version from the old' (Walch, 2017, p. 11).

The importance of the language of blockchain is a matter that this book will return to at a number of different points, not least because, as stated above, language is central to the regulatory and legislative enterprise. What is more, language clearly helps stakeholders define *the good* with regard to technologies and the contexts in which they are applied. Language does, to echo Walch, serve in some instances to 'obscure reality and lead to misunderstandings' (2017, p. 15), meaning that what amounts to a notion of the good proposed via the language of the blockchain acolyte or stakeholder involves scant substance. The good in such instances, like the blockchain projects to which it applies, is little more than vapour, and tells us far more about the desire of the entrepreneur or stakeholder behind the project than serve as a categorical solution to a proposed problem (Swartz, 2017, p. 83). Furthermore, the regulators' job is made difficult by having to confront waves of hyperbolic language and swim against the tide, so to speak, in order to discern the facts 'buried beneath a muddle of impenetrable gibberish' (Walch, 2017, p. 15). The *form of appearance* blockchain assumes and the language or vocabulary used to create those appearances is crucial to understanding blockchain. Blockchain corresponds in that regard to what Alexander Galloway (following Marx) refers to as a 'social hieroglyphic': 'something that does not announce on its surface what it *is* on the inside' (2004, p. 99). Therefore the social hieroglyphic must be '*denaturalized*, demystified' (Galloway, 2004, p. 99), a notion of particular relevance here. Demystifying blockchain could mean exposing fully the complexities of the inner workings (something beyond the scope of this book). Equally, however, it means challenging and exposing the fantasies and illusions of the blockchain ecosystem and in particular the ways that stakeholders (and regulators) become intoxicated by technological fantasies and illusions, how they generate faith and belief in the technology and the desire to preach as legitimate 'truths' techno-social futurities.

For those determined that blockchain is the solution to whatever problem their tech start-up has identified, the growth in user-friendly interfaces has been crucial to the promotion of technology, not least because it conceals the true complexity of the technology. Galloway has referred to this same phenomenon in the term of the Internet as one of 'continuity' (2004, p. 64). 'Despite being a decentralized network composed of many different data fragments', claims Galloway,

> the Internet is able to use the application layer to create a compelling, intuitive experience for the user [...] Continuity is defined as the set of techniques practiced by webmasters that, taken as a totality, create this pleasurable, fluid experience for the user.
>
> (2004, p. 64)

This means, I suggest, a point where blockchain is seamlessly integrated into any number of use-cases and the invisibility of its moving parts assured. Concealment of a technology's underlying complexity with user-friendly interfaces is obviously not new, but occurs with almost all mainstream technologies. It is largely seen as uncontentious and many consumers of technology undoubtedly want and indeed celebrate the effectiveness of a clean, well-designed interface. As Melanie Swan suggests,

> it is not necessary to know how TCP/IP works in order to send an email, and new technology applications pass into public use without much further consideration of the technical details as long as appropriate, usable, trustable frontend applications are developed.
>
> (2015, p.xiii)

Concealment of any technology's underlying complexity presents interesting questions, however, not least with regard to tensions between know-how and ignorance – that is, between those who understand how a certain technology works and those who do not. Concealment in the form of user-friendly interfaces not only disguises a technology's complexity, it creates a deliberate power imbalance between those who are able to manipulate and shape technology, and those who merely become subject, albeit to varying degrees, to the influence the technology has over them. As Jaron Lanier suggests: 'This is basically a way of saying that the better your computer skills are, the more right you have to be a genuine individual in control of your own digital life' (2014, pp. 290–291). Calling blockchain a ledger or spreadsheet whilst enabling them to be built and applied in a vast array of use-cases via user-friendly interfaces is yet another example of the integration of a technology into the social domain in ways that few understand. Education is certainly one option to mitigate increases in tension between know-how and ignorance, yet who comes to define the form and nature of that education, as I have argued, is itself contentious. In lieu of individuals and communities having the opportunity to educate themselves in detail about the technologies that shape their everyday lives, it is vital that a robust and informed regulatory regime maintains political oversight on behalf of the many who do not enjoy the level of computer skills necessary to reach conclusions as to the nature and value of technologies such as blockchain to their lives.

'Ledger' terminology and references are key to narrative constructions and a form of telling of blockchain already enmeshed in a logic of political economy. Blockchain is for many stakeholders a marvel that finally realises the true liberal economic potentialities promised by online, peer-to-peer and networked technologies that have yet to be delivered. A technology that will in the fullness of time become a user-friendly means of guaranteeing individual ownership of personal data, enabling value to be realised through self-exploitation of one's personal data, and, importantly, a mode of auto-accountability: what I refer to as *blockchain governmentality*, and which situates blockchain squarely within patterns of neoliberal reason and logic.

References

Althusser, Louis. 2008. *On Ideology*. London: Verso.

Blanchette, Jean-François. 2012. *Burdens of Proof: Cryptographic Culture and Evidence Law in the Age of Electronic Documents*. Cambridge: The MIT Press.

Bok, Sissela. 1982. *Secrets: On the Ethics of Concealment and Revelation*. New York: Pantheon Books.

Brown, Ian and Marsden, Christopher T. 2013. *Regulating Code: Good Governance and Better Regulation in the Information Age*. Cambridge: The MIT Press.

Casey, Michael J. and Vigna, Paul. 2018. *The Truth Machine: The Blockchain and the Future of Everything*. London: HarperCollins.

Deshpande, Advait, Stewart, Katherine, Lepetit, Louise and Gunashekar, Salil. 2017. *Understanding the landscape of Distributed Ledger Technologies/Blockchain: Challenges, Opportunities, And The Prospects For Standards*. Cambridge: RAND Corporation.

Diffie, Whitfield and Hellman, Martin E. 1976. New Directions in Cryptography. *IEEE Transactions on Information Theory*, Vol. 22, No. 6, pp. 644–654.

The Economist. 2015. The trust machine, 31 October–6 November.

Factom. 2014. *Factom: Business Processes Secured by Immutable Audit Trails on the Block-chain, Version 1.0*, 17 November. www.factom.org (accessed 27 February 2018).

Fenster, Mark. 2017. *The Transparency Fix: Secrets, Leaks, and Uncontrollable Government Information*. Stanford: Stanford University Press.

Galloway, Alexander R. 2004. *Protocol: How Control Exists after Decentralization*. Cambridge: The MIT Press.

Giddens, Anthony. 1990. *The Consequences of Modernity*. Cambridge: Polity.

Government Office for Science. 2016. *Distributed Ledger Technology: beyond block chain*. www.gov.uk/government/uploads/system/uploads/attachment_data/file/492972/gs-16-1-distributed-ledger-technology.pdf (accessed 9 February 2016).

Haber, Stuart and Stornetta, W. Scott. 1991. How to Time-Stamp a Digital Document. *Journal of Cryptology*, Vol. 3, No. 2, pp. 99–111.

Hall, Stuart. 2016. *Cultural Studies 1983: A Theoretical History*. Edited by Jennifer Daryl Slack and Lawrence Grossberg. Durham: Duke University Press.

Harper, Colin. 2018. Making Sense of Proof of Work vs. Proof of Stake. *Coin Central*. 24 January. https://coincentral.com/making-sense-of-proof-of-work-vs-proof-of-stake/ (accessed 25 May 2018).

Harvey, David. 2005. *A Brief History of Neoliberalism*. Oxford: Oxford University Press.

Jameson, Fredric. 2002. *The Political Unconscious: Narrative as a Socially Symbolic Act*. London: Routledge.

Katsh, Ethan and Rabinovich-Einy, Orna. 2017. *Digital Justice: Technology and the Internet of Disputes*. Oxford: Oxford University Press.

Knobel, Andres. 2017. Technology and online beneficial ownership registries: Easier to create companies and better at preventing financial crime. *Tax Justice Network*, 1 June. https://papers.ssrn.com/sol3/papers.cfm?abstract_id=2978757 (accessed 8 May 2018).

Lanier, Jaron. 2014. *Who Owns the Future?* London: Penguin.

Latour, Bruno. 2002. Morality and Technology: The Ends of the Means. Translated by Couze Venn. *Theory, Culture & Society*, Vol. 19, No. 5/6, pp. 247–260.

Lessig, Lawrence. 2006. *Code: Version 2.0*. New York: Basic Books.

Morozov, Evgeny. 2014. *To Save Everything, Click Here: Technology, Solutionism and the Urge to Fix Problems that Don't Exist*. London: Penguin.

Nakamoto, Satoshi. 2008. *Bitcoin: A Peer-to-Peer Electronic Cash System*. https://bitcoin.org/bitcoin.pdf (accessed 18 January 2018).

Pasquale, Frank. 2015. *The Black Box Society: The Secret Algorithms that Control Money and Information*. Cambridge: Harvard University Press.

Ponicano, Jonathan. 2017. Blockchain Tops $4.5 Billion In Private Funding This Year, But Deal Growth Stalls. *Forbes*, 22 September. www.forbes.com/sites/jonathanponciano/2017/09/22/blockchain-tops-4-5-billion-in-private-funding-this-year-but-deal-growth-stalls/#1bb344ef74c6 (accessed 27 February 2018).

Proulx, Serge. 2012. Information Technology as Political Catalyst: From Technological Innovation to the Promotion of Social Change. *Connecting Canadians: Investigations in Community Informatics*. Edited by A. Clement, M. Gurstein, G. Longford, M. Moll and L. Shade. Edmonton, AB: AU Press, pp. 105–116.

Rouvroy, Antoinette and Stiegler, Bernard. 2016. The Digital Regime of Truth: From the Algorithmic Governmentality to a New Rule of Law. *La Deleuziana – Online Journal of Philosophy*, No. 3, pp. 6–29. www.ladeleuziana.org/2016/11/14/3-life-and-number/ (accessed 14 May 2018).

Rowley, Jason. 2018. 2018 VC Investment into Crypto Startups Set to Surpass 2017 Tally. *TechCrunch*, 3 March. https://techcrunch.com/2018/03/03/2018-vc-investment-into-crypto-startups-set-to-surpass-2017-tally/ (accessed 14 May 2018).

Swan, Melanie. 2015. *Blockchain: Blueprint for a New Economy*. Sebastopol: O'Reilly.

Swartz, Lana. 2017. *Blockchain Dreams: Imagining Techno-economic Alternatives after Bitcoin. Another Economy is Possible*. Edited by Manuel Castells. Cambridge: Polity Press, pp. 82–105.

Tapscott, Don and Tapscott, Alex. 2016. *Blockchain Revolution: How the Technology behind Bitcoin is Changing Money, Business and the World*. London: Portfolio Penguin.

Walch, Angela. 2017. Blockchain's Treacherous Vocabulary: One More Challenge for Regulators. *Journal of Internet Law*, Vol. 21, No. 2, pp. 9–16.

Interlude I: Supplementing the memory economic

... Wampum, memex, transcopyright, blockchain ...

Blockchain technology is a highly reliable witness to ideas and events; in that sense it bears no relation to the fallibility of human memory whilst maintaining an inescapable dialogue with it. Blockchain records and (re)presents data, appends and witnesses, (de)materialises and (re)configures, and does so in ways that both reflect existing Internet capabilities and intensify them, for purposes that are primarily economic, but nevertheless result in social, cultural and political consequences.

As a product of human ingenuity blockchain supplements human memory only as far as it supplements hypertext, the Internet, online applications, all networked capabilities already at play with configuring memory and memorialisation across time and space. In so doing blockchain offers a potent contribution, a new verse in social narratives and ontological pathologies on (the problematic of) forgetting, of forgetfulness and of the reflexive efforts of techno-social subjects and communities to cope with and to live up to the demands of information saturation and overload. To do so in an attempt to preserve knowledge, structure truth, and discern meaning from the white noise of global information networks and the blur of the mass data unconscious toward which we all now enunciate and gesture.

Blockchain (inter)weaves techno-social becoming and forges new paradigms of forgetfulness, not new capacities for remembering. It continues long-standing traditions of human technique and experiment aimed at supplementing but above all *preserving* memory; making memory better, more expansive, more accountable, more visceral, more powerful, but always outside being. Blockchain is not the first and it will not be the last technology practically employed or conceptually devised for these ends, nor will it be the last technology to adapt the perceived failures and missed opportunities of its forerunners.

Wampum

Wampum is a small, short, tubular bead, made from the quahog clam shell. The white beads are made from the inner whorl of the shell, and the purple beads come from the dark spot or 'eye' on the shell.

Dating back one thousand years, wampum and other material components (e.g., bark fibers, sinew, hemp fibers, string – or other weaving materials) have been used by Woodlands Indians for ceremony and as records of important civil affairs (e.g., alliances, treaties, marriage proposals, ceremonies, wars, etc.) by stringing the wampum beads together on individual strands or weaving them into belts. Thus wampum serves as a sign technology that has been used to record hundreds of years of alliances within tribes, between tribes and between the tribal governments and colonial government.

According to Tehanetorens, the coastal Indians were the first to make and use wampum, but through trade with other tribes, it travelled to the interior and western regions of the continent. Post-contact, wampum was also appropriated by American colonists, who used it as their first form of currency in colonial 'America'. Further, it was the wampum of the Iroquois Confederacy (Mohawks, Oneidas, Onondagas, Senecas and Cayugas) that influenced the democratic thought that led to the Constitution of the United States. Wampum strings and belts served to engender further diplomatic relations, and their presentation was a gesture that required reciprocity on the part of the recipient. Consequently, accepting a gift of wampum meant that the recipient accepted its implied message and responsibility. Wampum records are maintained by regularly revisiting and re-'reading' them through community memory and performance, as wampum is a living rhetoric that communicates a mutual relationship between two or more parties, despite the failure of one of those parties to live up to that promise (which we know was the result of most wampum treaties with the colonists). Thus wampum embodies memory, as it extends human memories of inherited knowledges via interconnected, nonlinear designs with associative message storage and retrieval methods.

(Haas, 2007, pp. 78–81)

Memex

Consider a future device for individual use, which is a sort of mechanized private file and library. It needs a name, and, to coin one at random, 'memex' will do. A memex is a device in which an individual stores all his books, records, and communications, and which is mechanized so that it may be consulted with exceeding speed and flexibility. It is an enlarged intimate supplement to his memory [...]

Most of the memex contents are purchased on microfilm ready for insertion. Books of all sorts, pictures, current periodicals, newspapers, are thus obtained and dropped into place. Business correspondence takes the same path. And there is provision for direct entry. On the top of the memex is a transparent platen. On this are placed longhand notes, photographs, memoranda, all sorts of things. When one is in place, the depression of a lever causes it to be photographed onto the next blank space in a section of the memex film, dry photography being employed.

There is, of course, provision for consultation of the record by the usual scheme of indexing. If the user wishes to consult a certain book, he taps its code on the keyboard, and the title page of the book promptly appears before him, projected onto one of his viewing positions. Frequently used codes are mnemonic, so that he seldom consults his code book; but when he does, a single tap of a key projects it for his use. Moreover, he has supplemental levers. On deflecting one of these levers to the right he runs through the book before him, each page in turn being projected at a speed which just allows a recognizing glance at each. If he deflects it further to the right, he steps through the book 10 pages at a time; still further at 100 pages at a time. Deflection to the left gives him the same control backwards.

A special button transfers him immediately to the first page of the index. Any given book of his library can thus be called up and consulted with far greater facility than if it were taken from a shelf. As he has several projection positions, he can leave one item in position while he calls up another. He can add marginal notes and comments, taking advantage of one possible type of dry photography, and it could even be arranged so that he can do this by a stylus scheme, such as is now employed in the telautograph seen in railroad waiting rooms, just as though he had the physical page before him.

(Bush, 1945)

Transcopyright

My style of hypertext would allow you to create your own mesh of insightful structures in a live document, as you explore. A document is not a file and nor is it necessarily a sequence. It is a structure. The central feature of the Xanadu system I proposed in the 1960s is that when a document quotes another, it pulls in the actual text from the source, wherever that lives. I call this 'transclusion'.

That implies that anyone posting a Xanadu document grants the world a licence to quote from it, charging the reader a one-time fee if they wish – a principle I call 'transcopyright'. The links are two-way: each document links back to all the places that quote it. And, crucially, it can all be dynamic. Every change you make is immediately propagated and clarified and resolved. The document is never out of date.

Transclusion would make a huge difference. You could follow through from a comment someone put on your page to see at once what they said to everyone else, and then ask 'Is is [*sic*] it only me you love or are you spamming everyone else?'

With transcopyright, artists could start to make a living. I have a friend who hears her albums played on the radio and the musicians' collecting societies say they can't pay her because the number of plays is 'statistically insignificant'. Micro-sales might be a huge market, but we don't know until we try.

(Nelson, 2006, pp. 54–55)

References

Bush, Vannevar. 1945. As We May Think. *The Atlantic Monthly*, July. www.theatlantic.com/magazine/archive/1945/07/as-we-may-think/303881/ (accessed 18 May 2018).

Haas, Angela M. 2007. Wampum as Hypertext: An American Indian Intellectual Tradition of Multimedia Theory and Practice. *Studies in American Indian Literatures*, Vol. 19, No. 4 (Winter), pp. 77–100.

Nelson, Ted. 2006. It Could All Be So Much Better. *New Scientist*, 16 September, pp. 54–55.

2 A regulatory conundrum

Introduction

> Code is no more neutral than regulation, with each subject to monopoly and capture by commercial interests.
>
> (Brown and Marsden, 2013, p. xix)

> [L]aw and legal reason not only give form to the economic, but economize new spheres and practices. In this way, law becomes a medium for disseminating neoliberal rationality beyond the economy, including to constitutive elements of democratic life. More than simply securing the rights of capital and structuring competition, neoliberal juridical reason recasts political rights, citizenship, and the field of democracy itself in an economic register.
>
> (Brown, 2015, pp. 151–152)

> The current patchwork of regulation applied to businesses using decentralized ledger technology is compromised by its inability to adapt to the technology, its inefficient mechanisms for responding to market and governance failures, and it overwhelming tendency to quash innovation in the name of preventing crime and protecting consumers.
>
> (Reyes, 2016, p. 233)

Over the course of the next two chapters we will examine the regulating of blockchain technology, the blockchain ecosystem and the forms of conduct the technology produces or will potentially produce. Whilst regulating blockchain is not a straightforward matter, it can be guaranteed that the ecosystem and its aims and products will eventually become the subject of and shaped by the force (or lack thereof) of regulations. At present national jurisdictions are competing in the hope of becoming what Kevin Warbach has called, 'the Silicon Valley of the crypto economy' (2018, p. 40), and this is, I argue, not a positive step for long-term regulatory need or requirement. As within each jurisdiction, as well as straddling many of them, are numerous private commercial actors seeking to leverage the competitive furore surrounding the so-called fourth industrial revolution by providing legal and regulatory solutions to the problems it is creating as well as those it has inherited. As Jake Goldenfein and Andrea Leiter maintain: 'Groups like the

Ethereum Legal Alliance, Mattereum, Open Law, Clause.io, Agrello, the R3 Consortium, Common Accord, and Legalese' are defining 'the entire envelope of computational legal conduct' on blockchain (2018, p. 144).[1]

Classic regulatory conundrums turn on the extent to which regulatees are compliant or can be made to be compliant in the future. Where they are not, and this is already evident amid the excitement of new technologies such as blockchain, regulators try to 'minimise resistance *ex ante* or have a strategy for dealing with it *ex post*' (Brownsword and Goodwin, 2012, p. 62). Regulators traditionally draw on different combinations of law (case law, legislation, judicial review, etc.), regulation (existing forms of regulation or substantive and general regulatory principles), and governance (non-legal but not necessarily less formal modes of command and control), in order to achieve *ex ante* and *ex post* regulatory outcomes. Insofar as those are distinguishable options that can mixed and matched as the regulatory setting requires, the three give structure to new regulatory regimes or alternatively mobilise existing structures capable of absorbing certain regulatory targets: behaviours, forms of conduct and the material effects of technology.[2] Further, 'social solidarity can play different roles in regulation', claims Tony Prosser:

> one is to create the essential social underpinning of mutual trust and expectation which is necessary for markets to function [...] the second role of the social solidarity-based approach is, however, to prevent or limit the socially fragmenting role of markets.
>
> (2010, p. 16)

In the United Kingdom mainstream regulatory patterns extend across a wide range of public, private, as well as hybrid regulatory environments. These include: financial services (banking, markets and insurance); utilities (water, gas, electricity); communications (fibre broadband infrastructure, Internet, etc.); and transport (railway infrastructure and delivery, etc.) (Prosser, 2010). This has led to a regulatory mesh that covers a heterogeneity of private and public regulatory needs. Forty years of neoliberalism in Britain and around the world has, however, greatly impacted regulatory environments, and in particular the force regulators are able to bring to those environments. During this period, as Stuart Hall stresses, regulators have 'lacked teeth, political courage, leverage or an alternative social philosophy, and were often playing on both sides of the street' (2017, p. 327). Hence in the blockchain and wider technology sectors, to recall Warbach, governments and regulators have become enamoured with the economics of forging the next Silicon Valley in their jurisdiction, rather than critically confronting the social and political ramifications of technology and fulfilling meaningful, socially

---

1 Mattereum is a particularly interesting case because it was established by Vinay Gupta who has been vocal about the 'chaos' of entrepreneurial practices in the blockchain ecosystem and, specifically, the dominant role played by 'rule by entrepreneur', namely, loose forms of self-regulation (2017).

2 For an outline of the 'regulatory environment' broken down into composite parts of regulation, law and governance, see: Brownsword and Goodwin, 2012, pp. 24–26.

aware regulatory needs. The issues Hall identifies are central to the analysis in this chapter, including the extent to which government, law and regulators have allowed and are continuing to allow free-market economic principles and the managerial doctrines of public choice theory to act as guide in reaching conclusions and developing regulatory frameworks. In order to foster a regulatory environment that favours generosity over self-interest would require greater seismic shifts in regulatory theories and practices than those either relevant to the blockchain ecosystem or, indeed, able to be addressed by this book. Nonetheless, approaching the regulation of blockchain as *politically* necessary, as this book ultimately aims to do, gives, as Hall argues with regard to challenging neoliberalism more broadly, 'resistance content, focus and a cutting edge' (2017, p. 318).

Mainstream regulators are not well positioned at present to enable or empower 'alternative social philosophies' (Hall, 2017, p. 327), namely, those geared towards community and generosity rather than markets, greed and self-interest. In a shamelessly loaded question, Brown and Marsden ask whether there are 'solutions that may be effective ex ante to ensure the development of technologies that do not act against the public interest, without stifling innovation and introducing bureaucratic interventionist regulation to an area that has blossomed without it?' (Brown and Marsden, 2013, p. 33). Their response is to accept that this would mean technology companies being forced to avoid 'the economic determinism of belief in the invisible hand of the market' (Brown and Marsden, 2013, p. 33). Regulating blockchain, especially via forms of regulation rooted in public interest, political feasibility and democratic oversight, must not retreat from challenging the hegemony of commercial and consumer models that Brown and Marsden highlight albeit in a rather unfavourable light. A process of hegemony premised on the rights of 'private capital to "grow the business", improve share value, pay dividends and reward its agents with enormous salaries, benefits and bonuses' (Hall, 2017, p. 319), and driven by those who advocate stimulating consumption because 'they want neither to hear nor speak about the end of consumerism' (Stiegler, 2010, p. 4).

'Regulatory competition is said to provide the flexibility for jurisdictions to develop standards to match the local requirements (whether political or technical)', claim Murray and Scott, 'the capacity to innovate in regulation while encouraging states to adopt rules of minimum necessary burden on business or others (because of the threat that such regulatory clients might shift their business elsewhere)' (2002, pp. 509–510). At stake from continued ineffectual public interest regulation, or as a direct result of putting private interest ahead of public interest so that 'no clear boundary separates the state from the private entities with which it works to regulate and deliver services' (Fenster, 2017, p. 91), is, therefore, the further triumph of and auto-deferral to the specious logic of free markets, with all the corresponding erosion of the state's capacity for intervention and reduction of political feasibility that entails. Whilst it may be argued that 'regulatory history is replete with evidence of the practical difficulties resulting from shoehorning decentralized ledger technologies, related applications and the businesses that offer products and services related to them into a regulatory scheme first designed for centralized technologies' (Reyes, 2016, p. 191), a case for state-led regulation must nevertheless be made, and, moreover, threats of regulatory arbitrage, as raised by Murray and Scott, called out and confronted. 'The state regulates by determining the parameters of the technical system and the correlative evolution of the social systems through negotiation, forecasting and planning, that is, through long-term organization of technological and industrial becoming', argues Bernard Stiegler, more importantly, and in agreement with the position outlined above, 'it must equally ensure the possibility of research independent of private investment, which is short-termist when compared with intergenerational social time' (2010, p. 100). This is not at present a position reflective of blockchain regulatory debates or actions, but this chapter aims to open up just such debates.

Regulating blockchain

In *The Regulatory Enterprise*, Tony Prosser proposes two regulatory visions at once in dialogue and polar opposition (2010, p. 4), as well as acknowledging a degree of hybridity constituting regulatory environments and spaces of control, something which influential voices in technology regulation, namely Lawrence Lessig, have been accused of underplaying in order to assert the argument 'that there is considerable novelty to the nature of law in Cyberspace' (Murray and Scott, 2002, p. 504). There is a 'major distinction', claims Prosser, 'between regulation as infringement of private autonomy and regulation as a collaborative enterprise' (2010, p. 4), and this, I suggest, is applicable to the blockchain regulatory conundrum.[3] For present purposes the former, an emphasis on autonomy, can be said to accord with a vision of blockchain put forward by the ecosystem based on neoliberal market-complementing regulation, economic efficiency and self-interest, and what Prosser further refers to as 'regulation for economic efficiency and consumer choice' (2010, p. 18). In his discussion of liberty and trust

---

3   The distinction is made more apparent when the nature of different blockchains is taken into consideration. Namely, *permissioned ledgers*, which, as the name suggests, are designed for use on closed, private systems by those with the requisite permissions (e.g. to create a 'transparent' and 'immutable' information and data audit trail *within* the confines of a global corporation); in contrast to permissionless ledgers like the Bitcoin blockchain which maintain a public character and are therefore more open to scrutiny. A great deal of research, development and subsequent discussion surrounding actual use-cases for blockchain technology has now moved on to the role of permissioned ledgers for back-office functions in, for example, banking systems. The irony of this given the initial libertarian aspirations the technology was said to engender (i.e. the avoidance of centralised financial institutions) is unmistakable. As David Golumbia remarks, this irony is symptomatic of 'a reassertion of the political power that the blockchain is specifically constructed to dismantle' (2016, p. 76; see also, Herian, 2016, 2018). Moreover, as Lana Swartz has argued, the 'incorporative blockchain' of back-office functions is no longer pursuing the libertarian dream of holistically remaking society, but is in fact quite 'boring' (Swartz, 2017, p. 96), in the sense that it has very quickly fallen into step with the needs and desires of big business.

within a (neo)liberal moral and legal framework, Joseph Raz defines autonomy or the 'capacity for valuable autonomous life' as a 'double-side duty' (or what might otherwise be deemed a deliberate contradiction), requiring 'government to stand back and let people have the choice as to how to conduct their own lives', but equally government taking 'active steps, where needed, to ensure that people enjoy the basic capacities (physical and mental) and have the resources to avail themselves of an adequate range of options available in their society' (1996, p. 113). On the other hand, the latter, regulation as a collaborative enterprise, enables political, social or distributive feasibility, community and generosity (Cohen, 2011, pp. 217–219), or what Prosser aligns to 'regulation for social solidarity' and 'regulation as deliberation' (2010, p. 18). A fourth regulatory framework highlight by Prosser concerns the protection of rights (2010, p. 18); regulation rooted in domestic and transnational legislative frameworks, as well as international law and treaties, which do not necessarily favour either the polarity of markets and self-interest or community and generosity unless predisposed to do so by law.

Cutting across each of the positivist regulatory frameworks, however, is a natural law tradition and a potential for equity that aims at mollifying the harder edges of the regulatory enterprise and arguably underscoring the deliberative conditions that Prosser touches on. It is here that we can locate 'the good' in relation to blockchain, although it is important, not least given regulatory uncertainty that is central to the blockchain regulatory conundrum, to understand the role the good plays when applied to the regulation of blockchain, rather than simply notions of the good free-flowing from the blockchain ecosystem as a product of particular techno-economic concepts and use-cases – a notion of the good that arguably accords with 'an empty space into which human choice may move' (Murdoch, 2001, p. 95). Notions of the good drawn from *inter alia* Plato, Aristotle and Hobbes are instructive here, as is, with particular regard to Prosser's fourth regulatory framework, translation of the good as a moral determination of justice to a regime of enforceable (contractual) rights. In the background, however, it is important to remember the problems created by attempting to pin down the good. As Iris Murdoch maintains, the concept of the good 'remains obscure and mysterious', and we all 'see the world in the light of the Good, but what', she asks, 'is the Good itself?' (2001, p. 95).

While Plato and Aristotle rejected the good as rooted in subjectivism, both maintain the import of human nature in defining what goods are or ought to be. For Plato the role of human nature 'is not to define or set the good, but merely to define what the possibilities of human achievement are' (Murphy, 2011). Similarly, Aristotle holds that,

> what makes it true that something is good is not that it stands in some relation to desire but rather that it is somehow *perfective* or *completing* of a being, where what is perfective of completing of a being depends on the being's nature.
>
> (Murphy, 2011)

In contrast Hobbes forefronts desire in determinations of the good, and it is this form that arguably best describes the sorts of regulatory process that will be discussed later, notably around self-regulation. Subjectivist theories of the good make true what is good as that which is desired or liked, and thus the good for Hobbes always returns to notions of self-preservation which manifest clearly in, for example, efforts to forestall legislation that restricts the global investment practices of technology titans like Google, and lead them instead to enter into self-regulation pacts (Deibert and Rohozinski, 2010, p. 10) in order to retain control within the limits of self-interest.

Also, brief mention of the shift from good to right is important here because it is fundamentally a continuation of an enlightenment colonisation of economic rationality over all social life, whereby contract is the ultimate arbiter of human interrelatedness negating the need for honesty or trust to flourish outside of contractual domains and agreements. Conditions, moreover, which are further reinforced by a suite of contractual remedies that insist on performance as well as compensation and damages. Equity as body of law, in this sense, arguably preserves contractual domains whilst countermanding the resilience of non-contractual social relations and status. The importance of contract in the blockchain context cannot be overstated, not least because of the importance placed on the burgeoning field of so-called 'smart contracts' (as well as 'secret contracts') as a new and potentially global modern contractual regime-in-waiting. Smart contracts are certainly not capable of supplanting contract law as we presently find it, but the hope of many stakeholders is that they soon will. Melanie Swan, for instance, addresses the matter via her usual problem/solution matrix. 'Contracts do not make anything possible that was previously impossible', she claims, 'rather, they allow common problems to be solved in a way that minimizes the need for trust. Minimal trust often makes things more convenient by taking human judgement out of the equation, thus allowing complete automation' (2015, p. 17). For Swan, therefore, the journey from an ethics rooted in human discretion (morality, equity, natural law and so on), to enlightenment social rationalisation in the form of contract is *perfected* by blockchain, to recall the Aristotelian notion of the good, and the opportunity for full automation of contractual agreements and the rendering *autonomous* of all forms of human interrelatedness over which contract has long principally held sway. And recalling Hobbes, Swan also suggests that 'smart contracts impact not just contract law, but more broadly the notion of the social contract within society' (2015, p. 17).

We will return to smart contracts again briefly later. For the time being, however, it is important to note that what Swan and others in the blockchain ecosystem are proposing is not so much radical due to novelty – contract long ago shifted the texture of social interactions and as an offline and off-chain technology has been supremely successful, perhaps more so than blockchain and smart contracts are ever likely to be. Instead, radicalism is to be found in the apparent attempt within the blockchain ecosystem to forge a linkage between a metaphysic of 'the good' and the instrumental performativity inherent to contractual status. Moreover that this connection should be made by machines and software *automatically* and *autonomously* rather than as a precondition of human needs, rights and desires, thus skewing and intertwining the logic of 'the good' and contract. 'A technological innovation may know long periods of stagnation or regression', Félix Guattari argues, 'but there are few cases in which it does not "restart" at a later date' (1995, p. 40). The suggestion here is not that the technology or mode of legal technique of contract has not been anything but alarmingly present throughout modernity. What has amounted and continues to amount to the good, in comparison, is more contentious. Yet smart contracts may well indicate a *restart* of contract and especially in the performativity of *contracting*, as implied by Guattari, through (re)alignment with 'the good', although the consequences of this remain unknown and potentially hard to determine.

The current task of understanding what *regulating blockchain* means or ought to mean is occurring against a backdrop of continuing struggles to achieve stable regulation and governance of commercial platforms, within networks and in consideration of interoperability and the broader architecture of the Internet. Few, it might be said, would argue that Internet regulations have succeeded in producing universally held 'good' behaviour or conduct. The questions, problems and so on that blockchain brings to the fore are not easily abstracted from concerns that continue to plague regulation of Internet-based networks and systems, and from the perspective of capital these concerns often coagulate around perceived and actual systemic inefficiencies that technologies bring to bear. There is a phylogenetic evolution of network technologies, in which blockchain can be included, exposed to formal and informal (customary) standards and benchmarks for improving efficiency gains in business (and beyond), with any subsequent determinations of effectiveness those technologies herald linked directly and primarily to net gains in economic efficiency. This emphasis on efficiency is arguably a product of neoliberalism generally, although Michael Power attributes it more specifically to the audit culture that has matured during the last 40 years of neoliberalism. 'At the level of these technologies', claims Power, 'practitioners constantly debate the efficiency of different methods and seek to elaborate cost-efficient solutions to the problem of providing assurance' (1997, p. 7). 'Accordingly', he concludes 'even audit techniques are surrounded by sub-programmes and meta-discourses about their potential. *Technical practice cannot be disentangled from the stories which are told of its capability and possibility*' [emphasis added] (1997, p. 7).

Further, as Brownsword argues:

> one of the facts of regulatory life is that there is no easy way out of deep moral disagreement. It is a problem that has taxed moral and political philosophers; and it is a problem that will continue to plague the regulation of new technologies.
>
> (2008, p. 294)

Shortcomings in Internet regulation remain stubbornly apparent some 30 years into the mass adoption of the technology (Brown and Marsden, 2013; Mueller, 2013; Pasquale, 2015; Srnicek, 2017). The hows and whys of blockchain regulation now form part of, but have also arguably intensified, the broader regulatory conundrum started by the Internet. There are a number of reasons for this claim. Of most interest here, however, is one that concerns the co-evolution of technology and economy and, importantly, associated cultural and political ramifications, and how regulatory environments, enterprise and rationale address them. If, for example, it is true that the 'economy is an expression of its technologies' (Arthur, 2009, p. 193), it is equally so, I claim, that technologies are the expression of economic will, and the present blockchain moment is both illustrative *and* symptomatic of the latter, rather than the former.

Disrupting regulation

The emergence of so-called blockchain 'disruption' within the contemporary political and economic moment calls to mind Joseph Schumpeter's notion of *creative destruction* (Schumpeter, 2010). In the hands of quasi-libertarian, self-interested and, what Vinay Gupta (2017) has called, 'chaotic' entrepreneurs, this creative destruction has led, in the main, to myriad attempts at re-imagining (*not* disrupting) legacy financial systems over the last decade using cryptocurrencies within the scope of capitalism. The desire now is to repeat the process in an array of non-currency-based, normatively civic arenas such as e-voting, land registries and health records (Tapscott and Tapscott, 2016). In practice this means growth in blockchain-based private/public partnerships, or to put it another way, an upsurge in tendering for *privatisation* of forms of public administration that will put many more future data controllers beyond direct political accountability (private corporate actors not being publicly elected officials). So-called blockchain 2.0 and 3.0 projects are thus following a model of evolving capital-led projects: from those of a classical liberal economic age in which capital was front and centre in all modes of business, commerce and industry, to the more ambiguous and obscure role capital now plays in the strategies of misdirection and sleights of hand of neoliberalism. Amid shifts in economic/regulatory models the role of regulators has been amplified by the perverse matrix of behaviours and attitudes these technologies have created and continue to create. But regulation is also being denied, resisted and sent into retreat based on the idea that centralised government authorities and regulators are ill-equipped and ill-prepared for the task of dealing with technology or high levels of chaos and white noise emanating from the blockchain ecosystem.

The so-called 'wait and see' or the somewhat more proactive 'wait and monitor' approaches to regulation adopted by the likes of the European Commission (Singh, 2017) are symptomatic not of a reasonable approach to blockchain, but, I argue, of an unwillingness by governments to muster the energy, let alone the resources, to challenge private self-interest. 'Drawing up regulations for blockchain at this early stage would be a mistake', argued *The Economist* in 2015:

> the history of peer-to-peer technology suggests that it is likely to be several years before the technology's full potential becomes clear. In the meantime

regulators should stay their hands, or find ways to accommodate new approaches within existing frameworks, rather than risk stifling a fast-evolving idea with overly prescriptive rules.

(2015, p. 13)

Narratives of regulatory weakness such as the one presented by *The Economist* and disseminated by technology ecosystems like that of blockchain are being accepted by governments and regulators as fundamental truths. Further, practices of rhetoric and persuasion have enabled competition and markets to intercede and translate regulatory frameworks and techniques in their own image. Standardisation, for example, whilst considered *contra* the interests of devotees of free markets who 'characterize regulation as simply an unnecessary cost to business', is nevertheless only good at the end of the day for delivering economies of scale that will be of benefit to ever larger markets (Zetzsche et al., 2017, p. 52).

Again there is nothing new about any of this. What is happening around blockchain is merely a continuation of regulatory trends that have remained constant for at least 40 years, except, perhaps, during the collapse of public confidence wrought by the 2008 financial crisis which forced governments to change tack from fewer to more (apparent) regulations (Zetzsche et al., 2017, pp. 47–50). In the context of technology, the change in regulatory bias notably occurred within financial services and created the outgrowth of FinTech (financial technologies) and RegTech (regulatory technologies) respectively. However, this resulted in greater commitments by governments to innovationist narratives and working with a reserve army of entrepreneurs prepared to play in 'sandboxes'. This sandbox culture as the *sine qua non* of contemporary regulatory standoffishness at the state level has ultimately spawned the problematic regulatory conundrum with which we are now faced, one in which innovationism and solutionism have been legitimised.

Attempts by entrepreneurs to leverage personal, self-interested gains through the re-imaging of various legacy systems, are occurring at the fuzzy edges of transnational regulatory understanding and leading to the threat of regulatory disorientation, whereby focus is stuck on 'centralized actors in a decentralized ecosystem' and therefore 'will not be able to keep pace' (Reyes, 2016, p. 221). Jurisdictions have as a consequence reacted at different speeds, some slow, others with more urgency, especially in the case of cryptocurrency regulation, which has included in some cases outright bans on the trading and possibly also on the use of cryptocurrency.[4] But as yet the majority of jurisdictions have said little and done less to define or impose limits on blockchain specifically, nor on its ecosystem or the conduct produced by it. This 'wait and see' approach, it would appear, is a

---

4 The UK and EU are both presently considering the need to regulate cryptocurrency in order to address problems of anonymity apropos money laundering and tax evasion. Other nations, South Korea for instance, are also planning to ban cryptocurrency trading for the same reasons. See for example: Kollewe, 2017.

longer-term project, a fact that is only welcome if that means serious critical scrutiny of the technology is undertaken in the meantime (Walch, 2017, p. 14).

Where it is a problem, however, is twofold: first, where the wait and see policy is beholden to forms of innovationism or creates a vacuum that innovationism quickly fills – something often made clear by calls from entrepreneurs and other stakeholders for government not to stifle innovation;[5] second, in allowing a lag between law, regulation and governance and blockchain to grow in the interim. Both problems, which largely intersect, repeat the shortcomings and mistakes of Internet regulation which have led to the explicit dominance of big data business and the mass commercialisation of cyberspace on the one hand, and a parallel ungovernable 'dark net' on the other. Whether the problem is seen as central (legitimate and notionally legal big data business), or peripheral (dark web as shadow or black markets), there is a clear shared dialogue between the innovative capabilities of the technologies in use. Ironically, if we follow Ilkka Tuomi's (2002) definition of innovation as relating to technologies that lead to tangible change in social practices, it is more likely than not that the peripheral uses innovate first and further. Milton Mueller (2017) reinforces this point, whilst also simultaneously celebrating innovation and highlighting failures in Internet regulation and governance. 'It has become a cliché', says Mueller,

> to note that the 'unified and unfragmented space' created by the victory of the Internet protocols was filled not only with *innovative economic and social activity*, but also with the crimes and conflicts that accompany human interactions in every other space.
>
> [emphasis added] (2017, p. 11)

Thus, Mueller concludes, '[a]long with the innovations, efficiencies, and creative new forms of entertainment and interaction came thieves, bullies, fraudsters, child abusers, spies, vandals' (2017, p. 11).

Whilst blockchain may not be considered a particularly risky technology in terms of potential threats or harms it poses to individuals or communities – compare this with, for example, cautionary tales surrounding 'the malign aspect of technology' (Arthur, 2009, p. 215) that includes perceived threats from bioengineering, artificial intelligence and nanotechnologies (Brownsword, 2008) – this does not mean that *no* threats or harms exist. Instead these manifest in other, more subtle ways. There are, for instance, conceivable threats and harms posed by the blockchain ecosystem in further entrenching and disseminating neoliberal ideology. For neoliberal stakeholders and those complacent about the ill effects of social and political control wrought by 'free-market' economics, this is unlikely to

---

5   The European Commission is illustrative again here, where both Eva Kaili and the German European People's Party group Member of the European Parliament Jacob von Weizsäcker have backed regulatory approaches that do not 'regulate too early, so as to avoid stifling innovation' (Singh, 2017).

sound like a threat at all. For this class of stakeholder blockchain remains, for the better, 'an institutional technology to decentralize the governance structures used to coordinate people and economic decision making' (Aste et al., 2017). If, however, neoliberal ideology is grounded in what Stuart Hall called the anachronism of 'the free, possessive individual, with state cast as tyrannical and oppressive', whereby the state 'must not intervene in the "natural" mechanisms of the free market, or take as its objective the amelioration of free-market capitalism's propensity to create inequality' (2017, p. 318), then what is at stake in the regulatory decisions that foster or mitigate *more* neoliberalism in the blockchain context ought to be clear, questioned and ultimately challenged, because they *do* represent threats and the potential for harm.

G.A. Cohen is less forgiving than Hall in the language he chooses to criticise markets, but the conclusions the two reach are nevertheless in accord:

> The immediate motive to productive activity in a market society is typically some mixture of greed and fear, in proportions that vary with the details of a person's market position and personal character. In greed, other people are seen as possible sources of enrichment, and in fear they are seen as threats. These are horrible ways of seeing other people, however much we have become habituated and inured to them, as a result of centuries of capitalist development.
>
> (2011, pp. 217–218)

Cohen is robust in his critique of free-market ideology, and although he also deals at length with the more germane issue of regulation in his criticism of John Rawls, it is his 'antimarket' discourse that provides a vocabulary for tackling the blockchain regulatory conundrum as it is understood here, and in particular to feed the double meaning of this section of the chapter, where *disrupting regulation* concerns the ability of regulation to disrupt, as well as be disrupted. It offers, therefore, a principled basis for thinking about blockchain regulation not from the point of view of neoliberal free-market ideology, a position Cohen claims is motivated by 'greed and fear' (2011, p. 218), but from commitments to 'fellow human beings and with a desire to serve them while being served by them' (2011, p. 218). Cohen continues:

> I mean, here, by 'community', the antimarket principle according to which I serve you not because of what I can get out of doing so but because you need my service. That is antimarket because the market motivates productive contribution not on the basis of commitment to one's fellow human beings and a desire to serve them while being served *by* them, but on the basis of impersonal cash reward [...] The genius of the market is that it recruits shabby motives to desirable ends, and, in a balanced view, both sides of that proposition must be kept in focus. Generosity *and* self-interest exist in everyone. We know how to make an economic system work on the basis of self-interest. We do not know how to make it work on the basis of generosity. But that does

not mean that we should forget generosity: we should still confine the sway of self-interest as much as we can.

(2011, pp. 217–219)

Cohen's call 'to confine the sway of self-interest' resonates closely with the regulatory enterprise required in the blockchain context, but also more generally as well. Finally, regulating blockchain as it is defined here asks whether blockchain is a necessary technology in a given context versus alternative technologies or even, perhaps, whether the option of no technology at all is or might be the most appropriate response. This approach recalls the question of why nobody has found a use for blockchain in the ten years of its existence (Stinchcombe, 2017). Moreover it echoes a pragmatic turn by the United States Bureau of the Fiscal Service (BFS) towards evaluations of blockchain use and relevance in a given context. For example, on the BFS website under the heading 'Determine if Blockchain is a Good Fit' is the following framework:

> To help you determine if blockchain is a potential solution, you can apply criteria to your use case. If you answer 'yes' to several of these questions, a blockchain solution may be worth considering:
>
> - Do you need a structured central repository of information?
> - Is more than one entity reading or writing transactions to a database?
> - Is there less than total trust between parties/entities in the ecosystem? (for example, one user will not accept the 'truth' as reported by another user)
> - Are central gatekeepers introducing costs and /or 'friction' when verifying transactions (for example, manual verification)?
> - Are there routine or logical interactions that occur that could be programmed to self-execute (for example, smart contracts)?
>
> (BFS, 2018)

GDPR vs blockchain

Ahead of an in-depth look at regulation it is important to discuss a particular and notable manifestation of the blockchain regulatory conundrum, namely the General Data Protection Regulation (GDPR) introduced by the European Union (EU) in May 2018 to replace the 1995 Data Protection Directive. The regulation represents an extraordinary and in some cases unwelcome new reality in the blockchain ecosystem as a continuation of the EU's 'particularly strong constitutional tradition of privacy protection' and development of EU data protection law (Brown and Marsden, 2013, p. 59). What is more, GDPR actually performs a number of functions that data sovereignty models on blockchain perform, most notably in terms of giving back control of personal data to data subjects (European Commission, 2018), thereby arguably undermining many blockchain business models. The EU's influence in this regard extends far beyond the boundaries of the Union, which thus implies a far-reaching impact of the GDPR for blockchain use-cases that do not specifically, intentionally or directly involve personal data of EU citizens. 'The EU has successfully influenced other regional privacy laws by restricting the transfer of personal data from member states to countries without adequate privacy protection', Brown and Marsden point out, and this 'determination of "adequacy" overseen by the European Commission, in practice requires other states to introduce most of the key protections [from EU data protection directives and regulations] into their own national laws' (2013, p. 59).

It is important, albeit briefly, to note GDPR here even though potential impacts remain speculative at the time of writing, because the regulation is likely to impact a wide range of blockchain use-cases in the EU and beyond. Key questions for the GDPR versus blockchain debate begin with the matter of control of personal data, specifically who within the context of a blockchain application is controlling data and thus accountable for its administration within the scope of the regulation. As Jacek Czarnecki maintains:

> The controller determines the purposes and means of the processing of personal data. Does such an entity exist at all in the context of a distributed blockchain? We can potentially treat transaction-confirming miners as controllers (in the case of the proof-of-work consensus) – something that in the case of large public blockchains will be unfeasible in practice.
>
> (2017)

Control equally concerns jurisdiction, in terms of the jurisdiction in which a data-controlling party (blockchain node or miner for example) is located and thus the possible or extent of the laws governing them. Winston Maxwell and John Salmon also point to the impact upon issues of control wrought by the different varieties of blockchain, namely permissioned, permissionless and so on (2017, pp. 16–19). The impact of the GDPR on use-cases flowing from the ecosystem is certainly not negligible, and impact assessments will likely be necessary for use-cases relating to permissionless, public blockchains, as well as those for civic service management of sensitive data such as health records (Maxwell and Salmon, 2017, p. 21). The necessity of impact assessments for private or enterprise blockchain is less clear, however, as Andries Van Humbeeck maintains:

> An important aspect of GDPR on blockchain is the fact that personal data is not to leave the EU. This is a major problem with public blockchains, since there is no control on who hosts a node. This is less an issue when it comes to private or permissioned blockchains.
>
> (2017)

In this sense the GDPR is arguably already performing a broad-ranging *ex ante* regulatory function that some blockchain stakeholders will view as counterproductive to innovation.

Rights for 'data subjects' under GDPR include: access to personal data and supplementary information, which involves submission of a subject access request

(SAR); objections to certain forms of processing including direct marketing and for research and statistics; rectification of inaccurate and incomplete personal data; erasure of personal data, otherwise known as 'the right to be forgotten'; the restriction of processing of personal data; rights relating to profiling and automated decision making, a right that could impinge upon the 'invisible' machine-to-machine capabilities that blockchain is able to facilitate via smart contracts; and claims for compensation for damage caused by a data breach. Further, limitations on transferring data and information outside of the EU other than for prescribed reasons, places restrictions on the free flow across geographical and jurisdictional space. Many of the rights and restrictions the GDPR introduces contradict the ways in which existing global computer networks operate, and this includes blockchain.

Of the new rights, the right to be forgotten (Art. 17) is one which does not sit comfortably with what for many stakeholders are core and desirable features of blockchain, namely the ability of 'immutability' to create 'transparency' in order to foster 'trust'. It is important to note that 'erasure' is not an absolute right to be forgotten under the terms of the legislation, however, and if, for example, the data involves defence of a legal claim or has overriding public interest then a data controller can refuse to comply with the right. 'The goal of GPDR is to "give citizens back the control of their personal data", whilst imposing strict rules on those hosting and "processing" this data, anywhere in the world', says Van Humbeeck, and

> one of the things GDPR states is that data 'should be erasable'. Since throwing away your encryption keys is not the same as 'erasure of data', GDPR prohibits us from storing personal data on a blockchain level. Thereby losing the ability to enhance control of your own personal data.
>
> (2017)

For Van Humbeeck this is the paradox of GDPR and blockchain. Maxwell and Salmon describe the issue further:

> One of the design features of blockchain architecture is that transaction records cannot be changed or deleted after-the-fact. A subsequent transaction can always annul the first transaction, but the first transaction will remain in the chain. The GDPR recognises a right to erasure. The broad principle underpinning this right is to enable an individual to request the deletion or removal of personal data where there is no compelling reason for its continued processing. What constitutes 'erasure' is still open to debate. Some data protection authorities have found that irreversible encryption constitutes erasure. In a blockchain environment, erasure is technically impossible because the system is designed to prevent it.
>
> (2017, p. 15)

The right to be forgotten linked to the erasure of personal data thus strikes at the heart of the immutability of blockchain. Following the logic above, once immutability is brought into question or falls completely through general imple-mentation of mechanisms for undoing chains, this brings into question both the creation of transparency and the ability to foster trust. And, some will argue, without the ability to foster trust or at least to do so without the evil necessity of having to rely on institutional middlemen like banks or government, what is the point of blockchain?

For use-cases to remain viable, an industry in workarounds that exploit cracks in the detail of the GDPR has been in business since the reality of what GDPR would entail began to emerge in the blockchain ecosystem in early 2017. 'Smart contracts will contain mechanisms governing access rights', claim Maxwell and Salmon, 'therefore the smart contract can be used to revoke all access rights, thereby making the content invisible to others, albeit not erased' (2017, p. 15). Meanwhile, 'a popular option to get around this problem is a very simple one', says Van Humbeeck, 'you store the personal data off-chain and store the reference to this data, along with a hash of this data and other metadata (like claims and permissions about this data), on the blockchain' (2017). But, as Van Humbeeck also admits, the term 'workaround' is a clear acknowledgement of the regrettable position the GDPR puts the ecosystem in, and that 'compromise is rarely good for business' (2017). This is an illustration of the point that classic regulatory conundrums turn on the extent to which regulatees are compliant or can made to be compliant in the future. As Stuart Biegel maintained with regard to the Internet but in terms arguably appropriate for the present discussion:

> Under current conditions, given the highly participatory nature of online activity and the distributed, anarchic design of cyberspace itself, there are a host of ways to get around most restrictions that may be imposed. In addi-tion, new architectural changes can often be countered by other code-based solutions. Thus a proposed regulatory approach may not be possible unless those that have the ability to resist agree to go along with the plan.
>
> (2003, p. 361)

At the time of writing the ramifications of the GDPR versus blockchain debate remain inconclusive. What is obvious already, however, is a desire for blockchain stakeholders to exploit, as best they can, uncertainties existing within the four corners of the GDPR using *know-how* or as Biegel suggests 'the ability to resist'. Thus while the regulation is forcing compliance to some extent, it is by no means watertight and concerns for regulators ought to surround greater desires to undermine the regulations rather than comply with them. Test cases in the coming months and years will be necessary for the further interpretation of the regulation and these are guaranteed to emerge as stakeholders push blockchain concepts and use-cases to the limits of compliance. Quite what 'compliance' means in terms of blockchain is, of course, itself yet to be meaningfully or authoritatively defined by regulators. The enterprise of regulating blockchain apropos traditional frameworks is where we turn next.

References

Arthur, W. Brian. 2009. *The Nature of Technology: What It Is and How It Evolves*. London: Penguin.

Aste, Tomaso, Tasca, Paolo and Di Matteo, Tiziana. 2017. Blockchain Technologies: The Foreseeable Impact on Society and Industry. *Computer*, Vol. 50, No. 9 (September), pp. 18–28.

Biegel, Stuart. 2003. *Beyond our Control? Confronting the Limits of Our Legal System in the Age of Cyberspace*. Cambridge: The MIT Press.

Brown, Ian and Marsden, Christopher T. 2013. *Regulating Code: Good Governance and Better Regulation in the Information Age*. Cambridge: MIT Press.

Brown, Wendy. 2015. *Undoing the Demos: Neoliberalism's Stealth Revolution*. New York: Zone Books.

Brownsword, Roger. 2008. *Rights, Regulation, and the Technological Revolution*. Oxford: Oxford University Press.

Brownsword, Roger and Goodwin, Morag. 2012. *Law and Technologies of the Twenty-First Century*. Cambridge: Cambridge University Press.

Cohen, G.A. 2011. *On the Currency of Egalitarian Justice, and Other Essays in Political Philosophy*. Edited by Michael Otsuka. Princeton: Princeton University Press.

Czarnecki, Jacek. 2017. Blockchains and Personal Data Protection Regulations Explained. *Coindesk*, 26 April. www.coindesk.com/blockchains-personal-data-protection-regulations-explained/ (accessed 20 April 2018).

Deibert, Ronald and Rohozinski, Rafal. 2010. Beyond Denial: Introducing Next-Generation Information Access Controls. *Accessed Controlled: The Shaping of Power, Rights, and Rule in Cyberspace*. Edited by Ronald Deibert, John Palfrey, Rafal Rohozinski and Jonathan Zittrain. Cambridge: MIT Press.

The Economist. 2015. The Trust Machine, 31 October–6 November.

European Commission. 2018. *25 May – GDPR tightens data protection rules for companies and gives people back control*. European Commission. https://ec.europa.eu/unitedkingdom/news/25-may-%E2%80%93-gdpr-tightens-data-protection-rules-companies-and-gives-people-back-control_en (accessed 25 May 2018).

Fenster, Mark. 2017. *The Transparency Fix: Secrets, Leaks, and Uncontrollable Government Information*. Stanford: Stanford University Press.

Goldenfein, Jake and Leiter, Andrea. 2018. Legal Engineering on the Blockchain: 'Smart Contracts' as Legal Conduct. *Law and Critique*, Vol. 29, No. 2 (July), pp. 141–149.

Golumbia, David. 2016. *The Politics of Bitcoin: Software as Right-Wing Extremism*. Minneapolis: University of Minnesota Press.

Guattari, Félix. 1995. *Chaosmosis: An Ethico-Aesthetic Paradigm*. Translated by Paul Bains and Julian Pefanis. Bloomington: Indiana University Press.

Gupta, Vinay. 2017. European Parliament blockchain presentation May 2017. *YouTube*. www.youtube.com/watch?v=xEFVuccuHI8&t=4s (accessed 1 February 2018).

Hall, Stuart. 2017. *Selected Political Writings: The Great Moving Right Show and Other Essays*. Edited by Sally Davison, David Featherstone, Michael Rustin and Bill Schwartz. Durham: Duke University Press.

Herian, Robert. 2016. How Blockchain Could Make Trusts More Transparent. *Coindesk*, 13 April. www.coindesk.com/blockchain-trusts-more-transparent/ (accessed 16 January 2018).

Herian, Robert. 2018. Blockchain and the Distributed Reproduction of Capitalist Class Power. *MoneyLab Reader 2: Overcoming the Hype*. Edited by Inte Gloerich, Geert Lovink and Patricia de Vries. Amsterdam: Institute of Network Cultures, pp. 43–51.

Kollewe, Julia. 2017. Bitcoin: UK and EU plan crackdown amid crime and tax evasion fears. *The Guardian*, 4 December. www.theguardian.com/technology/2017/dec/04/bitcoin-uk-eu-plan-cryptocurrency-price-traders-anonymity (accessed 12 January 2018).

Maxwell, Winston and Salmon, John. 2017. A Guide to Blockchain and Data Protection. *Hogan Lovells*, September. www.hlengage.com/_uploads/downloads/5425Guide toblockchainV9FORWEB.pdf (accessed 20 April 2018).

Mueller, Milton. 2013. *Networks and States: The Global Politics of Internet Governance.* Cambridge: MIT Press.

Mueller, Milton. 2017. *Will the Internet Fragment? Sovereignty, Globalization and Cyberspace.* Cambridge: Polity.

Murdoch, Iris. 2001. *The Sovereignty of Good.* London: Routledge.

Murphy, Mark. 2011. The Natural Law Tradition in Ethics. *The Stanford Encyclopaedia of Philosophy.* https://plato.stanford.edu/entries/natural-law-ethics/ (accessed 25 April 2018).

Murray, Andrew and Scott, Colin. 2002. Controlling the New Media: Hybrid Responses to New Forms of Power. *The Modern Law Review*, Vol. 65, No. 4 (July), pp. 491–516.

Pasquale, Frank. 2015. *The Black Box Society: The Secret Algorithms that Control Money and Information.* Cambridge: Harvard University Press.

Power, Michael. 1997. *The Audit Society: Rituals of Verification.* Oxford: Oxford University Press.

Prosser, Tony. 2010. *The Regulatory Enterprise.* Oxford: Oxford University Press.

Raz, Joseph. 1996. Liberty and Trust. *Natural Law, Liberalism, and Morality.* Edited by Robert P. George. Oxford: Oxford University Press, pp. 113–129.

Reyes, Carla L. 2016. Moving Beyond Bitcoin to an Endogenous Theory of Decentralized Ledger Technology Regulation: an Initial Proposal. *Villanova Law Review*, Vol. 61, No. 1, pp. 191–234.

Schumpeter, Joseph A. 2010. *Capitalism, Socialism and Democracy.* Abingdon: Routledge.

Singh, Rajnish. 2017. EU must work to enable blockchain technology. *The Parliament Magazine*, 7 November. www.theparliamentmagazine.eu/articles/opinion/eu-must-work-to-enable-blockchain-technology (accessed 31 March 2018).

Srnicek, Nick. 2017. *Platform Capitalism.* Cambridge: Polity.

Stiegler, Bernard. 2010. *For a New Critique of Political Economy.* Cambridge: Polity.

Stinchcombe, Kai. 2017. Ten Years in, Nobody has Come Up with a Use for Blockchain. *Hacker Noon*, 22 December. https://hackernoon.com/ten-years-in-nobody-has-come-up-with-a-use-case-for-blockchain-ee98c180100 (accessed 31 January 2018).

Swan, Melanie. 2015. *Blockchain: Blueprint for a New Economy.* Sebastopol: O'Reilly.

Swartz, Lana. 2017. Blockchain Dreams: Imagining Techno-Economic Alternatives after Bitcoin. *Another Economy is Possible.* Edited by Manuel Castells. Cambridge: Polity Press, pp. 82–105.

Tapscott, Don and Tapscott, Alex. 2016. *Blockchain Revolution: How the Technology behind Bitcoin is Changing Money, Business and the World.* London: Portfolio Penguin.

Tuomi, Ilkka. 2002. *Networks of Innovation: Change and meaning in the age of Internet.* Oxford: Oxford University Press.

US Bureau of Fiscal Services (BFS). 2018. https://fiscal.treasury.gov/fsservices/gov/fit/blockchain.htm.

Van Humbeeck, Andries. 2017. The Blockchain-GDPR Paradox. *Medium*, 21 November. https://medium.com/wearetheledger/the-blockchain-gdpr-paradox-fc51e663d047 (accessed 20 April 2018).

Walch, Angela. 2017. Blockchain's Treacherous Vocabulary: One More Challenge for Regulators. *Journal of Internet Law*, Vol. 21, No. 2, pp. 9–16.

Warbach, Kevin. 2018. Trust, But Verify: Why the Blockchain Needs the Law. *Berkeley Technology Law Journal*, 16 (forthcoming).

Zetzsche, Dirk A., Buckley, Ross P., Barberis, Janos N. and Arner, Douglas W. 2017. Regulating Revolution: From Regulatory Sandboxes to Smart Regulation. *Fordham Journal of Corporate & Financial Law*, Vol. 23, No. 1, pp. 31–103.

3   Regulatory tradition

Introduction

> When we say that emerging technologies should be understood as being situated in a particular regulatory environment, the essential idea is that, when we act – whether we act as developers and commercial exploiters, or as users and appliers, of particular technologies – we do so in a context that has a certain coding for action, a coding that signals whether various acts are permitted (even required) or prohibited, whether they will be viewed positively, negatively or neutrally, whether they are incentivised or disincentivised, whether they are likely to be praised or criticised, even whether they are possible or impossible, and so on.
>
> (Brownsword and Goodwin, 2012, p. 27)

A regulatory tradition surrounds the Internet which it would be wrong or even impossible to ignore with regard to blockchain. A variety of networked technologies are rightly subject to, albeit to different degrees, pressing questions concerning their effect on human behaviour. Blockchain does not change this fundamental regulatory paradigm, nor, as the Internet continues to show, the need for standard setting and information gathering concerning the regulatory environment in order to ensure effective regulation is maintained. The aim, as Andrew Murray and Colin Scott contend, is to 'locate problems of controlling the new media squarely within well established analyses of problems of regulatory control' (2002, p. 516). Further, that such analysis 'encourages us to look at all the mechanisms of control which already subsist within the target system and to find ways to stimulate or steer those indigenous mechanisms towards meeting the public interest objectives of regulation' (Murray and Scott, 2002, p. 516).

Stuart Biegel envisages a framework for regulation that is: 'neutral and broad-based, one which recognizes that the term includes case decisions, legislation, relevant policies, administrative agency activity, international cooperation, architectural changes, private ordering, self-regulation, and any other methods that might be employed to control various portions of cyberspace' (2003, pp. 356–357). 'By defining regulation in this broad and objective manner', Biegel concludes:

> we can more precisely identify the contours of the debate for individual problem areas. A definition that recognizes that regulation can include everything

from action by the powers-that-be to steps that can be taken by individual Netizens is essential here. Cyberspace regulation is not necessarily something that is invariably carried out by *someone else*, but rather a series of steps that anyone can accomplish on an individual basis in particular circumstances. A broad definition recognizes the variety of meanings and the range of manifestations inherent in the term.

(2003, p. 357)

There is much to commend in both Murray and Scott's and Biegel's regulatory outlines and motivations, not least as attempts to demonstrate the necessity for offline regulation to evolve in the uncertain and ill-defined realm of online networks, rather than be simply jettisoned as outmoded and unfit to serve the novel and unique contours of cyberspace. This differs, for instance, from more essentialist views on cyberspace regulation put forward by the likes of Lawrence Lessig. 'Cyberspace demands a new understanding of how regulation works', argues Lessig, it 'compels us to look beyond the traditional lawyer's scope – beyond laws, or even norms. It requires a broader account of "regulation," and most importantly, the recognition of a newly salient regulator [...] Code' (2006, p. 5). Recognition that regulation would have to address or autonomously respond to a multiplicity of regulatory needs and contexts online, and was thus unlikely to fit a single, monolithic definition, continues to hold in the context of blockchain (De Filippi and Wright, 2018, p. 51). This does not mean the blockchain regulatory process, in whatever form it eventually takes, can or should be considered neutral, however. That is fundamentally naive and on that point in particular I disagree with Biegel. Insistence on neutrality only achieves denial of or distraction from the inevitability of messy human involvement *qua* politics (and ethics) that necessarily constitute the regulatory process as human. Motivation for this denial or distraction is a parallel need or desire to affirm regulation pursuant to economic reason, logic and rationalisation. As a general backdrop to questions of blockchain regulation therefore, Biegel's definition is relevant but regulation can be understood here more generally as 'the intentional activity of attempting to control, order or influence the behaviour of others' (Black, 2002, p. 25), which necessarily carries political and ethical principles and burdens that ought to be shared by the community as whole, whether on- or offline.

According to Brown and Marsden there are three existing and conflicting approaches to Internet regulation from a technical and legal policy perspective: 'continued technological and market-led self-regulation, reintroduction of state-led regulation, and multistakeholder coregulation' (2013, p. 2). Emerging blockchain regulatory environments are unlikely to denude existing regulatory modalities or strategies, but rather draw on them. Regulating blockchain, whatever forms it takes and Latinate nominations it is given in the medium to long term, will inevitably reference existing regulatory frameworks; or, put another way, will reference regulatory knowledges derived from both the mainstream as well as the margins, in order to develop and progress implementations in private and public sectors alike caught within the force field of capitalist and neoliberal reason. As Goldenfein and Leiter argue:

the legal quality of these environments need not be identified or identifiable immediately, but is more likely to develop over time and remains a site of contestation. The governing values of the environment are yet to be established. There is accordingly a great deal at stake in how we characterise these systems and in the normative trajectory of their engineering.

(2018, p. 142)

Mainstream theories and practices informed by the regulatory tradition and conventional wisdom of regulators are important measures for understanding the nature and (re)definition of regulatory environments in response to the emergence of new technologies such as blockchain. Regulation, after all, even in its most rigid form will invariably try to bend before it breaks, and there is always a degree of play in the joints of most regulatory environments. New technologies rarely warrant a regulatory *tabula rasa*, but it would be unrealistic for existing regulation to always or easily accommodate the demands new technologies bring. 'Each time a new technology appears, or an established technology assumes a fresh significance or moves forward in some way, we should not, so to speak, have to reinvent the wheel', argues Roger Brownsword, 'even if we do not need to reinvent the regulatory wheel, we do need to refine our regulatory intelligence to bring it into alignment with the characteristics of each particular technology' (2008, p. 290). A problem afflicting both new regulation and, to echo Brownsword, the refinement of regulatory intelligence is the extent to which both have been captured and dominated by theories of economic reason and those of so-called 'new public management' (Hood, 1991) in recent decades via a broader neoliberal colonisation of regulatory theory and practice. This has led to the prominence of markets and competition *as* regulation, via emphasis on 'cost control, financial transparency, the automatization of organizational sub-units, the decentralization of management authority, the creation of market and quasi-market mechanisms [...] the enhancement of accountability [and] the creation of performance indicators' (Power, 1997, p. 43). Using technologies such as blockchain, the desire of neoliberalism is to replace 'the presumed inefficiency of hierarchical bureaucracy with the presumed efficiency of markets' (Power, 1997, p. 43).

To summarise before moving on: there are three key areas of regulatory interest that will be explored. First, blockchain within traditional mainstream regulatory frameworks, most notably those of the Internet and e-commerce, as a subset of Internet regulation. Discussion here will focus on *self-regulation* as the prevailing mode, but will also explore other key areas applicable to blockchain in the short to medium term based on the lessons learnt (or missed) in other areas of network regulation, notably multistakeholder co-regulation and coded regulation of cyberspace. Second, regulating blockchain for community and generosity, not self-interest: this is arguably a sub-species of the form of regulation outlined above, but also acts as a foil to dominant notions residing within the regulatory mainstream, notably neoliberal free-market principles. In order to prevent the topic from being too abstract, however, this section will begin by examining multistakeholder governance as a mode of regulation by civil society that emerges in the face of failures in the market and the legitimacy of self-regulation. Third, block-chain as regulator: this position will be dealt with last and arguably transcends the previous two positions, something that will be made more apparent in the following chapter exploring blockchain as a means of enforcing tax liabilities that off-shore trusts and financial management presently help avoid.

Self-regulation

Self-regulation is an important place to focus with regard to blockchain because evidence points towards the blockchain regulatory enterprise as already beholden to so-called market-complementing regulation, in the sense that self-regulation or 'rule by entrepreneur' (Gupta, 2017) are dominant approaches. Moreover, self-regulation with regard to blockchain fits general trends and narratives of fluid management practice within technology sectors that celebrate risk, build 'sand-boxes', and treat failure as a cornerstone of resilience in the construction of a more successful economic self through enterprise. As blockchain acolyte Rachel Botsman states:

> [e]very innovator wants to be first over the line, and it's no different with the quest for the ultimate blockchain technology. Inevitably, there will be glitches along the way because that's how innovation comes into being and grows resilient, just as a body develops its immune system by being exposed to bugs and viruses. The blockchain's enormous potential means developers and investors are taking a classic 'fail fast, fail forward' approach.
>
> (2017, p. 231)

Following Botsman it is perhaps instructive to consider themes and keywords from embryology, engineering and cybernetics that consider self-regulation as, for example: 'the process of cell reorganization or readjustment that occurs in the restoration of an organic defect or incompleteness'; 'a quantity that expresses the degree of imperfection of a device or system'; 'any systematic behaviour within a system that tends to restrict fluctuations of any variable' (Bullock and Stallybrass, 1977, p. 533). The three descriptions above can and do apply to regulation more generally, but it is the articulation of adaptability within the ecosystem where the resonance with self-regulation is perhaps strongest.

Monroe Price and Stefaan Verhulst argue, 'there is no single definition of self-regulation that is entirely satisfactory, nor should there be', yet self-regulation 'rarely exists without some relationship between the industry and the state' (2000, p. 58). This latter point is crucial because it not only indicates the possibility of government imposing 'sledgehammer regulation' (Brown and Marsden, 2013, pp. 32–33), or 'the heavy hand of the law' (Tapscott and Tapscott, 2016, p. 297), but also warranted and unwarranted retreats by government due to, amongst other things, the idea disseminated by technology stakeholders and lobbyists warning government against stifling innovation that regulation is too demanding, challenging or complex. Forms of self-regulation, including quasi self-regulation (or regulated self-regulation), exists on a continuum with state-led regulation and multistakeholder co-regulation (Brown and Marsden, 2013, p. 12). As species of self-regulation the prevailing approaches to blockchain regulation fit squarely within recent paradigms of Internet regulation (Marsden, 2000, p. 6) and long-standing traditions of liberal political economy traceable to the ideas of Adam Smith, David Hume and Adam Ferguson (Lemke, 2012, p. 43). What the liberal tradition of Smith *et al.* advocated for which is of particular significance here was the de-legitimation of the State as regulator by mobilising economic reason 'to assess whether governmental action is necessary and useful or superfluous and harmful' (Lemke, 2012, p. 43). Returning to the rather more recent matter of approaches to Internet regulation therefore, it is perhaps unsurprising to find the virtues of self-regulation extolled as absolutely and necessarily distinct from state or government regulation:

> Given the competing societal interests in controlling content on the Internet, meaningful and effective self-regulation is more effective than the exclusive exercise of government authority. Self-regulation has a greater capacity to adapt rapidly to quickening technical progress and to the transnational development of the new communications medium. In addition to flexibility, self-regulation presents the benefits of greater efficiency, increased incentives for compliance, and reduced cost. A carefully structured programme of self-regulation, often developed in co-operation with government, is in harmony with the new technology, mirroring the Internet itself as a global, essentially private and decentralised network of communication.
>
> (Price and Verhulst, 2000, p. 75)

Most striking about Price and Verhulst's celebration of self-regulation is that their call for rapid adaption needed to keep pace with 'quickening technical progress' within the context of the Internet at the turn of the millennium, mirrors arguments that obtain within the blockchain ecosystem today. This span of at least 30 years in which self-regulation has been considered the *lingua franca* of technology regulation highlights two possible, and at first blush seemingly opposing, options. First, self-regulation has remained a dominant regulatory theme and method because it is effective within the economic limits of what it is expected to achieve. Continuing application of self-regulation in regulating blockchain is therefore deemed legitimate and justifiable because of the precedent set by the Internet. Second, regulators or more specifically state-led regulation has never got a grip on networked technologies and has either given up trying to do so in any meaningful way, or been beaten back by entrepreneurs and other stakeholders of technological solutionism and innovationism lobbying for greater regulatory latitude and freedom *qua* self-regulation, and the desire to assert greater control over their '*regulatory footprint*' (Currie et al., 2017). As Carla Reyes suggests, the promotion of innovation and adaptability might well be key aspects of regulating decentralised ledger technology, but 'these self-regulatory proposals elevate this criterion over all others' and doing so, 'discounts the actual market failures that have occurred since the introduction of decentralized ledger technologies' (2016, p. 220). Far from being in opposition therefore, both options are clearly interlinked or two sides of the same coin. There has been, in short, a triumph of the *self* in regulation, perhaps even over it. And this is, once more I argue, symptomatic of neoliberalism.

A key question for existing paradigms of self-regulation is the scope of effectiveness, which refers to economic considerations and the importance of cost-benefit analyses in establishing regulatory norms, deciding on their adjudication and enforcement. Reyes has argued that: 'History intimates that the self-regulatory approach is unlikely to sufficiently resolve the market failures that will ultimately allow illicit and fraudulent uses of decentralized technologies to occur' (2016, p. 194). Price and Verhulst meanwhile believe self-regulation is crucial for necessary rapid adaption to occur in the domain of networked technologies. Highlighted a moment ago, the durability of self-regulation, coupled with evidence of law and regulatory lag resulting from the failure of other attempts at regulation (state-led regulation or multistakeholder co-regulation) to close the governance gap 'between what the technologists and advanced users know of the medium and political responses' (Brown and Marsden, 2013, p. 7), suggests Price and Verhulst are either correct or that self-regulation has simply triumphed in the conflict against 'command and control' state-led regulation and multistakeholder co-regulation.

The decentralised and distributed nature of blockchain and other networked technologies appears to make self-regulation a given for many stakeholders based on the assumption that it provides the most suitable or 'natural' regulatory option to fit a plurality of possible contexts that often transcend formal regulatory boundaries and jurisdictions. 'Decentralization', Swan enthusiastically proclaims, 'is an idea whose time has come' (2015, p. 91), and thus, the Tapscotts conclude, 'government should approach regulating technologies cautiously, acting as a collaborative peer to other sectors of society. They must participate as players in a bottom-up governance ecosystem rather than enforcers of a top-down regime of control' (2016, p. 297). Michael Power identifies two strands of governance. First, governance that 'concerns the effectiveness of market based controls, in the sense of the ability of an active takeover market to "discipline" managers into maximizing a firm's value' (1997, p. 41). Second, governance that 'relates to the effectiveness of regulatory initiatives to penetrate the organization and ensure compliance with rules via specifically designated officers, audit committees, and other internal representatives' (1997, p. 41). Applied to the blockchain ecosystem it can be argued that most blockchain initiatives remain too immature at present to fulfil Power's second governance criterion, but with regard to the first it is clear that market competencies at the forefront of decisions within the blockchain ecosystem have led to a greater onus on self-regulation.

Self-regulation, in this instance, is perhaps better referred to and understood as what Julia Black calls 'decentred regulation', namely, regulation no longer 'tied exclusively or even predominantly to the state' (2002, p. 2), but which is equally modelling the ideological designs set for it by stakeholders of the blockchain ecosystem. 'At the conceptual core of a decentred understanding', Black further explains, 'are five central notions: complexity, fragmentation, interdependencies, ungovernability, and the rejection of a clear distinction between public and private' (2002, p. 4), a set of criteria that is brought into sharp focus when read against what Swan calls the issue that 'blockchain technology raises with regard to government regulation', namely, 'the value proposition offered by governments and their business model' (2015, p. 90). A fundamental flaw in alternatives to self-regulation has been to focus on centralised actors in a decentralised ecosystem, meaning regulators, as Reyes argues, 'will not be able to keep pace' (2016, p. 221) either with technology or technology-led behaviours or, indeed, the flexibility and fluidity of decentred, self-regulation. The accusation Reyes is making – and it is one that corresponds with broader issues of regulatory lag – is that state-led regulation in particular has been too rigid in its appraisal of the landscape of fast-developing technological contexts. Julia Black attributes this failure to the following reasons:

> Complexity, fragmentation of knowledge and of the exercise of power and control, autonomy, interactions and interdependencies, and the collapse of the public / private distinction are the central elements of the composite 'decentred understanding' of regulation. Together they suggest a diagnosis of regulatory failure which is based on the dynamics, complexity and diversity of economic and social life, and in the inherent ungovernability of social actors, systems and networks.
>
> (2002, p. 8)

Turning to the nature of self-regulation, the question arises of whether an over-emphasis on the self in regulation engenders a form of fragmentation, particularly where 'an essentialist approach to self-regulation would require that all the elements of regulation – formation of norms, adjudication, enforcement and others – be self-generated' (Price and Verhulst, 2000, p. 58). 'The fragmentation of the neoliberal self begins when the agent is brought face to face with the realization that she is not just an employee or student', offers Mirowski as a example, 'but also simultaneously a product to be sold, a walking advertisement, a manager of her résumé, a biographer of her rationales, and an entrepreneur of her possibilities' (2014, p. 108), to which can be added the regulator of her technologies. Self-regulation applies to individuals in the sense of Mirowski's example, but equally describes a form of regulation within and across industries, institutions and so on. 'Observations of fragmentation relate to [...] autonomy and ungovernability of actors (or systems)', claims Black, and autonomy

> is not used in the sense of freedom from interference by government, rather it is the idea that actors will continue to develop or act in their own way in the absence of intervention. Actors or systems are self regulating, and regulation cannot take their behaviour as a constant.
>
> (2002, p. 6)

A key problem of self-regulation (at least given the scope of neoliberal reason) begins, I suggest, with basic questions of human capacity: how can a person, industry, institution and so on expect to be and do all things necessary to sustain itself at once, and what might the consequences be of critical failure or lack of motivation to maintain the *self*? The neoliberal self, Mirowski continues,

> has to somehow manage to be simultaneously subject, object, and spectator. She is perforce *not* learning about who she really is, but rather provisionally buying the person she must soon become. She is all at once the business, the raw material, the product, the clientele, and the customer of her own life. She is a jumble of assets to be invested, nurtured, managed, and developed; but equally an offsetting inventory of liabilities to be pruned, outsourced, shorted, hedged against, and minimized. She is both headline start and enraptured audience of her own performance.
>
> (2014, p. 108)

What Mirowski describes is not only interesting in terms of unravelling the nature of self-regulation with neoliberalism, but equally, as earlier discussions here have shown, how blockchain can be seen as a useful tool for helping to achieve the ultimate goal of a more efficient neoliberal self. This is of course ironic given the self-regulation in question here concerned blockchain in the first place. Where better, therefore, for the self-regulating blockchain entrepreneur to look for a means to improve their chances of 'success' and become the 'enraptured audience' of their own performance, than to the very technology to which they are beholden?

Key to the paradigm of self-regulation and enabling self-regulatory actors and systems is the insistence of markets and market logics. This makes self-regulation a prime organisational form within the neoliberal project through the creation of forms of market-complementing regulation, and by facilitating the corresponding retreat of more proscriptive and prescriptive forms of *ex ante* and *ex post* regulations deemed less flexible and opposed to innovation as a symptom *par excellence* of the agile neoliberal subject. As the (re)turn to self-regulation by the blockchain ecosystem attests, it is now commonplace for markets and competition to act as regulators, and they are for stakeholders the most efficient way to organise data, knowledge, indeed all forms of social and cultural production. Through endless transacting and jostling for economic 'leverage' of one's peers, markets forge themselves out of the blockchain 'space', something that paradoxically shifts the fundamental premise of peer-to-peer equanimity associated with blockchain I argue, and reminds us that power obtains within networks and systems regardless of whether those systems and networks are sold as models for new equitable economies. Technologies like blockchain thus mirror markets as brute shapers of raw and unorganised data, and stakeholders promote these technologies as civilising forces for shaping knowledge and being, as they do all forms of data, and, more crucially, as the best means for preparing data for the inevitability (the always already) of the market. Given the insistence and inevitability of markets within techno-economic spheres, however, blockchain can equally be said to act as a cultivator or form of data culturalism for market-ready actors.

Many different contemporary technologies and technological applications are designed to model and reproduce market conduct in more effective and efficient ways. Indeed, most if not all major online platforms including Amazon, Facebook, Airbnb, Google, eBay, Uber, are marketplaces in spite of their varied attempts at accentuating aspirational traits in their advertising and user interfaces to detract from this. While it may be stating the obvious, especially in the case of *de facto* marketplaces such as Amazon and eBay, given the power and influence of these businesses, not only in terms of brute capital and equity holdings (the traditional path to power), but also the huge amount of data each holds on their users – the 'gold of the 21st century' (European Commission, 2018) – the potential for 'insight' and 'influence' the data allows in a variety of social contexts, it is important to note their instrumentality in the totalisation of free-market logics and ethics. What is more, the *further embeddedness* (these companies clearly did not start the trend but nonetheless embrace it) of the 'primary virtues' of competition and markets (Harvey, 2005, p. 65) they each represent. As network-based, techno-social infrastructures, this small clutch of companies have all, to a greater or lesser extent, achieved or come very close to achieving the most prized aims of neoliberalism: to render competition and markets the common sense of contemporary social life, whilst burying political subjectivity within a morass of economic reason thus making it indistinguishable. While markets and technology are closely intertwined, technologies have inevitably remained products of market forces, not the other way round.[1] More important still, technologies and markets, as well as the presumed need for humanity to engage in competition in all walks of life, are rooted in a combination of conscious strategies, libidinal drives and unconscious desires that recall the importance of analysis of their affects through psycho-politics – something we will return to at the end of this book.

As already discussed, self-regulation privileges the 'internal regulation' of individual entrepreneurs over the 'external congruence' of government or State (Lemke, 2012, p. 43). Given such a broad and potentially deeply subjective regulatory measure therefore, how is the matter of regulatory legitimacy realised or upheld? 'A key challenge presented by [...] novel governance mechanisms', claim Murray and Scott, 'is how to deploy them in such a way that [they] are perceived as legitimate' (2002, p. 516). One response is, as we have seen, that markets provide the ultimate arbiter where moral, prudential, or practical issues of regulation arise (Brownsword and Goodwin, 2012, p. 29). Another, as Lemke has argued, that regulatory action is no longer concerned with 'legitimacy or illegitimacy, but success or failure' (2012, p. 43); that to be considered or rewarded as, for instance, a successful entrepreneur in effect transcends any problematic in the

---

1   Ellen Meiksins Wood draws an important distinction between commerce and capitalism, and, notable in the example of the Dutch Republic during the seventeenth century, describes a close relationship between commerce, commercialisation and technologies that enabled the Dutch to maximise market opportunities (2017, p. 93).

legitimacy of self-regulation. '[T]he routinization and standardization of denial of a true invariant self has become a hallmark of modern life', argues Philip Mirowski, '[i]t is the sheer ordinariness of the expectation that the self should provide no obstacle to success because it is supple, modular, and plastic that is the germ of everyday neoliberalism' (2014, p. 108).

'Legitimacy is one of the oldest concepts in political theory', claim Brownsword and Goodwin,

> It concerns questions of justification of the exercise of power by those over whom that power is exercised. Political legitimacy can be classified into two dimensions. The first concerns the source of authority, or how the government has come to be in power. For example, we no longer accept as legitimate a government that has come to power by deposing a democratically elected government in a military coup. Similarly, we do not accept a government as legitimate where it is imposed by a foreign occupying power. Rather, we generally hold that the source of authority for a government is the will of the people, its self-determination, however that might be expressed or measured. Where the source of power is illegitimate, the exercise of power of what the (illegitimate) government then does once in power is also deemed illegitimate, even were it to be generally perceived as acting for the social good.
>
> (2012, p. 173)

Regulatory discourse would clearly err in legitimacy were it to assume that all states or governments around the globe who command and control the research, development and production of new technologies are democratic. Brownsword and Goodwin make this point clearly, as do Murray and Scott: 'Judgements on the appropriate balance between democratic and other forms of legitimation are likely to differ within different political cultures' (2002, p. 516). What Brownsword and Goodwin do not touch on, however, are the external pressures on government that can (and do) have delegitimising effects on the ability of government to function in an equitable, fair or just public manner. The effect of neoliberalism on democracy and regulatory legitimacy alike has been to re-imagine and re-constitute both through endless processes of austerity and efficiency, whilst simultaneously delegitimising thought and practice deemed inefficient and via technology thriving on 'the fetishistic denial of democracy's failure, its inability to secure justice, equity, or solidarity even as it enables millions to access information and make their own opinion known' (Dean, 2009, p. 42). Neoliberalism has turned questions of legitimacy into measures of success.

Self-regulation of technologies that transcend private interest and impact public civic life, if they are to be taken seriously and considered legitimate, must go hand in hand with political accountability and oversight that does not begin and end with the brute economics of individual self-interest. This means rejecting conceptualisations of systems of private ordering 'as protective of individual freedom and the freedom of contract', and thinking of them instead as communal systems that invite 'a public dimension and thus mechanisms for the protection of public interest' (Goldenfein and Leiter, 2018, p. 143). This notion is clearly at odds with the tradition of self-regulation. For some that would be an end to the argument, indeed the prevalence of self-regulation suggests there is little space for argument at all. Instead, however, what would it mean to place civic and public interest first? Political accountability and oversight ought, after all, to act as means of legitimating the adoption and declaration of a regulatory position; the monitoring of responses to that position; the pressure exerted to ensure compliance; and finally, to decide when enforcement steps are taken against regulatees who do not comply (Brownsword and Goodwin, 2012, p. 35).

The churn of global political affairs coupled with the colonisation of the social by capital and economic reason has placed democracy under increasing pressure in recent decades both in the West and elsewhere. And with the aid of new technologies democracy risks ceding more ground to explicit forms of authoritarianism (Bogost, 2017), as well as far more subtle forms of elite interest and power.[2] What passes for 'democracy' or 'politics' in a neoliberal framework requires pause to consider what complexions of democracy and politics are really being argued for, however, and in particular whether economic theories of 'democracy' are being recreated and promoted as a priority (Mirowski, 2014, p. 58). In other words it is very difficult to discern anything beyond existing, totalising economic ontological conditions. The raw and traumatic realisation of economic totality lies in just how far economic reason has interwoven and interpellated all levels of contemporary social life, and that modern capitalist democracies are predicated on weak political visions of individual success. Escaping or countermanding neoliberal realities is as a consequence hard to achieve, especially as new technologies like blockchain geared towards the aims of neoliberalism proliferate and reinforce its base.

The alternative is, as Stuart Hall framed it, forms of democracy that do not 'erode the foundations of a just and responsible conduct of public affairs' and do not create an ethos within which irresponsibility can thrive (2017, p. 25). Uncoupled from its close neoliberal ties blockchain could arguably achieve what Hall calls for as it is capable of recording the ill gains that constitute capitalist societies and reflecting them back. Yet, the present deployment of blockchain as a means of strengthening the cause of economic reason, constantly puts it into question with regard to the parallel role hoped for it in strengthening politics and democracy. Specifically suggestions by blockchain evangelists that new forms of collaborative democracy can be built on blockchain with incentives to reward civic participation modelled on the Bitcoin mining function (Tapscott and Tapscott, 2016, p. 214) are a real concern because this is precisely the type of perversion of the political in order to gratify the economic that will lead to impoverishment of political processes. In a world of blockchain politics risk becoming entirely

2   At the time of writing news is breaking of the supposed data breach involving the private company and political strategist organisation Cambridge Analytica, which used data derived from Facebook, without full consent from users, in order to shape election campaigns (Trump in 2016), and thus intervene in the democratic process in questionable and concerning ways.

subservient to market logics and competition, whether directly and unashamedly as has been evident from years of privatisation and so-called 'new public management' (Hood, 1991), or indirectly as a result of alternative co-operative consensus models on blockchain that fail entirely to shake off the yoke of neoliberal economic reason.[3]

Multistakeholder co-regulation

> 'Stakeholders' get to make and even enforce the rules and anyone who isn't or can't be a 'stakeholder' – well tough luck!
>
> (Gurstein, 2014)

Multistakeholder co-regulation (MS) or mutlistakeholderism, a somewhat pejorative term that we will see shortly reflects some of the more negative aspects of this regulatory approach, is yet another species of regulation that has long standing in the field of Internet and network technologies. MS speaks, in particular, to globalising models of consensus building around both the application layers of a network and the deeper transport and network architecture and fabric on top of which applications, including blockchain, run. Multistakeholder is a term, Michael Gurstein claims,

> used within the Internet sphere to describe (more or less appropriately) the decision-making processes of various of the Internet's technical bodies (the IETF [Internet Engineering Task Force], the IAB [Interactive Advertising Bureau], ICANN [Internet Corporation for Assigned Names and Numbers]).
>
> (2014)

Brown and Marsden further highlight the regulatory pluralism built around influential and 'often stridently independent Internet engineers and technologists, who play a significant role in the standards and other regulatory processes, particularly

---

3   This is arguably the case with FairCoin, which despite championing co-operation over competition, nonetheless reproduces and promotes a number of neoliberal-like ideas and strategies such as gift economies and the prerequisite of efficiency as a measure of the success of the 'post-capitalist' economy the coin fosters (König and Duran, 2016). Brett Scott nevertheless maintains that the approach of FairCoin is to be generally welcomed as a reaction to prevailing economic trends:

> A project like Faircoin [...] starts from the assumption that, while formal market systems may be a source of economic growth and individual enhancement, they are simultaneously the source of social inequality, individual alienation and community disintegration. Thus, rather than trying to find narrow solutions to individual hardship, initiatives like Faircoin seek to create alternative economic systems that bypass normal markets, and that rewrite the deep level rules of economic engagement. In particular they place heavy emphasis on the basis of economic life being mutual cooperation and solidarity, rather than individual competition for narrow economic success.
>
> (2016, p. 10)

in the infrastructure technology but also in content, applications and services'
(2013, p. 12). It is fair to say that global network technologies that in many
senses ignore legal jurisdiction and national boundaries alike require, as a necessity, novel approaches to regulation and governance that are able to account for
a variety of transnational factors and biases. This includes working with considerations of levels of overall adoption of a technology in particular jurisdiction
or nation, as well as forms of behaviour produced by adoption more generally
within a specific culture.

In order to achieve the requisite flexibility and evolving consensus, MS draws
on different areas of expertise and experience, from government to business, as
well as wider public discourse and citizenry. This has, as Brown and Marsden
point out, often placed MS at odds with traditional regulation, and it has been
criticised for being 'an extremely tenuous chain of accountability' that draws on
participants within 'international fora and nongovernmental organization stakeholders' (2013, p. 3). Moreover, as Gurstein argues, the MS model 'is in fact the
transformation of the neo-liberal economic model which has resulted in such
devastation and human tragedy throughout the world into a new form of "post-
democratic" governance', and he points, in particular, to the collective work
of the Aspen Institute including 'numerous Internet luminary co-authors and
collaborators' (2014).

There are two main functions of MS of interest here as potential and already
operative modes of blockchain regulation.[4] First, MS involves consensus across
jurisdictions in order to collectively define the nature and form regulation takes in
a range of different macro-technical and macroeconomic circumstances. This is in
many ways a larger scoping exercise within what is otherwise normal procedural
regulation at the state level, yet draws on business and industry to help inform and
shape regulatory strategies and policies and, indeed, can even exclude government
from certain aspects of the regulatory process. Mentioned above, ICANN, the
private incorporated arm of US government management and administration of
the Internet Domain Name System (DNS), has been important in forging competition and markets for domain names globally, and often cited as the proto-
typical multistakeholder organisation operating at the global level of Internet
governance. For Ethan Katsh and Orna Rabinovich-Einy domain names and
therefore ICANN are the ultimate focus of Internet regulation, and this begins
from practical, topographical and categorical requirements for navigating cyberspace,
which enable subsequent business on the Internet to be conducted:

> Domain names, which are linked to internet protocols (IP) addresses such as
> 128.20.0.1, are like street addresses and are *the only piece of the internet that
> must be regulated*. This is handled by the Internet Corporation for Assigned
> Names and Numbers (ICANN), which was established in 1998. Domain

4 The All Party Parliamentary Group on blockchain (APPG blockchain) in the UK Parliament is an attempt at a multistakeholder model of policy development and potential
governance.

names provide us with an essential map – perhaps even the street structure itself – in the infinite global city that is the internet. Without domain names, we would have the equivalent of a city without recognizable street names, and it would be difficult to locate anything. Without regulation of domain names, there might be more than one entity with the same domain name. In that case, we would also not know how to locate what we are looking for.

[emphasis added] (2017, p. 62)

Meanwhile, Milton Mueller views the role of ICANN as more problematic: 'ICANN can do effective governance', Mueller points out in criticising the lionisation of ICANN within the MS model, because it has 'exclusive control of resources that are essential to the functioning of the Internet' (2017, p. 118). Yet, it is clear that ICANN falls short in fulfilling the promise of MS not only in terms of the limited breadth of its international stakeholder inclusion (it is almost exclusively US-centric, a position that admittedly reflected the early and more pronounced domestic and commercial development and adoption of the Internet within the US, but is undeniably out of date now),[5] but also in terms of its marginalisation of wider civic inclusion and democratic oversight. The MS model that ICANN represents is therefore contentious from the point of view of public interest and political feasibility. '[A]meliorative views of multistakeholder models overlook the most critical feature of existing, functioning multistakeholder governance institutions', claims Mueller:

non-state actors are elevated to the same status as governments in the making of public policy. Indeed, they may even limit or exclude governments from certain roles. (ICANN's bylaws, for example, do not allow government officials to be board members).

(2017, p. 116)

Second, MS operates on a smaller scale *within* rather than across individual jurisdictions, regulatory groups and regimes. In this case the process involves an array of different voices, competencies, knowledges and skillsets from across the socio-political, economic, cultural and academic spectrum, much as it does at the international level. Yet this latter type promotes an even greater pluralism in the regulatory and decision-making processes, and thus exists, at least for Brown and Marsden, within the remit of civil society because it introduces or attempts to introduce the citizenry into the regulatory-making process, something that cannot be practically or meaningfully achieved at the global level. An interesting facet of MS at this level is the way it mediates between forms of self-regulation and, as will discussed shortly, forms of autonomous code-based regulation. As Mueller argues: 'Nation-states are too large to make information policy and access decisions for

5 For instance, nearly 50% (13 of the 28) members of the ICANN policy development team are based in the US, and there is only one from the UK (see: www.icann.org/p olicy#staff).

the diverse array of individuals and groups within a society, and too small and conflict-prone to make optimal decisions for the global Internet as a whole' (2017, p. 128), the option of MS in this context therefore appears an effective choice in order to achieve a broad range of compliance needs.

Again, however, it is questionable the extent to which domestic fora are committed to civic ends or public interest in the way Brown and Marsden imply. The APPG blockchain within the UK Parliament, for instance, points to the fact that MS groups pertaining to be rooted in government and civic interest still foreground the interests of commerce, business and, above all, markets and competition. Thus public interest is a second-hand consideration, or one that can be satisfied, stakeholders believe, via the 'trickle-down' successes of business as first-order considerations. Michael Gurstein describes similar concerns:

> While there are clear and well-regarded opportunities for participation by private sector stakeholders, technical stakeholders and civil society stakeholders in the Internet policy forums (marketplace) there is no obvious 'stakeholder' in the process with the task of representing the 'public interest'. Thus no one has the responsibility for ensuring that the decision-making processes are fair and not subverted or captured and that the range of participants is sufficiently inclusive to ensure a legitimate and socially equitable outcome. Nor in the multistakeholder model, as in the neo-liberal economic model is there any external regulatory framework to protect the general or public interest in the midst of the 'liberalized' (i.e. non-regulated) interactions and outcomes resulting from the interactions between individual sectional interests.
>
> (2014)

Pushing back against narrowly defined MS groups, whether at the global or domestic level, brings with it the counter-threat of regulatory groupings becoming too big and thus arguably administratively unworkable and untenable. Yet tailoring groups to fit a range of macro and micro regulatory needs also raises the issue of who ultimately chooses the groupings and the nature of their membership. Following what Gurstein describes above, it is hard to believe groups would include advocates of public interest generally or to the exclusion of private interest more specifically, with pragmatic economic determinations instead leading to more members who are unwilling to 'rock the boat' when public interest is not met. 'In the MS model there is no promotion of the public interest', claims Gurstein, 'rather somehow the public interest is a (magical) bi-product/outcome of the confluence (or consensus) processes of each individual stakeholder pursuing their particular individual interest (stake)' (2014).

Mueller is also no supporter of broad-based MS models:

> One of the fallacies of multistakeholder ideology is to assume that the global Internet governance institutions will become more responsive and better able to govern the Internet properly by including more and more people from a greater diversity of backgrounds. To multistakeholder evangelists, the answer

to every problem is simple: more participation from more people! This is a dangerous mistake.

(2017, p. 120)

Whilst it might be possible to agree with Mueller's evaluation, what he is advocating does not dispel the fear that public interest advocates, under his model, would necessarily be any more welcome. Indeed, he quickly turns from disparaging 'multistakeholder evangelists' to a default neoliberal setting of free-market evangelism which absolutely does not concern itself with public interest or civil models of regulation. 'Multistakeholder models are a feasible way out [from the threat of over-politicisation of regulation]', argues Mueller, 'if we view them as competitors to and substitutes for state power; only if they have some basis for contractual power; and only if their scope of governance is inversely correlated to the size of the community they engage' (2017, p. 121).

Much of what has been discussed in this section has drawn on the experience of Internet regulation. Indeed, as described at the start of the chapter, the Internet is an obvious and not unreasonable place to start to look for emerging trends in blockchain regulation and governance. As influential voices in the blockchain ecosystem, the Tapscotts point to lessons learnt from Internet regulation in moving forward with comparable blockchain regimes. Unsurprisingly perhaps, and with clear echoes of Mueller's position, the Tapscotts view MS as the way forward in the long term. 'We believe effective regulation and, by extension, effective governance come', they claim, 'from a multistakeholder approach where transparency and public participation are valued more highly and weigh more heavily in decision making', and for 'the first time in human history', they conclude, 'nonstate, multistakeholder networks are forming to solve global problems' (2016, p. 298). Further, like Mueller, the Tapscotts suggest that we 'no longer need government officials to convene for the rest of us to align our goals and efforts' (2016, p. 298). Although in highlighting 'businesses, academia, NGOs [nongovernmental organisations], and other nonstate stakeholders' (2016, p. 298) as the obvious sources for building the blockchain MS model, they equally, if unintentionally, affirm Gurstein's complaint of public interest a (magical) bi-product of individual consensus building.

The Tapscotts are not, however, entirely in favour of MS. Instead they reserve judgement based on regulatory needs flowing from the blockchain ecosystem that, in their estimation, exceed those of the Internet. Therefore, whilst 'the Internet governance model is a good template' and the 'multistakeholder network worked for the Internet', they claim (although this is clearly debatable, as the earlier discussion showed), 'we need to recognize that there will be a greater role for regulation of blockchain technologies' (2016, p. 298). The answer to the blockchain regulatory conundrum at least in the short to medium term is, for the Tapscotts, a fluid MS governance and regulatory model that straddles Internet and emerging blockchain regimes, and draws experience directly from individuals who have long been at the forefront of Internet governance, not least within ICANN (2016, p. 300). The closed circle of regulatory influence, one might say, is therefore made complete, or at the very least nears a state of completion within the Tapscotts' logic, and far from pushing against Internet regulatory norms and traditions they are instead embracing them. As with many other areas of blockchain it is, as I have repeatedly argued, business as usual therefore, and that business is neoliberalism.

Code-based regulation

> In real space, we recognize how laws regulate – through constitutions, statutes, and other legal codes. In cyberspace we must understand how a different 'code' regulates – how the software and hardware (i.e., the 'code' of cyberspace) that make cyberspace what it is also regulate cyberspace as it is.
>
> (Lessig, 2006, p. 5)

Discussion of code-based regulation within the blockchain context struggles to dodge the influence of Lawrence Lessig, as Primavera De Filippi and Aaron Wright demonstrate in their exergue to Lessig's work, *Blockchain and the Law* (2018). As suggested previously, however, Lessig's essentialist perspective that posits cyberspace as a regulatory environment which, by virtue of its difference and novelty, lies outside the boundaries of traditional or offline regulatory ideas, systems and procedures ('regulate cyberspace as it is') is not one viewed here as reflective of the reality of network regulation, and thus not entirely accurate. Not least because, whilst Lessig's code as law theory has been influential in narrow techno-legal contexts, the dominance of forms of traditional regulation that circulate industries and actors offline (self- and market-complementing regulation in particular), have been translated online – in many senses in order to literally 'follow the money' – revealing that code-based regulation (or code as law) is far from the predominant or, more importantly, desirable form of regulation for network technologies, but only part of a suite of regulatory options. 'Lessig's work is of great value for reminding us of the importance of architecture as a basis for regulation', claim Murray and Scott (2002, p. 500) in their discussion of Lessig's influence on Internet regulation, and this cannot be denied with regard to blockchain. Indeed, it could be argued that notions of architecture find fresh prominence in regulatory considerations of decentralised and disintermediated controls that blockchain affords. Yet, while Lessig ought to be and is acknowledged here, as well as through a number of the sources that inform the discussion here on code-based regulation and technology regulation more generally, it is not considered necessary to rehearse his theories in order to bring new regulatory insight to light where blockchain is concerned, but instead to take a broader view of blockchain regulatory enterprise as a species of network regulation which does not begin and end with Lawrence Lessig.

The idea that systems or networks can be auto-regulating, and particularly in contrast to the messy contingencies of human *self-regulation* and *multistakeholderism*, including the potential for both to create and not be able to resolve market failures, has long been a central theme in Internet regulatory debates. 'Code-based change at various levels of the Internet architecture', argues Biegel, 'has emerged as potentially the single most powerful regulatory strategy available' (2003, p. 362), and code-based regulation draws on notions that stem from approaches to regulating a wide variety of different systems and processes (Reyes, 2016). Before moving on it is worth revisiting the definitions presented earlier with regard to self-regulation as they are of relevance here, namely those from across embryology, engineering and cybernetics: 'the process of cell reorganization or readjustment that occurs in the restoration of an organic defect or incompleteness'; 'a quantity that expresses the degree of imperfection of a device or system'; 'any systematic behaviour within a system that tends to restrict fluctuations of any variable' (Bullock and Stallybrass, 1977, p. 533). As a precursor to the consideration of alternative models of code-based auto-regulation, these definitions demonstrate how, in particular, regulation exists or is capable of existing *within* bodies or systems rather than being imposed upon them either *ex ante* or *ex post* by external forces. By removing the possibility that external forces can corrupt or themselves be corrupted also feeds notions of the improved security and efficiency of internal regulatory modalities. Biegel further enfolds this within a model of 'architecture based regulation', and does so in terms that resonate with blockchain discourse emanating from the ecosystem:

> Consistent with the online world's decentralized, anarchic structure, architecture-based regulation can occur at various points in the system, and just about anyone from the powers-that-be to individual users can help set it in motion. Not only is architecture-based regulation potentially the most effective form of regulation currently available, but – to the extent that it can be accomplished by bypassing the legal system – it may also very well be the easiest to set in motion. Thus, otherwise libertarian commentators who typically argue that the government should stay out of cyberspace are finding that they are actually looking to the government to establish limits on what persons and groups might be able to accomplish through it.
>
> (2003, p. 193)

Carla Reyes follows this regulatory theme through a proposal of what she calls an 'endogenous model of regulation' (Reyes, 2016, p. 222) specific to the context of blockchain. The endogenous model, according to Reyes, 'simultaneously governs from within and without, and sidesteps the ex ante/ex post regulatory choice by building compliance into the protocol' (2016, p. 222). Furthermore, 'endogenous regulation leads to an approach that is iterative, cooperative, focused on the functional purposes for enacting regulation, and implemented from within the market requiring regulation' (Reyes, 2016, p. 222). In essence, Reyes's proposal takes as its starting point formal regulatory modes – including legislation, rules, directives, customs, doctrines, principles, as well as the capacity for discretion and flexibility *qua* natural law and equity – and embeds these in protocols at the point a blockchain application is built (coded or programmed), or a broader distributed ledger architecture is mobilised on top of which multiple commands (e.g. smart contracts) might run and execute. What Reyes's proposal does not advocate is 'using smart contracts to create code of law that enables the regulation of private actors and decentralized autonomous organizations' (2016, p. 227). Smart contracts are at once a point of true radical potential in blockchain, as a connection between an intertwined 'the good' and contractual status. Moreover, as Melanie Swan maintains, this connection should be made by machines and software *automatically* and *autonomously* rather than as a precondition of human needs, rights and desires, thus skewing and intertwining the logic of 'the good' and contract. In contrast to Reyes's analysis of the role of smart contracts, yet maintaining the same basic regulatory logic, Quinn DuPont and Bill Maurer talk of the significant changes that 'cryptocontracts' (smart contracts) are bringing to system administration, especially with regard to the Ethereum blockchain. 'Cryptocontracts tend', they claim, 'to build social and functional properties *within* the system, whereas traditional contracts require a cadre of individuals to perform these things outside the contract' (2015).

As with Reyes's proposal and other concepts of code-based regulation, the key to the effectiveness of system oversight lies in constant autonomous adjustments to changing sets of conditions and emergent sets of commands and protocols. There is, in other words, a higher level of efficiency within a smart contracting regulatory context, one that is in constant state of action/ reaction, than is possible in traditional offline and off-chain contracting or regulatory regimes. The binary nature of smart contract regulation, one that eschews any form of discretion including, notably, human discretion, is not attractive in all circumstances, but could, I suggest, find use in strict liability regulatory regimes. This regulatory measure is not one that seems all that attractive to the blockchain ecosystem, however, although perhaps for good reason if it is viewed as counter-innovative and threatens a degree of constraint that is unpalatable to advocates of free-market logics of technological flourishing. Instead regulators such as the Financial Conduct Authority in the UK acknowledge that smart contracts 'with predetermined codified rules to automatically ensure firms' compliance when reporting data' could 'significantly improve *our* access to data', which would in turn, 'allow *us* to identify areas of emerging risk more efficiently and improve the speed and accuracy of our response' [emphasis added] (2017, p. 20). In other words, smart contracts could be used to regulate more effectively and thus, in the minds of some stakeholders, represent the realisation of Marshall McLuhan's prophecy of technological reversal: 'an empowering technology turned into a mechanism of co-option and enslavement' (Moulthrop, 1991).

The 'first and primary target for regulation-through-code' or 'technology-assisted regulation', says Reyes, 'is the technology itself' (2016, p. 228). The key aim being to address the law or regulatory lag that occurs ordinarily when regulation has to chase technological advances by 'filling the gap' (Reyes, 2016, p. 222), whilst not simply enabling further informal self-regulation in the form of coded regulation that has no formal basis in law, but insisting on thorough and formal regulatory oversight. 'This is a proposal', Reyes concludes, that regulators undertake the dual task of enacting a law or regulation via statute, and then implementing that statue through code, so that it is endogenously incorporated into the decentralized ledger technology or application running on top of the technology.

(2016, p. 228)

'The proposal here is not' claims Reyes, 'for allowing the industry to self-regulate through rules created by use of the blockchain or other similar technologies' (2016, p. 227). This particular problematic feature of existing technological regulation that Reyes sees endogenous regulation potentially addressing is certainly prominent within wider technological ecosystems, as the earlier discussions of self-regulation revealed and the recent European Union General Data Protection Regulation (GDPR) also shows. Moreover, so is the insistence on technology-assisted regulation from 'within the market requiring regulation' (2016, p. 227), but here Reyes is clearly less concerned.

The question I would like to conclude with here is why the market needs to be heeded at all in the context of Reyes's endogenous regulation and by extension any (re) imagining of code-based regulation? If endogenous regulation comes *a fortiori* the market, surely it risks devolving to a mere species of self-regulation, rather than remaining a species of state-led regulation or regulation defined under political and democratic mandate in the public interest as proposed initially by Reyes, and thus also risks losing its teeth. Reyes, in other words, assumes without question the legitimacy and rationality of market regulation, and in so doing loses favour here because such regulation would not ultimately foster co-operative outcomes, as Reyes initially claims, but seek out competitive ones. Again, however, the fact that endogenous regulation of the type advocated by Reyes must act as a species of market-complementing regulation tells us a great deal about the pervasiveness of market bias in this model and the regulatory regime more generally, and the high probability of neoliberal influence underpinning it and the future of blockchain regulation.

To add more context to the question of whether or not market or competitive regulatory interventions are needed or relevant in the context of code-based regulation, it is worth briefly examining the regulatory schema devised by Andrew Murray and Colin Scott (2002), in particular for the purposes of understanding how hybridity in regulatory control systems occurs and its varied effects. For Mark Fenster, hybridisation 'promises collaboration among regulators and interested parties, and therefore better regulations based on information that private entities willingly share with regulators, as well as more willing compliance' (2017, p. 91). Murray and Scott define regulatory control systems as models incorporating standard setting, information gathering and behaviour modification (2002, p. 502). For present purposes, the control system proposed is analogous to that described above – namely, a smart contracting regulatory context that is in a constant state of action/reaction, where action relates to standard setting and information gathering, and reaction to behaviour modification and standard setting. Thus a cyclical, adaptable and efficient regulatory process is formed that is able to control the context in which it is deployed, at least in theory.

Murray and Scott read these elements of control systems against four different forms of control system: hierarchical control (law and other formalised rules); community-based control (social norms); competition-based control price/quality ratio (and equivalents with non-market decisions); design-based control (inbuilt design features and social administrative systems) (2002, p. 504). It will be noted that the control systems Murray and Scott describe accord with the various areas of regulation discussed more widely during this chapter, and therefore it is not only with regard to code-based regulation that they apply. However, I introduce them here because of the convenience of using the schema to isolate and examine individual features of the different regulatory control systems, and thus bring into question the need, as Reyes has it, for code-based regulation to align to market-complementing characteristics. As stated earlier, I dispute this need. Code-based regulation, which parallels what Murray and Scott refer to as design-based control and involves inbuilt design that interacts with the regulatory environment in which it is deployed, can work in hybrid with competition-based control or market-complementing regulation, but it can equally work with hierarchical control (we will explore this further, for example, in the discussion on blockchain *as* regulator), or community-based control, or different combinations across all four control systems. In other words, there is no default relationship between code-based and market-complementing regulation that is not intentional, whether this is due to arguments of economic efficiency or for ideological reasons, that is, to promote a greater competitive field in which neoliberalism can flourish. As mentioned above, there is a high probability of neoliberal influence determining the future of blockchain regulation, a suggestion implied by Murray and Scott when they claim that among 'the widely observed hybrid forms are competition law and co-regulation and enforced self-regulation' (2002, p. 505). Whilst hybridity of regulatory types may help temper the influence and force of any one individual form of regulation therefore, whether that is formal law, self-regulation, multistakeholder co-regulation or code-based regulation, the present regulatory landscape into which blockchain has emerged based on Internet regulatory trends, points towards the dominance of competition and markets as default modes of regulatory control. Something advocates of alternative regulation must address urgently.

Conclusion

Blockchain not only continues the regulatory conundrums faced by the Internet and other networked technologies but problematises them further by creating novel choke points enmeshed in a contentious ethics of political economy, namely the desires and needs of the neoliberal project to 'leverage' socioeconomic shifts blockchain promises. A practical way in which to address problems facing regulatory authorities over blockchain is to look at those points representing the intertwined and monetisable arenas so coveted by the entrepreneurial class. These include forms of pervasive network decentralisation supporting 'immutable' audit trails of big data that enable greater scalability and efficiency in universal data exchange. As blockchain hype begins to subside, reaches an equilibrium of ordinariness, and begins to disappear into everyday practices, regulatory authorities, whether global or transnational governance bodies, or forms of multi-stakeholder regulation and self-regulation will be faced with the task of imposing limits on systems and processes that are deeply embedded in techno-social and techno-economic practices and thus largely invisible. It is important to figure out therefore what shape regulation will take sooner rather than later; to, in effect, learn from mistakes that have plagued (and continue to plague) the Internet and other areas of technological growth and innovation. Bringing to the fore regulatory possibilities that maintain sufficient democratic accountability of commercial practices will be crucial to the regulatory enterprise to come.

As this chapter has shown, the starting point for assessing potential forms of regulation is traditional. However, the regulatory landscape for evolving technologies can benefit from critical and more marginal approaches that push beyond traditional framework and conventional wisdom, including those that reveal the role that fetishism and erotics play within the blockchain ecosystem, and, importantly, what these psychic phenomena tell us about blockchain conduct and how the technology 'is part of the deeper order of things' (Arthur, 2009, p. 216). Where once the mantra for regulators may have been 'follow the money', neoliberalism has made any clear sense of the work of for-profit self-interested capitalists in commercial domains such as blockchain ambiguous. Instead, I argue, the desire of entrepreneurs ultimately identifies where regulators need to be looking, and regulators must, therefore *follow the desire*. This is an approach that actually continues key areas of traditional regulatory environments where the focus is on individual and group behaviour and the products of those behaviours. Extending the regulatory enterprise to considerations not simply of behaviour or behavioural economics but more specifically to focus on the undercurrent of digital production, transaction and exchange as embodiments, condensations, materialisations of libidinal drives and unconscious desires, signals the critical work psycho-politics can do in determining regulatory approaches capable, I argue, of cutting through the illusions and fantasies of stakeholders in the blockchain ecosystem. We will return to this theme in the concluding part of this book.

References

Arthur, W. Brian. 2009. *The Nature of Technology: What it is and how it evolves.* London: Penguin.

Biegel, Stuart. 2003. *Beyond our Control? Confronting the Limits of Our Legal System in the Age of Cyberspace.* Cambridge: The MIT Press.

Black, Julia. 2002. Critical Reflections on Regulation. *Australian Journal of Legal Philosophy*, 27, pp. 1–37.

Bogost, Ian. 2017. Cryptocurrency Might be a Path to Authoritarianism. *The Atlantic*, 30 May. www.theatlantic.com/technology/archive/2017/05/blockchain-of-command/528543/ (accessed 25 January 2018).

Botsman, Rachel. 2017. *Who Can You Trust? How Technology Brought Us Together – and Why It Could Drive Us Apart.* London: Portfolio Penguin.

Brown, Ian and Marsden, Christopher T. 2013. *Regulating Code: Good Governance and Better Regulation in the Information Age*. Cambridge: MIT Press.

Brownsword, Roger. 2008. *Rights, Regulation, and the Technological Revolution*. Oxford: Oxford University Press.

Brownsword, Roger and Goodwin, Morag. 2012. *Law and Technologies of the Twenty-First Century*. Cambridge: Cambridge University Press.

Bullock, Alan and Stallybrass, Oliver, eds. 1977. *The Fontana Dictionary of Modern Thought*. London: Fontana/Collins.

Cross, Michael. 2017. Blockchain deal bodes ill for conveyancers. *The Law Society Gazette*, 16 October. www.lawgazette.co.uk/news/blockchain-deal-bodes-ill-for-conveyancers/5063242.article (accessed 15 January 2018).

Currie, Wendy L., Gozman, Daniel P. and Seddon, Jonathan J.M. 2017. Dialectic tensions in the financial markets: a longitudinal study of pre- and post-crisis regulatory technology. *Journal of Information Technology*. https://doi.org/10.1057/s41265-017-0047-5 (accessed 10 May 2018).

De, Nikhilesh. 2018. German Central Bank: Cryptocurrencies Must be regulated on a Global Scale. *Coindesk*, 15 January. www.coindesk.com/german-central-banker-cryptocurrencies-must-be-regulated-on-a-global-scale/ (accessed 16 January 2018).

De Filippi, Primavera and Wright, Aaron. 2018. *Blockchain and the Law: The Rule of Code*. Cambridge: Harvard University Press.

Dean, Jodie. 2009. *Democracy and Other Neoliberal Fantasies: Communicative Capitalism and Left Politics*. Durham: Duke University Press.

DuPont, Quinn and Maurer, Bill. 2015. Ledgers and Law in the Blockchain. *Kings Review Magazine*, 23 June. http://kingsreview.co.uk/articles/ledgers-and-law-in-the-blockchain/ (accessed 25 April 2018).

European Commission. 2018. *25 May – GDPR tightens data protection rules for companies and gives people back control*. European Commission. https://ec.europa.eu/unitedkingdom/news/25-may-%E2%80%93-gdpr-tightens-data-protection-rules-companies-and-gives-people-back-control_en (accessed 25 May 2018).

Fenster, Mark. 2017. *The Transparency Fix: Secrets, Leaks, and Uncontrollable Government Information*. Stanford: Stanford University Press.

Financial Conduct Authority (FCA). 2017. *Distributed Ledger Technology: Feedback Statement on Discussion Paper 17/03*. Financial Conduct Authority. December. www.fca.org.uk/publication/feedback/fs17-04.pdf (accessed 6 February 2018).

Goldenfein, Jake and Leiter, Andrea. 2018. Legal Engineering on the Blockchain: 'Smart Contracts' as Legal Conduct. *Law and Critique*, Vol. 29, No. 2 (July), pp. 141–149.

Gupta, Vinay. 2017. European Parliament blockchain presentation May 2017. *YouTube*. www.youtube.com/watch?v=xEFVuccuHI8&t=4s (accessed 1 February 2018).

Gurstein, Michael. 2014. The Multistakeholder Model, Neo-liberalism and Global (Internet) Governance. *Gurstein's Community Informatics*, 26 March. https://gurstein.wordpress.com/2014/03/26/the-multistakeholder-model-neo-liberalism-and-global-internet-governance/ (accessed 24 April 2018).

Hall, Stuart. 2017. *Selected Political Writings: The Great Moving Right Show and Other Essays*. Edited by Sally Davison, David Featherstone, Michael Rustin and Bill Schwartz. Durham: Duke University Press.

Harvey, David. 2005. *A Brief History of Neoliberalism*. Oxford: Oxford University Press.

Hood, Christopher. 1991. A Public Management for all Seasons. *Public Administration*, Vol. 69, No. 1, pp. 3–19.

Katsh, Ethan and Rabinovich-Einy, Orna. 2017. *Digital Justice: Technology and the Internet of Disputes*. Oxford: Oxford University Press.

König, Thomas and Duran, Enric. 2016. FairCoin V2 White Paper Draft. *FairCoin*. www. fair-coin.org (accessed 14 April 2018).

Lemke, Thomas. 2012. *Foucault, Governmentality, and Critique*. Boulder: Paradigm Publishers.

Lessig, Lawrence. 2006. *Code: Version 2.0*. New York: Basic Books.

Marsden, Christopher T. 2000. Introduction: Information and communications technologies, globalisation and regulation. *Regulating the Global Information Society*. Edited by Christopher T. Marsden. London: Routledge, pp. 1–40.

Mirowski, Philip. 2014. *Never Let A Serious Crisis Go To Waste: How Neoliberalism Survived the Financial Meltdown*. London: Verso.

Moulthrop, Stuart. 1991. You Say You Want a Revolution? Hypertext and the Laws of Media. *Postmodern Culture*, Vol. 1, No. 3. https://muse.jhu.edu/ (accessed 25 April 2018).

Mueller, Milton. 2017. *Will the Internet Fragment? Sovereignty, Globalization and Cyberspace*. Cambridge: Polity.

Murray, Andrew and Scott, Colin. 2002. Controlling the New Media: Hybrid Responses to New Forms of Power. *The Modern Law Review*, Vol. 65, No. 4 (July), pp. 491–516.

Power, Michael. 1997. *The Audit Society: Rituals of Verification*. Oxford: Oxford University Press.

Price, Monroe E. and Verhulst, Stefaan G. 2000. In search of the self: Charting the course of self-regulation on the Internet in a global environment. *Regulating the Global Information Society*. Edited by Christopher T. Marsden. London: Routledge, pp. 57–78.

Reyes, Carla L. 2016. Moving Beyond Bitcoin to an Endogenous Theory of Decentralized Ledger Technology Regulation: an Initial Proposal. *Villanova Law Review*, Vol. 61, No. 1, pp. 191–234.

Scott, Brett. 2016. *How Can Cryptocurrency and Blockchain Technology Play a Role in Building Social and Solidarity Finance?* Working Paper 2016 2011. Geneva: United Nations Research Institute for Social Development.

Swan, Melanie. 2015. *Blockchain: Blueprint for a New Economy*. Sebastopol: O'Reilly.

Tapscott, Don and Tapscott, Alex. 2016. *Blockchain Revolution: How the Technology behind Bitcoin is Changing Money, Business and the World*. London: Portfolio Penguin.

Wood, Ellen Meiksins. 2017. *The Origin of Capitalism: A Longer View*. London: Verso.

4 Blockchain the regulator

Introduction

> The archons are first of all the documents' guardians. They do not only ensure the physical security of what is deposited and of the substrate. They are also accorded the hermeneutic right and competence. They have the power to interpret the archives. Entrusted to such archons, these documents in effect speak the law: they recall the law and call on or impose the law.
>
> (Derrida, 1996, p. 2)

> Transparency and power do not get along well.
>
> (Han, 2015, p. 47)

> Surely confidence in the tax system would be better served if we had greater transparency?
>
> (Hodge, 2016, p. 70)

> The extent to which regulatory technology increases transparency by reducing autonomy remains open to debate.
>
> (Currie et al., 2017)

Blockchain as *archon*, 'receiver general of the finances' (Mercier, 1772, pp. 169–176), *Custos Rotulorum* (a legally mandated keeper of records) (Styles, 1980, p. 222), or simply regulator, all are interesting visions of or prospects for blockchain that fulfil the greater public interest requirements argued for thus far in this book by placing the technology in the hands of those who check opportunism and disproportionate private self-interest, especially when it strays into the civic domain. Yet this remains far from an unproblematic vision of blockchain because it necessitates high standards from the regulatory guardians to fulfil their duty in the public interest, maintain legitimacy and not allow corruption of practices or technologies. Furthermore, additional concerns obtain over transparency in public expenditure where government information and communications technology (ICT) projects are concerned and the ability, as Margaret Hodge, former chair of the Public Accounts Committee puts it, 'to follow the taxpayer's pound' (2016, Chapter 2). Transparency, as earlier discussions in this book have highlighted, is often presented as an end in itself, and thus where it can be demonstrated as operative the belief follows that it is politically effective and morally justifiable. Yet notable paradoxes involved in drives to create more transparency in contemporary information networks and systems and calls for increased transparency and accountability 'often translate into heightened levels of surveillance and controls inevitably facilitated through numerous technologies and the affordances they create' (Currie et al., 2017).

The likelihood of private businesses developing, building and maintaining multiple blockchain-led regulatory infrastructure projects on behalf of publicly and politically accountable bodies in the near future is without doubt. This will inevitably have an impact on the shape of transparency narratives in terms of regulation by introducing a closer and thus problematic relationship between self-interest (i.e. the guiding profit motive of business) and the regulatory enterprise. IBM, for example, has already developed a 'Blockchain for Government' resource, one built around much of the rhetoric identified and explored throughout this book, as the following passage attests:

> To build trust, governments strive to be as open, transparent and collaborative as possible and blockchain may be a key tool. To demolish bureaucracy, they seek to streamline citizen interaction, financial transactions and contract management. All too often, they fall short of their own ambitions on both counts.
>
> In a recent IBV Study 'Building trust in government: Exploring the potential of blockchain for government' 200 government leaders in 16 countries were surveyed on their experience and expectations for blockchain. The study concluded that this technology offers the opportunity to tackle the trust and bureaucracy challenges head on. Researchers found a significant percentage of trailblazer governments are launching projects that apply blockchain to transform regulatory compliance, contract management, identity management and citizen services.
>
> Blockchain offers a new approach to enhancing transparency and collaboration between governments, business and citizens. By registering assets and recording ownership changes on a distributed shared ledger, the quest for transparency and right to privacy needn't be at odds. Important information can be shared widely, seamlessly engendering true openness. Transactions can be verified close to real time and combined with the extensive use of privacy services make fraud and cybercrime very difficult. Smart contracts – once verified and deployed – will always execute. Reneging on a contract becomes a thing of the past. This all goes towards amplifying transparency, building trust and breaking down bureaucracy between government, business and citizens.
>
> (Palfreyman, 2017)

IBM can be seen to be proposing more private/public partnership ICT infrastructure projects, yet at a granular level the issue, as the passage above attests, is one of private corporations also taking hold of and shaping narratives of transparency and trust, and in particular what technologies are needed to facilitate it. IBM opt for blockchain, as do many other actors, but aside from the specifics of the technology involved it is important to remember that the ethos of both transparency and trust advocated is being produced by private self-interest on behalf of the public interest. This is nothing more than an extension of the privatisation of government services and functions via blockchain, and this ought rightfully to be of concern as it has been with regard to other technologies, systems and so on whose private contractualised development has been explicitly encouraged by successive governments of all stripes in Western capitalist nations during at least the last 40 years. Stuart Hall claimed privatisation comes in 'three sizes: (1) straight sell-off of public assets; (2) contracting out to private companies for profit; (3) two-step privatisation "by stealth" where it is represented by unintended consequences' (2017, pp. 332–333). Blockchain could, I suggest, potentially be mobilised via any one of the three avenues, but the more pressing concern is whether or not government is leading on the issue of technological development or being led by the likes of IBM, and thus selling public interest.

Notions of blockchain as a neutral 'tool' at the disposal of governments or regulators, where regulatory legitimacy and the ability to call regulators to account based on their deployment of the technology, as well as on many or all subsequent failures within the regulatory regime, are all important factors. Regulators will generally support technological interventions to automate compliance if it can be shown to achieve greater operational efficiency (Currie et al., 2017). But where technologies such as blockchain are integrated into the environment as regulatory instruments, requires, as Roger Brownsword and Morag Goodwin maintain, that 'regulators are called to account, not so much for their failure to create the right kind of environment for new technologies, but for their over-reliance on technological tools' (2012, p. 46). Moreover, there ought to be significant concern with regard to the continued expansion of a culture of audit, which via blockchain regulatory implementations risks disseminating economic reason *qua* neoliberal rationality far beyond financial services and into every corner of contemporary social life. Blockchain could, as Melanie Swan contends, 'become the lingua franca archival mechanism for the whole of society's documents' (2015, p. 21).

If what Swan contends were to be the case it would require blockchain to assume a position of archival guardianship and command over documents that intensifies, extends and indeed problematises questions of regulatory legitimacy. Jacques Derrida relates the authority of the archive to the role played by the *archons*, Greek superior magistrates, expected not only to guard the documents but to assume 'right and competence' over their interpretation, meaning the documents ultimately spoke the law (1996, p. 2). The archons, originally from *arkheion*, meaning house or domicile, represented jurisdiction in the form of dwelling, and a place where documents and the archive dwelled permanently, marking the 'institutional passage from the private to the public', but 'not always from the secret to the nonsecret' (Derrida, 1996, pp. 2–3). While it is reasonable to think about blockchain's regulatory capacities not being limited to overcoming challenges such as arcane practices in financial services and in many other documented sectors and compliance environments as well therefore, blockchain as regulator should not be expected to automatically bring to light, to render transparent, all that is deemed (unnecessarily) secretive.

Unearthing the regulatory potential of blockchain to check private and commercial opportunism and interests rather than promote them, as well as bolster the resolve of governments and regulatory authorities to achieve such ends is not easy because it goes against the tide of dominant blockchain narratives, as well as conceptual development to some degree. To recall the earlier discussion, as a regulator blockchain is an example, I argue, of 'blockchain for no good' because it exists outside prioritisations of self-interest and private advantage and therefore does not correspond to 'the good' of market and competition norms. Notionally blockchain as regulator would be turning against its maker in the sense that the technology would be used to constrain rather than promote capitalist and neoliberal agendas, and thus undermine the interests of blockchain stakeholders. By focusing attention instead on prioritising public interest and political feasibility blockchain-led regulation would be of benefit to both governments and taxpayers as it 'drastically reduces the potential for tax controversy, including tax audits, as most tax controversy today comes from arguing over transactions in an historical context' (Flynn, 2016). 'The blockchain removes the requirement for someone to question corporate taxes (or underlying commercial transactions)', argues Channing Flynn, 'because the government and the taxpayer should instantly be on the same verifiable page as to what transactions were just processed a moment ago, and every subsequent moment. It's a just-in-time system' (2016).

The main thrust of this proposal is of course not itself neutral politically, but alludes to the use of blockchain to achieve aims that presently exist outside global politico-economic frameworks and norms. The irony of blockchain's libertarian credentials being refocused on supporting centralised authorities and government revenue protection aims is noteworthy, but pushed further to incorporate socialist aims is perhaps not as deep an irony as it first appears. 'The tantalizing open question for those inspired by this [socialist/anarchist] tradition', argues Brett Scott, 'is whether blockchain systems can be a basis upon which people can easily interact with distant strangers for collaboration at scale' (2016, pp. 15–16). Scott continues:

> Blockchain systems – at least superficially – offer a vision of large-scale egalitarian self-organization far beyond the scale of ordinary anarchist attempts at building cooperative communes. In this vision, the objective is to replace hierarchal centralized institutions with decentralized ones, but the point of doing this is not to once-and-for-all perfect a means for naturally self-interested individual humans to contract with each other. Rather it is to allow naturally social beings to flourish and collaborate with each other in a spirit of cooperation, not individualistic competition.
>
> (2016, pp. 15–16)

The proposal for blockchain as regulator is one that echoes Scott and examples explored thus far in this book, including Wampum and Mercier's tax trunk.

Moreover it is a proposal that corresponds with David Harvey's call to locate within the 'existing bundle of technologies, saturated as they are in the mentalities and practices of capital's search for class domination [...] the emancipatory potentialities that somehow have to be mobilised in anti-capitalist struggle' (2014, p. 110), to which can also be added the potentialities to check the onward march of neoliberalism. In lieu of a thoroughgoing vision of blockchain socialism what blockchain can do now, within the politico-economic status quo, is help governments and regulators confront aggressive forms of tax avoidance and evasion and thus tip the balance, if marginally, in favour of public and democratic interest.

Key regulatory needs that blockchain could fulfil in existing processes for tackling tax crimes are twofold and involve a combination of regulation around (standard setting and information gathering) and enforcement of specific provisions of UK criminal legislation. First, this chapter will explore the defence contained within the *Criminal Finances Act* 2017 (hereafter 'the Act') that individuals and companies, otherwise known as 'relevant bodies', may have for failing to prevent facilitation of UK and foreign tax evasion offences.[1] That is, of being able to show that *reasonable prevention procedures* were in place at the time the offence was committed in order to avoid *inter alia* potentially unlimited fines. Second, and connected to the matter of the 2017 Act by virtue of the notion of 'a culture of secrecy' that the two rely on, blockchain's role in mandatory registries of private individual or corporate financial interest, income and asset ownership, with the aim of better policing offshore trusts. Both examples benefit from secure, auditable and transparent environments in which key financial information can be managed to confront any slippage in information asymmetries and shared in order to more effectively highlight but also in theory prevent instances of and a growth in potential arenas for tax evasion and avoidance.

As mentioned, what links the two parts of this chapter is consideration of a long-standing culture of financial secrecy that ultimately works against public interest by undermining the tax regime upon which public services and democratic regimes rely. If blockchain could work to deter individual or corporate involvement in aggressive forms of tax management, thus changing the culture around acceptance of tax liabilities rather than simply operating as means of evidence gathering for *ex post* prosecutions, this would be, it is believed here, a desirable and radical outcome. Moreover, it echoes the spirit of the 2017 Act, as HM Revenue and Customs (HMRC) maintain:

> The new offence [...] does not radically alter what is criminal, it simply focuses on who is held to account for acts contrary to the current criminal law. *It does this by focussing on the failure to prevent the crimes of those who act for or on behalf of a corporation, rather than trying to attribute criminal acts to that corporation.*
>
> [emphasis added] (2016, p. 4)

1 S.45–46 *Criminal Finances Act* 2017.

Relying on the 'transparency' and audit functions of blockchain will not auto-matically dissuade individuals, corporations, institutions and so on from engaging in aggressive tax management planning and strategies, including forms of avoid-ance or evasion. The battle against the creation of specious legal mechanisms that disguise property holdings, funds and other assets off shore, thus distancing the nature of liabilities from the scrutiny of tax authorities and in many cases deliber-ately obscuring them, has no obvious end and blockchain alone no solution. This is in spite of the blatant illusion that these legal mechanisms represent being openly acknowledged by many authorities, and even underpinned by international collective 'wealth management' organisations such as STEP (Society of Trust and Estate Practitioners). As Brooke Harrington maintains: 'While STEP and many wealth management practitioners see the use of offshore finance as legitimate and necessary, most outside the industry see it as a transparent scam' (2016, p. 131). The irony of Harrington's use of 'transparent' in this context is not lost here, but points to a notion that will be discussed in more detail later in the chapter, namely, transparency as a false hope for solving the problems of financial secrecy and aggressive tax management.

Blockchain may offer an opportunity to recalibrate the power play between those who would engage in aggressive tax strategies and planning, and those charged with regulating or constraining them, by, for example, more effectively enforcing tax liabilities *ahead* of settlement on trust, rather than relying on bring-ing trustees to account post-settlement. In many senses the proposal set out here for blockchain as regulator answers Lana Swartz's question of what it would mean 'for the radical blockchain moment if it were allowed to be boring?' (2017, p. 102). For technologists, venture capitalists and entrepreneurs the idea of using blockchain to constrain rather than promote private enterprise and celebrate lib-eral economic reason is likely not just 'boring', but utterly off point.[2] Blockchain, it will be suggested here therefore, creates conditions not simply for an 'Internet of value', which is so precious a concept for the likes of Michael Casey and Paul Vigna (2018), but an Internet of *regulated* value where competition is not allowed to dominate socioeconomically, but is tempered by greater public and democratic oversight, and improved political feasibility of public interest blockchains.

Blockchain: reasonable prevention procedure?

Before turning to look more closely at the broader culture of secrecy vis-à-vis aggressive tax management practices which ultimately commands the need to explore blockchain as potential regulatory monitor of tax liabilities, we will explore the narrow definition of blockchain as a means to reasonable prevention procedure

---

2   Two well-known venture capitalists in Silicon Valley, Marc Andreessen and Fred
    Wilson, who have previously backed Airbnb, Facebook and Twitter, have been parti-
    cularly vocal with regard to government and regulators taking a very light touch as
    blockchain evolves in order to enable the 'unlimited potential' of the technology
    (Politico Magazine, 2016).

under the 2017 Act. For present purposes it is not necessary to trace the full background of the 2017 Act, but rather to understand the immediate relevance of the defence. Section 45 of the Act sets out the defence as follows:

45 Failure to prevent facilitation of UK tax evasion offences

(1) A relevant body (B) is guilty of an offence if a person commits a UK tax evasion facilitation offence when acting in the capacity of a person associated with B.

(2) It is a defence for B to prove that, when the UK tax evasion facilitation offence was committed –

    (a) B had in place such prevention procedures as it was reasonable in all the circumstances to expect B to have in place, or

    (b) it was not reasonable in all the circumstances to expect B to have any prevention procedures in place.

(3) In subsection (2) 'prevention procedures' means procedures designed to prevent persons acting in the capacity of a person associated with B from committing UK tax evasion facilitation offences.

Following this outline the Act continues to define tax evasion, an important feature of the present discussion that we will return to shortly. First, however, how does the notion of reasonable prevention procedures arise in the 'relevant body' *qua* corporate body? Moreover, what is the significance of these procedures beyond the clearly stated aim of the Act to mitigate the culpability of individuals of companies caught engaging in tax evasion? There are three stages that apply to both the domestic and foreign tax evasion facilitation offences, and HMRC describe them as follows:

Stage one: the criminal tax evasion by a taxpayer (either an individual or a legal entity) under existing law.

Stage two: the criminal facilitation of the tax evasion by an 'associated person' of the relevant body who is acting in that capacity.

Stage three: the relevant body failed to prevent its representative from committing the criminal facilitation act.

Defence: where the relevant body has put in place 'reasonable prevention procedures' to prevent its associated persons from committing tax evasion facilitation offences (stage two), or where it is unreasonable to expect such procedures, it shall have a defence.

(2016, p. 6)

The offence against which reasonable procedures could offer a defence, namely tax evasion, is not created by the 2017 Act but rather continues to build on previous offences found in other legislation, including s.72 of the *Value Added Tax Act* 1994 and s.106A of the *Taxes Management Act* 1970, as well as supplementary material that s.51 ('Consequential Amendments') of the 2017 Act outlines. In terms of the defence there is a clear lineage that can be traced to the *Bribery Act* 2010, in which it was determined that businesses that have 'adequate procedures' in place to prevent bribery activities can rely on those protocols as a defence under the law.

The potential of the defence to mitigate the liability of a corporation was tested in *Serious Fraud Office v Standard Bank Plc (Now known as ICBC Standard Bank plc)* [2015] WL 10382767. In that case the bank in question was found wanting because there was no culture within the organisation able to recognise the significance of creating and maintaining the necessary procedures. More recently in *Director of the Serious Fraud Office v Eurasian Natural Resources Corporation Ltd* [2017] EWHC 1017 (QB), the defence was invoked not simply to show a corporate commitment to preventing bribery at a purely procedural level, but in order to present an image of being 'good corporate citizens' (at 137). In other words, contained within the defence is arguably a kernel of deterrent effect that not only promotes a means for corporations to mitigate their liability if and when they find themselves on the wrong side of the legislation, but, and perhaps more importantly, the nature of the defence itself prompts the need for deeper and more pervasive cultural change, and this is key to its relevance here.

Given the specific targeting of corporate cultures that may prove fertile ground for bribery and analogous fraudulent activity, the notion of adequate measures as a basis from which the defence under the 2017 Act takes its reasoning is entirely coherent. Both the *Bribery Act* and the 2017 Act maintain a show of force against the threat of corporations escaping liability in lieu of a prosecutable subject, namely the corporate body as such. In the past businesses have been hard to prosecute because of problems in determining that the directing mind of the corporation, notably the board of directors, either knew about or participated in any particular criminal act. The defence of adequate measures, like that of reasonable prevention procedures, places the onus on the directing mind of the corporation to take ownership of any preventative strategies against bribery, fraud or tax evasion occurring within their organisation. Failure to do so, as in the case of *Standard Bank*, leaves a corporation open to prosecution under the relevant Act.[3] If businesses and more specifically their boards are either unable or unwilling to create and maintain the necessary culture of preventative measures (as *Standard Bank* suggested), is there an argument for 'imposing' *ex ante* procedures on corporations, rather than relying on them to follow regulation or the letter of the law? And if so, what role might blockchain play in this?

There are a number of places to start looking for a potential role for blockchain in helping to enforce the 2017 Act. Returning to the three stages outlined above, it is clear that blockchain could operate within each stage or, indeed, across different combinations of them and thus as a 'reasonable prevention procedure'. The

---

3 This is notwithstanding the matter of deferred prosecution agreements raised in the case of *Standard Bank* as per *Crime and Courts Act* 2013 Sch.17 Pt 1 para. 7(1). Whilst deferrals are an important topic in their own right, it is not one that will be dealt with here.

first two stages relating to an individual or entity could each be subject to recording tax liabilities ahead of any interaction (e.g. financial transaction or trading of assets) with another individual or entity for the purposes of conducting business. Moreover, the global networked reach of blockchain matches the trans-jurisdictional nature of the offences contained with the 2017 Act, thus placing the technology on a strong footing for co-ordination of global monitoring, information gathering and enforcement. 'The new offences will be committed where a relevant body fails to prevent an associated person criminally facilitating the evasion of a tax', states HMRC, 'and this will be the case whether the tax evaded is owed in the UK or in a foreign country' (2016, p. 3), thus a need to maintain global, large-scale oversight is of concern when supporting the implementation and applications of technologies.

Further, following six guiding principles published by HMRC – risk assessment; proportionality of risk-based prevention procedures; top level commitment; due diligence; communication (including training); monitoring and review (2016, p. 15) – reveals where blockchain might be most effective, and two in particular, due diligence and monitoring and review, merit closer examination. First, HMRC states that an 'organisation applies due diligence procedures, taking an appropriate and risk based approach, in respect of persons who perform or will perform services on behalf of the organisation, in order to mitigate identified risks' (2016, p. 27). Due diligence is required across all sectors, but is pertinent to those industries that deal with clients or customers seeking out bespoke and potentially aggressive forms of tax management strategies and mechanisms. Risk is deemed higher in these instances therefore and those providing such services should maintain a greater level of due diligence of their customers, in what is now widely recognised as the 'know your customer' protocol, but equally of the practices undertaken on behalf of those customers. In other words, due diligence ought to be all-encompassing and thus secure, readily auditable and verifiable in order to ascertain whether risk from a particular customer or area of business is recognised and properly scrutinised, and when coupled with regulatory changes that increase pressure 'on working practices and individuals to maintain heightened levels of transparency' (Currie et al., 2017), the need for robust and well-tailored systems able to harmonise due diligence and compliance demands becomes of paramount importance. HMRC describe the procedures necessary to meet the needs of due diligence as follows:

> The due diligence procedures put in place should be proportionate to the identified risk. For example, it may be that the risk identified in given situations is so remote as to justify there being no procedures in place. Alternatively, an organisation may assess the risks as being substantial in relation to a particular associated person, or service, and so apply considerably greater scrutiny in that circumstance. Organisations may choose to conduct their due diligence internally, or externally, for example by internal audit teams or external consultants. *We recognise that the reasonableness of prevention procedures should take account of the level of control and supervision the organisation is able to exercise over a particular person acting on its behalf and the relevant*

body's proximity to that person. It is expected that the effectiveness of the organisation's procedures will be reviewed and where necessary the procedures will be amended.

[emphasis added] (2016, p. 27)

The passage emphasised above demonstrates a point of cultural determinacy. HMRC recognise that whilst individuals and corporations may be doing all they can to mitigate criminal activity, namely tax evasion, risk will always extend beyond the control of a 'relevant body' (e.g. a tax-related service provider), especially risk from those acting on behalf of that body. Andres Knobel of the Tax Justice Network talks only very briefly of blockchain in his article on the use of technology to develop beneficial ownership registries, but more generally recognises the need for registries that can more effectively supply authorities with vital information about asset ownership, as well as providing banks and others subject to anti-money-laundering regulations with the means to improve their due diligence procedures (2017, p. 8). Given the distributed nature of blockchain networks, coupled with the simultaneity of recording and updating across those networks, information needed to perform robust due diligence across all parties (both within and outside a relevant body) within the terms set out by HMRC is entirely feasible.

Second, and following closely behind the concept of blockchain-based due diligence, is monitoring and review. HMRC state that an organisation must monitor and review its 'prevention procedures and makes improvements where necessary' (2016, p. 30). Like due diligence, the process of monitoring and reviewing internal systems in order to ensure they meet the standard necessary for reasonable prevention of criminal activity is one that would benefit both from a degree of agility (in order to meet changing and evolving circumstances), as well as systems able to stand up to robust levels of audit and scrutiny. HMRC describes the procedures necessary for improved monitoring and review as follows:

> There are a range of approaches which a relevant body may wish to take when reviewing its monitoring mechanisms. A relevant body may wish to have its review conducted by an external party, or may choose to conduct its review internally. Organisations can review their procedures in a number of ways, for example:
> - By seeking internal feedback from staff members and looking to other financial prevention procedures
> - Through formalised periodic review with documented findings
> - Through working with other organisations, such as representative bodies or other organisations facing similar risks.
>
> This is not an exhaustive list and it is expected that organisations will choose the approach most suited to their needs. Relevant bodies may change their review process in light of developments, for example a relevant body may need to take a more formalised and detailed approach to reviewing its procedures, following criminal activity by persons associated with it.
>
> (2016, p. 30)

Again, like due diligence, monitoring and review concerns a variety of different actors working synchronously to create a culture in which tax evasion is unable to thrive or, it might be said, even be contemplated. Acknowledgment by HMRC that a body to review procedures post-criminal activity is desirable is an unfortunate reflection of the fact that existing systems can and always will be circumvented by those determined enough to evade their tax liabilities. Blockchain will not automatically change this fact and there are certainly no guarantees that the technology is either impregnable or unassailable. Within the terms set by HMRC for improved monitoring and review procedures, however, what is key is the need for robust and recognisable networks and this is something blockchain can provide within organisations, across domestic bodies and internationally. There is a heavy dose of multistakeholderism involved in this vision of blockchain, one in which the technology is expected to suture a range of different, perhaps even disparate, individuals, organisations and businesses together in order to create a robust regulatory network. It is therefore important to recognise, as the earlier discussion on multistakeholder co-regulation described, that flaws exist in this model for monitoring and review.

Further, it contains elements of what the Tapscotts refer to as a blockchain 'governance network' (2016, p. 307). On the detail, however, the Tapscotts come to this regulatory network from a different angle than the one proposed here, not least in their emphasis on 'governance' (instead of referring specifically to regulation), which reflects the important shift 'away from an exclusive or predominating focus on the state as the source of regulation' (Brownsword and Goodwin, 2012, p. 181). That is, a move away from government – 'the traditional authority of the sovereign state under international law' (Brownsword and Goodwin, 2012, p. 181) – towards formal and informal modes of governance – 'the collective outcome of a vast array of actors and mechanisms that act to set, implement or enforce norms at or across various national or transnational sites of authority' (Brownsword and Goodwin, 2012, p. 181). Generally, however, the Tapscotts describe a blockchain governance network that 'should strive to be inclusive and welcome participation from all relevant stakeholders [...] the network should be transparent, releasing all of its data, documentation, and meeting minutes for public scrutiny' (2016, p. 307). Whilst what they envisage makes sense within the scope of the notion of monitoring and review, notably on the bases of transparency and public scrutiny, the multistakeholderism or network governance the Tapscotts advocate would under the interpretation of HMRC procedures here necessarily combine hierarchical or government-led regulatory measures which would inevitably change the degree of autonomy the Tapscotts consider central to the business-led governance network model they prefer.

By failing to address fully the issue of beneficial ownership secrecy in the 2017 Act, which, for example, allows the formation of complex multi- and trans-jurisdictional mechanisms able to disguise ownership and liability for certain assets, the government is arguably not insisting via legislation on the wholesale deterrence of tax evasion at all, but merely raising up a minor threat of procedural compliance as an obstacle to slow but not ultimately prevent evasion and avoidance schemes. Nor therefore is the government relying on the Act to seriously foster a culture in which aggressive tax planning and management encompassing avoidance as well as evasion will be considered morally and ethically wrong by *all* sections of society. Whilst it would be taking the matter too far to suggest that the Act is, at least at this point in time, impotent when it comes to preventing tax evasion, the question remains: notwithstanding that tax evasion and avoidance would be incredibly hard to shut down completely, why and for what purpose or intent have certain lifelines for tax evaders been left open by the legislation? Moreover, with the potential for evasion ever present it can be argued that the seemingly lessor evil of avoidance (lessor because of its notional legality) remains eminently morally justifiable when it is or ought to be seen as anything but. Avoidance, whilst legal, can and does work against the intention of Parliament to provide a tax regime able to promote desirable objectives and outcomes on behalf of society as a whole.[4]

Reliance on prevention that the government is seeking from the 2017 Act is predicated, I suggest, on a singular and non-specific notion of criminality as a deterrent in and of itself. Given the discussion here is on criminal legislation this reference to criminality may appear axiomatic. But the point is a vital one if the government's commitment to combatting tax evasion is to be taken seriously: it points to a certain degree of fuzziness between deterrence and regulation that is robust, definite and serious about stopping evasion and avoidance. If tax evasion could be entirely prevented via technology surely that is better and more morally justifiable than legislation favouring deterrence *ex post* which creates further space for 'products' that enable high-wealth individuals and corporations to escape tax liabilities. If blockchain could achieve the desired and necessary deterrence that would prevent revenue loss and laundering then that would be, I claim, radical and 'blockchain for good'.

Arcana or cultures of financial secrecy

> Part of what wealth managers must do to protect clients and their fortunes is to break or obscure any link between the two. The goal of all the tactics and techniques is to separate individuals from their wealth, in the eyes of the law and of any outside observers, while still allowing clients the use and benefit of that wealth.
>
> (Harrington, 2016, p. 138)

> If secrecy is the problem, transparency is the solution.
>
> (Fenster, 2017, p. 6)

There can be little doubt that the 2017 Act is aimed at combatting domestic and foreign tax evasion, and this should be broadly welcomed despite the flaws highlighted a moment ago. As has been suggested, however, questions remain over

---

4   See for example: *Inland Revenue Commissioners v Willoughby (Peter Geoffrey)*; *Same v Willoughby (Ruth Marylyn)* [1997] 1 WLR 1071 at 1079.

whether the new powers given to HMRC will actually work in practice (Collins and Magill, 2016). Moreover, the Act lacks support from a broader tax service culture, such as that found in so-called 'offshore' territories or 'tax havens' including the Cayman Islands, where there is no political will or interest in formally tackling secrecy in beneficial ownership by insisting on publication of beneficial ownership registers, because it would undermine the commercial business interests upon which the state ultimately relies for economic survival.[5] It is clear that the legislative measures contained within the Act will not place tax authorities on a reasonable footing to move forward in order to stop or even significantly diminish further financial crimes linked with aggressive tax management and planning (Cobham, 2017; Fowler, 2017).

Secrecy is central to the bigger picture of aggressive tax planning and thus can ultimately be traced to the potential overall effectiveness of the 2017 Act. 'Power likes to cloak itself in secrecy', claims Byung-Chul Han, the 'praxis of *arcana* is one technique that power employs. Transparency dismantles the arcane sphere of power' (2015, p. 47). Cultures of secrecy are intertwined with elite financial worlds, and a meshwork of law and regulation both for and against the continued obscuring of economic power seems capable only of sustaining it through promotion of *inter alia* regulatory arbitrage and an endless variety of loopholes. In relation to the blockchain ecosystem in particular, arbitrage has been a clear and present strategy for many start-ups and other businesses looking to work with blockchain. For example, online news service TechCrunch suggest that:

> Venture fundraising activity in blockchain and blockchain-adjacent companies is highly concentrated in just a handful of countries, with the U.S. leading the way, and a small but growing percentage of companies are choosing to locate themselves in countries with friendly attitudes toward blockchain and cryptocurrency innovation.
>
> The two that stand out here are Singapore and Switzerland, each of which are home to (at least) four percent of the startups that raised venture funding over the last 14 months. Over the course of reporting on other stories, Crunchbase News has learned from investors and entrepreneurs that many Asia-focused blockchain companies and investors in Singapore and Hong Kong are increasingly attractive domiciles for Chinese firms leaving that country in the wake of regulatory crackdown. Japan and Malaysia are also popular locales in Asia for blockchain companies and funds, in part thanks to permissive regulatory environments.
>
> (Rowley, 2018)

The likelihood of meaningful transparency ever piercing, as Han would have it, 'the arcane sphere of power' is thus low because it involves in a quite literal sense

---

5   In the UK the coalition government under Prime Minister David Cameron promised in 2013 to introduce mandatory beneficial ownership registers for 'offshore' jurisdictions, but the policy has since been dropped (Sabbagh, 2018).

tax authorities and regulators hitting a moving target that is capable of skipping across multiple jurisdictions. Moreover a target that was never really there to begin with, but merely an illusory target: a mirage of fiscal affairs, of 'shell' corporations, and head-office facia. 'Wealth gets divided among a variety of OFCs [offshore financial centres] so as to conquer the legal authority of onshore states seeking to tax or regulate it', claims Harrington, continuing:

> The general approach is to apply legal regimes selectively to individual compo-
> nents of a client's wealth – a stock portfolio, a house, a business, or a yacht –
> with two objectives in mind. First, each asset should be placed in the jurisdic-
> tion most favourable to the client's interests, whether that be minimizing taxes
> or defeating the claims of creditors and heirs; whatever the goal, there is a jur-
> isdiction competing to distinguish itself in providing the best possible protec-
> tions from onshore authorises. Secondly, the assets must be dispersed as widely
> as possible, in as complex a structure as possible; this makes the full extent of a
> client's wealth, as well its true ownership, very difficult to assess. The intended
> effect is to erase clients and their assets from public view.
>
> (2016, p. 135)

If blockchain were to prove to be the technology for dismantling the arcane apparatuses Harrington describes on behalf of the public interest it would be a radical technology indeed given the scale of the problem estimated to be anywhere between US\$240 billion and \$500 billion annually (Solheim, 2016; Turner, 2017). But, again, understanding precisely what is being demanded of the tech-nology by a variety of stakeholders is crucial if radical ends are to be achieved rather than missed. After all, the stakeholders in question are likely to be asso-ciated, at least in some way, with the problematic of aggressive wealth manage-ment that blockchain is here described as potentially working to undo. Goldman Sachs, for example, is actively engaged in multiple blockchain projects (see: www. goldmansachs.com/our-thinking/pages/blockchain/); is at the forefront of debates over the future mainstream viability of cryptocurrencies (Cuthbertson, 2018); and one of four global banks questioned by the New York State financial regulator (NYDFS) following revelations in the Panama Papers over involvement in setting up shell companies used to hide assets and avoid tax (Barlyn, 2016). This is one example of how the offshore system is, as Nicholas Shaxson has argued, 'not a colourful outgrowth of the global economy, but instead lies right at its centre' (2012, p. 9), which also further explains Harrington's claim that the amount of wealth held offshore 'has surged by 25 percent since 2008, and there has been a dramatic increase in the use of shell corporations during this time' (2016, p. 207). More particularly this may be construed as a conflict of interest inasmuch as it involves relying on a technology (blockchain) that has been shaped for the global market by a stakeholder against whom the technology could, at least notionally, be turned.

Potential conflicts of interest are, however, only one issue with the effectiveness of blockchain as regulator in the context of tackling global financial secrecy *qua* tax avoidance and evasion. Andres Knobel (2017) also points out an important practical matter: the role technology and digitisation of documentation relating to asset ownership have in existing tax management systems and strategies is retiringly small. Offline paper documentation remains the norm precisely, Knobel claims, to defeat threats posed by the gathering and sharing mechanisms that otherwise feed online content and global data and information sharing, as well as for the practical purposes of physical destruction by, for example, fire. This is, after all, information intentionally hidden and obscured by wealth management professionals on behalf of their clients, sometimes legitimately but often not and, more to the point, under morally specious justifications. Therefore keeping sensitive information in hard copy, offline (or *off-chain*), ought to mean the threat of information leaks remain low and this is, generally speaking, the case. The Panama Papers, Bahamas Leaks and Paradise Papers are three examples of investigative journalism piercing the arcana to reveal important information in the public interest, yet this work remains the tip of a proverbial iceberg.[6] Instead there are as yet no jurisdictions that require fully digital or online beneficial ownership registers; that require both the legal owner and beneficial owner to be registered; that apply technology to ensure the accuracy of information; and are thus working to effectively ensure a very low risk of tax systems being abused or financial crimes from being routinely committed (Knobel, 2017, p. 5).

Akin to the rubbish in/rubbish out problem that haunts the effectiveness of digital databases and record-keeping, cultures of financial secrecy built on paper records will inevitably render pointless any technological interventions that are not accompanied by the enforcement of document digitisation requirements. Again, however, a lack of will by government authorities and regulators to enforce such digitisation policies clearly exists and does not appear set to change any time soon. The first stage of blockchain as regulator in this context, therefore, has actually very little to do with blockchain at all, but instead requires a change in wealth management culture that insists on paper records, as well as digital systems geared not towards aiding tax authorities and regulators but helping entrepreneurs rapidly incorporate in order to benefit from wealth management processes. Technologies provide affordances that presently provide net gains that work against and not on behalf of regulators and tax authorities. There is no transparency that reasonably creates trust at the broadest levels of the public, meaning a lack of trust in financial elites and government inspectors alike by a public who see no tangible shift away from cultures of secrecy.

As discussed in depth thus far, trust is seen by many commentators as the *sine qua non* of blockchain as a revolutionary and desirable technology, and trust appears alongside transparency in many accounts often without question or, at least, in some fairly fuzzy and ill-defined ways all of which are tuned to benefit and success as the inevitable outcomes of trust/transparency matrices. Returning briefly to the notion of blockchain as a means of audit and the regulatory implications this has in relation to trust, Michael Power states:

6   For more information see: https://offshoreleaks.icij.org/ (accessed 9 May 2018).

The idea of audit has become an essential condition for talking about the prospective realization of a regulatory programme [...] audit shapes public conceptions of the problems for which it is the solution; it is constitutive of a certain regulatory or control style which reflects deeply held commitments to checking and trust.

(1997, p. 7)

For the Tapscotts, blockchain is quite simply the 'trust protocol' (2016); whilst for Casey and Vigna the relationship between trust and transparency (openness) is more nuanced, but really no less well defined:

the overarching objective for all of us should be to encourage the evolution of an open, interoperable permissionless network. There's a reason we want a world of open, public blockchains and distributed trust models that gives everybody a seat at the table. Let's keep our eyes on the ball.

(2018, p. 173)

There is, however, reason to think that trust and transparency do not and cannot co-exist in the manner suggested by these blockchain acolytes, and that the relationship between the two is perhaps even antagonistic and counterproductive. As Han argues:

If I know everything in advance, there is no need for trust. Transparency is a state in which all not-knowing is eliminated. Where transparency prevails, no room for trust exists. Instead of affirming that 'transparency creates trust', one should instead say, 'transparency dismantles trust'. The demand for transparency grows loud precisely when trust no longer prevails. In a society based on trust, no intrusive demand for transparency would surface. The society of transparency is a society of mistrust and suspicion; it relies on control because of vanishing confidence. Strident calls for transparency point to the simple fact that the moral foundation of society has grown faulty, that moral values such as honesty and uprightness are losing their meaning more and more.

(2015, pp. 47–48)

To suggest that blockchain is conducive of trust *and* transparency is, on Han's account, highly questionable if not impossible therefore, and this is a problem if both are essential to build momentum behind regulatory frameworks and procedures. And where Han points to mistrust as a corollary of a transparent society, I suggest *post-trust* as a product linked specifically to blockchain which is nevertheless symptomatic of the same retreat of moral foundations Han highlights. Moreover, whilst not intended as such, Han highlights crucial and largely unspoken tensions that lie at the heart of a number of blockchain concepts and use-cases, namely, the fostering of transparency not in relation to trust, as some would believe and claim, but in the service of control. Again, therefore, control and in particular forms of social control built not around political but economic reason emerge as likely and arguably desirable ends of blockchain conceptualisations. This means blockchain as a double-edged sword: at once creating conditions that do not allow financial secrecy to thrive, and undermining privacy in favour of technological controls that could quickly spread to define norms of social organisation. The spectre of blockchain governmentality therefore haunts what might otherwise seem like innocuous and good-natured attempts at technologically solving a lack of openness and perceived unavailability for everybody to have a 'seat at the table' (Casey and Vigna, 2018, p. 173) in terms of techno-economic and techno-social inclusivity. Of course, histories of hegemony and power tell us that not everybody can even hope to have a seat at the table. Equity and equanimity would signal an end to power, but blockchain is unlikely to achieve this lofty aim.

There is a financial culture built on an unwillingness to disclose information requested for scrutiny in the public interest, and absolute unapologetic concealment and secrecy with the aim to intentionally avoid or evade liabilities, and this culture is unlikely to change due to regulation and threats of criminal sanctions heralded by the likes of the 2017 Act. The hope is that technologies such as blockchain will be able to enforce changes to that culture, but this must begin with the technology not reinforcing conditions for avoidance and evasion by working against instead of on behalf of public interest authorities. Yet the promises of transparency blockchain heralds might too easily be assumed as enough to effect the significant change in culture that is required, and this would be a mistake. Transparency is not the opposite of secrecy, and attempts at transparency that involve disclosure of huge volumes of information and data often preclude openness by creating the forest in which no tree can be seen. Technology 'is not only a mechanism for applying controls and increasing data and information transparency', claim Currie et al., 'it may also have potential to obfuscate or distort data and information' (2017).

'[I]n contrast to Plato's world of truth', Han states, 'today's society of transparency lacks divine light inhabited by metaphysical tension. Transparency has no transcendence. The society of transparency is see-through without light' (2015, p. 39). Regulatory technology 'as both a social and material artefact, is viewed as increasingly essential as a means to enhance surveillance and encourage ethical conduct and cultural change' (Currie et al., 2017), but as this chapter has shown, the matter is far from straightforward. Lest we forget, as well, the cryptographic basis upon which blockchain is in large part built is an ancient method of creating and, with more recent computational developments, particularising (using public keys, for example), while still ultimately enforcing secrecy and not undermining it. 'Secrecy', as Whitfield Diffie and Martin Hellman maintain in their landmark study that helped launch contemporary computer cryptography, 'is at the heart of cryptography' (1976, p. 654). It is possible to see why blockchain (or analogous technologies) present a challenge to the *arcana* of global financial services and practices, and here have been discussed just some of the ways these challenges could be implemented. But it would disingenuous given the spirit of this book to insist that blockchain is a panacea to the ills of financial crime and moral bankruptcy vis-à-vis aggressive financial planning strategies. Blockchain is, however, a good option.

Conclusion

The 2017 Act, if it is to be truly effective as a tool for cutting through the nefarious and anti-social practice of cheating the public revenue, must ensure that individuals and companies do not begin plans for maximising personal or corporate wealth with considerations or contemplations of tax evasion. To be deterred or prevented ahead of a criminal act rather than punished after it does not routinely translate into restrictions on individual rights and liberties as some might fear. In the context of tax evasion (and even to some extent avoidance, especially when what are nevertheless legally avoided tax liabilities could easily be met by those actively avoiding them), it is absolutely the case that unease or complaint over restricted rights and liberties that may well accompany the implementation of robust preventative systems and procedures, such as the example of blockchain suggested above, should not be presaged because there can rarely if ever be an honest justification for them. The 2017 Act will fail if it does not contribute significantly to dispelling the culture of secrecy that haunts it and instead simply resolves matters through financial penalties (even in the form of unlimited fines), or further swells the prison population. Both of these options have long been the answer to financial criminality that harms communities and the state but have yet to prevent it from continuing, developing or, indeed, evolving, and are arguably, therefore, no answer at all.

The 2017 Act emphasises, and the basis for the offence it creates is, the role of corporate failure in acknowledgement and prevention of tax evasion. In particular tax evasion by an 'associated person' in the corporate context who is able to slip through the net of preventative measures existing at the time of the criminal act. The law, as we have seen, makes business liable for the criminality of employees who encourage or assist tax evasion, including by clients or suppliers. Hence it is deemed important, and this can be interpreted as one of the key policy areas that shadow the legislation, that businesses ensure they have robust measures and procedures in place to deter and at best prevent tax evasion and avoidance from occurring. Blockchain has been described here in that capacity. If we take seriously the broad strengths and benefits of blockchain (e.g. as a more robust digital record and registry of beneficial interests than those presently in existence), blockchain is capable of transcending the provisions of the 2017 Act in order to effect cultural change around tax liability. If there is no way for tax to be evaded or avoided because of 'water-tight' systems for monitoring, among others things, liabilities attached to assets, then it seems more credible that a change in culture will occur. Of course, the notion of a 'water-tight' system in any context is always misguided and even dangerous if it becomes an end in itself – a dam is never left unmonitored. Andres Knobel points to the problem of over-reliance on technology in an example of the evolution of certain US states as tax havens that offer, 'less regulation, less paperwork and more online/fully digital processes' (2017, p. 9). In this instance the digital processes in question allow shell companies to quickly and easily be established for the purposes of aggressive tax management. Yet the same emphasis on technology coupled with a retreat from offline or off-chain regulation could itself be a description of where blockchain becomes not the first or last line of defence against tax evasion and avoidance, but the only line.

'There is a growing global acceptance among regulators that the burden of regulation has become too onerous', claim Currie et al., 'and that new "regtech" start-ups, often funded by venture capitalists, have the potential to reduce regulatory complexity and correspondingly barriers to engaging in regulated activities faced by new entrants' (2017). Whilst it may be an attractive politico-economic proposition in terms of value for money or efficiency to turn all matters of regulation over to technology and in particular technologies developed and produced by private self-interest in the form of entrepreneurs, tech start-ups and venture capitalists, this is a move that assumes systems and networks that will, at all costs, remain incorruptible and always serve the public interest. This is not a state of affairs that presently describes blockchain, not least due to the problematic of rubbish in/rubbish out as a continuing basis of systemic risk and failure at the heart of network models that technological solutionism supports. What is more, and reflecting on a number of the critical issues discussed throughout this book, it proposes a transcendent quality to blockchain that is aimed at justification for its implementation in a variety of regulatory contexts that does not necessarily start with questions of how to better serve human need. It risks, in other words, fetishisation of technology in the truest sense. More than that, fetishisation of the rituals contemporary computational and network technologies perform: the auto-harvesting, -recording, -analysis and -management of data for the production and imprimatur of epistemologies and ontologies that increasingly have no basis in human interrelatedness. 'The introduction of new technologies (blockchain, machine learning and artificial intelligence)', argue Currie et al., 'is further removing human beings from transactions and so creating new challenges for regulators to ensure appropriate systems of transparency, surveillance and accountability' (2017). Blockchain raises as many issues and questions as it answers. As part of a critical process and analysis of aggressive financial practices, however, blockchain may reveal its true potential.

References

Barlyn, Suzanne. 2016. NY regulator wants info from Goldman, banks on Panama firm dealings: Source. Reuters, 11 May. www.reuters.com/article/us-goldman-sachs-panama -new-york-idUSKCN0Y22JK (accessed 9 May 2018).

Brownsword, Roger and Goodwin, Morag. 2012. *Law and Technologies of the Twenty-First Century*. Cambridge: Cambridge University Press.

Casey, Michael J. and Vigna, Paul. 2018. *The Truth Machine: The Blockchain and the Future of Everything*. London: HarperCollins.

Cobham, Alex. 2017. Two days left to end financial secrecy in the UK's Overseas Territories? *Tax Justice Network*, 26 April. www.taxjustice.net/2017/04/25/two-days-bene ficial-ownership-breakthrough/ (accessed 13 September 2017).

Collins, Jason and Magill, Tori. 2016. Analysis – Corporate failure to prevent facilitation of tax evasion. *Tax Journal*, Vol. 1331, No. 12 (November). www.taxjournal.com/articles/corp orate-failure-prevent-facilitation-tax-evasion-10112016 (accessed 13 September 2017).

Currie, Wendy L., Gozman, Daniel P. and Seddon, Jonathan J.M. 2017. Dialectic tensions in the financial markets: A longitudinal study of pre- and post-crisis regulatory technology. *Journal of Information Technology.* https://doi.org/10.1057/s41265-017-0047-5 (accessed 10 May 2018).

Cuthbertson, Anthony. 2018. Bitcoin Trading Comes to Goldman Sachs After Investment Bank Hires First Cryptocurrency Trader. *The Independent*, 3 May. www.independent.co.uk/life-style/gadgets-and-tech/news/bitcoin-trading-latest-goldman-sachs-digital-asset-trader-investment-banks-a8334171.html (accessed 9 May 2018).

Derrida, Jacques. 1996. *Archive Fever: A Freudian Impression.* Translated by Eric Prenowitz. Chicago: The University of Chicago Press.

Diffie, Whitfield and Hellman, Martin E. 1976. New Directions in Cryptography. *IEEE Transactions on Information Theory*, Vol. 22, No. 6 (November), pp. 644–654.

Fenster, Mark. 2017. *The Transparency Fix: Secrets, Leaks, and Uncontrollable Government Information.* Stanford: Stanford University Press.

Financial Conduct Authority (FCA). 2018. *RegTech.* Financial Conduct Authority, 8 January. www.fca.org.uk/firms/regtech (accessed 26 February 2018).

Flynn, Channing. 2016. Preparing for Digital Taxation in a Blockchain World. *Bloomberg News*, 28 November. www.bna.com/preparing-digital-taxation-n73014447764/ (accessed 18 May 2018).

Fowler, Naomi. 2017. UK Parliament fails to tackle financial secrecy in its overseas territories. *Tax Justice Network*, 26 April. www.taxjustice.net/2017/04/26/uk-parliament-fails-tackle-financial-secrecy-overseas-territories/ (accessed 26 May 2018).

Hall, Stuart. 2017. *Selected Political Writings: The Great Moving Right Show and Other Essays.* Edited by Sally Davison, David Featherstone, Michael Rustin and Bill Schwartz. Durham: Duke University Press.

Han, Byung-Chul. 2015. *The Transparency Society.* Translated by Erik Butler. Stanford: Stanford University Press.

Harrington, Brooke. 2016. *Capital without Borders: Wealth Managers and the One Percent.* Cambridge: Harvard University Press.

Harvey, David. 2014. *Seventeen Contradictions and the End of Capitalism.* London: Profile Books.

Hodge, Margaret. 2016. *Called to Account: How Corporate Bad Behaviour and Government Waste Combine to Cost Us Millions.* London: Abacus.

HM Revenue and Customs (HMRC). 2016. *Tackling tax evasion: Government guidance for the corporate offence of failure to prevent the criminal facilitation of tax evasion* (draft). HM Revenue & Customs. October. https://assets.publishing.service.gov.uk/government/uploads/system/uploads/attachment_data/file/560120/Tackling_tax_evasion_-_Draft_government_guidance_for_the_corporate_offence_of_failure_to_prevent_the_criminal_facilitation_of_tax_evasion.pdf (accessed 27 April 2018).

Knobel, Andres. 2017. Technology and online beneficial ownership registries: Easier to create companies and better at preventing financial crime. *Tax Justice Network*, 1 June. https://papers.ssrn.com/sol3/papers.cfm?abstract_id=2978757 (accessed 8 May 2018).

Mercier, Louis-Sebastien. 1772. *Memoirs of the Year Two Thousand Five Hundred, Vol. II.* Translated by William Hooper. London: G. Robinson.

Palfreyman, John. 2017. Blockchain for government: Building trust, demolishing bureaucracy. *Blockchain Unleashed: IMB Blockchain Blog*, 1 February. www.ibm.com/blogs/blockchain/2017/02/blockchain-government-building-trust-demolishing-bureaucracy/ (accessed 27 April 2018).

Politico Magazine. 2016. Politico 50 List: Our guide to the thinkers, doers and visionaries transforming American politics in 2016. www.politico.com/magazine/politico50/2016/marc-andreessen-fred-wilson-jerry-brito (accessed 30 April 2018).

Power, Michael. 1997. *The Audit Society: Rituals of Verification*. Oxford: Oxford University Press.

Rowley, Jason. 2018. 2018 VC investment into crypto startups set to surpass 2017 tally. *TechCrunch*, 3 March. https://techcrunch.com/2018/03/03/2018-vc-investment-into-crypto-startups-set-to-surpass-2017-tally/ (accessed 14 May 2018).

Sabbagh, Dan. 2018. Labour backs push for public ownership registers in UK overseas territories. *The Guardian*, 1 May. www.theguardian.com/world/2018/may/01/labour-backs-push-for-public-ownership-registers-in-uk-overseas-territories (accessed 1 May 2018).

Scott, Brett. 2016. *How Can Cryptocurrency and Blockchain Technology Play a Role in Building Social and Solidarity Finance?* Working Paper 2016–2011. Geneva: United Nations Research Institute for Social Development.

Shaxson, Nicholas. 2012. *Treasure Islands: Tax Havens and the Men Who Stole the World*. London: Vintage.

Solheim, Erik. 2016. We're losing $240bn a year to tax avoidance. Who really ends up paying? *The Guardian*, 10 May. www.theguardian.com/global-development-professionals-network/2016/may/10/were-losing-240bn-a-year-to-tax-avoidance-who-really-ends-up-paying (accessed 1 May 2018).

Styles, John. 1980. 'Our traitorous money makers': The Yorkshire coiners and the law, 1760–1783. *An Ungovernable People: The English and their law in the seventeenth and eighteenth centuries*. Edited by John Brewer and John Styles. London: Hutchinson & Co, pp. 172–249.

Swan, Melanie. 2015. *Blockchain: Blueprint for a New Economy*. Sebastopol: O'Reilly.

Swartz, Lana. 2017. Blockchain Dreams: Imagining techno-economic alternatives after Bitcoin. *Another Economy is Possible*. Edited by Manuel Castells. Cambridge: Polity Press, pp. 82–105.

Tapscott, Don and Tapscott, Alex. 2016. *Blockchain Revolution: How the Technology behind Bitcoin is Changing Money, Business and the World*. London: Portfolio Penguin.

Turner, George. 2017. New estimates reveal the extent of tax avoidance by multinationals. *Tax Justice Network*, 22 March. www.taxjustice.net/2017/03/22/new-estimates-tax-avoidance-multinationals/ (accessed 26 May 2018).

Interlude II: Regulatory technology

Louis-Sebastien Mercier's tax trunk

As a regulator, blockchain fits the growing trend for regulatory technologies or 'RegTech' aimed at providing public and private sectors alike with 'solutions' for auditing and managing domestic and transnational financial data and information, as well as, potentially, a whole raft of other legal, political and social documents.[1] Regulatory technologies have emerged in order to enable, as effectively as possible, compliance to remain in step with rapid advances in computing in industry and finance in particular (Currie et al., 2017). Blockchain as regulatory technology relies largely on code-based mechanisms, such as those discussed in the previous chapter. Yet there are a number of practical, offline and off-chain considerations that are not easily side-stepped by the implementation of blockchain as regulator, not least the intransigence of paper record-keeping in key compliance sectors in which blockchain could effectively operate.

'Regulatory technologies, through the automated application of rules, have their own agency and ability to exert both constraining and constitutive effects', claim Currie et al. (2017), and in conjunction with other code-based regulatory approaches blockchain could or might assert agency of this kind. But regulatory technologies must 'co-exist with human actors and so are participants in socio-technical networks' (Currie et al., 2017), meaning the agency technologies are perceived to have is or ought to relate only to human need, rather than allowing forms of technological fetishism and ideological notions of solutionism and innovationism to dominate the regulatory enterprise. Louis-Sebastien Mercier, French writer and dramatist at the time of the French Revolution, imagined the following tax regime in *Memoirs of the Year Two Thousand Five Hundred, Vol. II*, based on a rudimentary regulatory technology:

> Tell me, I beseech you, how are your public taxes levied? For let the legis-lature be as perfect as it may, taxes, I think, must always be paid. As a full answer, the worthy man my conductor took me by the hand, and led me to a spacious place, formed by the termination of four streets. I observed an iron

1 The Financial Conduct Authority's website defines RegTech as 'new technologies developed to overcome regulatory challenges in financial services', www.fca.org.uk/firms/regtech (accessed 24 April 2018).

chest that was twelve feet high; it was supported on four wheels; there was a small opening at top, which was secured from the rain by a kind of awning; on this chest was wrote, 'Tribute due to the king representing the state'. Hard by was another chest, of a smaller size, with these words; Free gifts.

I saw several people with easy, cheerful, contented looks, throw sealed packets into the chest, as in our days they threw letters into the post-office. I was so astonished at this easy manner of paying taxes, that I made a thousand ridiculous inquiries [...]

That large coffer you see, they said, is our receiver-general of the finances. It is there that every citizen deposits his contribution for the support of the state. We are there obliged to deposit the fiftieth part of our annual income. He that has no property, or what is only just sufficient for his maintenance, is exempt [...] In the other coffer are the voluntary offerings, intended for useful designs, for the execution of such projects as have been approved by the public. This sometimes is richer than the other; for we love liberality in our gifts, and no other motive is necessary to excite it than equity and a love for the state [...]

There is a similar trunk in every quarter of the city, and in every city in the provinces, which receives the contributions of the country. How I said, do you leave it to the good-will of the people to pay their taxes? There must be then a great number that pay nothing, without your knowing it – Not at all; your fears are vain. In the first place, we give with a free will; our tribute is not by compulsion, but founded on reason and equity. There is scarce a man amongst us who does not esteem it a point of honour to discharge the most sacred and most legitimate of all debts. Besides, if a man in condition to pay should dare to neglect it, you there see the table on which the name of the head of every family is engraved, by which we should soon see who had not thrown in his packet, on which should be his seal. In that case he covers himself with an eternal infamy, and we regard him as you regard a thief; the appellation of a bad citizen follows him to the grave.

(Mercier, 1772, pp. 169–176)

Mercier's illustration of an equitable taxation system in which individual citizens willingly pay their fair shares in consideration of the benefits the state will offer in return stands in stark contrast to the extreme and often nightmarish complexities of tax systems in many states today. The beauty of Mercier's vision is really to be found, however, in the fundamental principles underpinning the social tax burden that are highlighted in the example of his happy taxpayers. Put simply, Mercier's characters view taxation as good and therefore not something to be evaded or avoided for personal gain.

The virtue of taxation, the notion of it not necessarily as 'the good' in and of itself but as a means to it, is often obscured in real life behind a fog of legal doctrines, codes and technicalities. And any potential good in taxation is also missed or disregarded in favour of reductionist narratives that malign tax as a 'burden' we could all happily do without. Indeed, narratives that paint a picture of taxation as the precise opposite of Mercier's vision. Even if we take a step back from tax as a virtue and assume instead that the state *needs* taxation to successfully operate and achieve projects and aims, this does not necessarily do away with negative ideas of taxation. It does, however, point to enforcement as necessary in lieu of citizens who willingly (even not exactly happily) pay their share of tax. As a consequence, a Mercier-like vision of a tax system founded not on compulsion, but on reason and equity, quickly fades away.

In recent years the scandal of the so-called Panama and Paradise Papers has shown there is a significant appetite for aggressive forms of tax avoidance which show no signs of retreating. High net-wealth members of society would rather invest in defending their wealth, by purchasing exclusive legal and accounting services for example, than invest in public services through tax contributions. Effecting a cultural change that would reduce the need for compulsion in favour of reason and equity may, therefore, simply be pie in the sky. Equally, any sense that technology can or will affect the necessary or desired cultural change in this context could also be pie in the sky. In light of Mercier's story of the tax trunk, what would it mean for blockchain to assume the role of 'receiver-general of the finances', however, and act as the large coffer in which every citizen deposits a contribution for the support of the state? Moreover, blockchain as the table on which the name of the head of every family is engraved, 'by which we should soon see who had not thrown in his packet'? That is, a role for blockchain in facilitating and enforcing revenue collection and the way registration regimes and record-keeping work on behalf of the state and in the public interest. This might include, for example, a blockchain-based register of beneficial ownership able to be readily shared amongst international tax authorities in real time to ensure compliance with tax liabilities and obligations. As a technological 'solution' to the 'problem' of aggressive forms of tax avoidance this use of blockchain would, I suggest, go some way to being a use-case of 'blockchain for good'.

References

Currie, Wendy L., Gozman, Daniel P. and Seddon, Jonathan J.M. 2017. Dialectic tensions in the financial markets: A longitudinal study of pre- and post-crisis regulatory technology. *Journal of Information Technology*. https://doi.org/10.1057/s41265-017-0047-5 (accessed 10 May 2018).

Mercier, Louis-Sebastien. 1772. *Memoirs of the Year Two Thousand Five Hundred, Vol. II.* Translated by William Hooper. London: G. Robinson.

Part II
Critical perspectives

5   Setting the scene

Introduction

> [T]echnology is a phenomenon captured and put to use.
>
> (Arthur, 2009, p. 51)

> Contrast taking turns in a loose way with respect to who buys the drinks with keeping a record of who has paid what for them. The former procedure is in line with community, the latter with the market.
>
> (Cohen, 2011, p. 218)

> Blockchain-based systems can infuse efficiency and integrity into document registries of all kinds and many other government processes. That's simply better asset management, reducing administrative costs to taxpayers while increasing revenues to governments.
>
> (Tapscott and Tapscott, 2016, p. 205)

Part of what Manuel Castells (2010) called the rise of network society, and falling within the scope of ubiquitous or pervasive computing and ambient intelligence promoted by the likes of IBM in the latter part of the twentieth century (Wright et al., 2006, pp. 7–9), distributed ledger technology (DLT) or blockchain is aimed at transforming thought and practice in information and communication technology and beyond.[1] As a technology which first came to prominence with the

---

1   Definitions of and the similarities and differences between distributed ledgers and blockchains are key to understanding the technology and what it is expected or anticipated to achieve. The definitions found in the growing blockchain literature not only contextualise the technology but, I argue, politicise it as well. How blockchain is defined and in particular in some cases distinguished from DLT via differing terminology and vocabulary will be dealt with at length at various points in this book. Important to the process of critique in this instance, however, is not to attempt a closed or definitive definition of the technology. This is not possible given that the vocabulary used in and around the 'blockchain ecosystem' is unstable and highly contestable in legal, political, economic, cultural and technological terms. For the time being it can be acknowledged here that DLT and blockchain are not directly interchangeable but that blockchain is most likely a sub-set of DLT. Thus, whilst characteristics are shared between the two, there are important differences as well.

cryptocurrency Bitcoin after 2010, blockchain's potential stems from factors inherent to the technology, but also latent in the politico-economic assumptions and conditioning that surround and permeate blockchain conceptualisations and implementations, including the promise of the technology with regard to data 'immutability', 'transparency', and improved 'disintermediation' and 'decentralisation' for networked economies.[2] Blockchain is a new idea in the old techno-economic saga of capitalist modernity, one in which the political is concealed in and by the technological networks, and the ethical and cultural transformed and (re)produced in endless cyclical processes conforming to economic reason. 'One of the defining features of intelligent networks', argues Alexander Galloway, 'is an ability to produce an apparatus to hide the apparatus' (2004, p. 75), and in blockchain capitalism is mapping already existing financial networks atop new technological networks in a matrix that conceals and transforms the human into a modality of pure economic, calculable and auditable rationality. As a metropolitan entrepreneurial model of information technological revolution, blockchain supports Manuel Castells's claim that the critical ingredient for technological innovation and development 'is not the newness of the institutional and cultural setting, but its ability to generate synergy on the basis of knowledge and information, directly related to industrial production and commercial applications' (2010, p. 67).

Like myriad computational technologies that have come before it set to work in the fast and furious domains of capital, stakeholders expect blockchain to 'leverage' key advantages on behalf of business both global and domestic. This is the seemingly innocuous counterpoint to blockchain politics: a technology of pure instrumentality, a *neutral* technology. The impetus behind blockchain research and development during its mainstream emergence since 2015 has been predicated on satisfying the desires and needs of business. However, there is nothing apolitical or neutral about this positioning of blockchain as a technology in the service of business and commercial private interest. Among other things blockchain is expected to drive efficiencies in back-office functions, harmonise and simplify cross-organisational transacting and improve data assurance, to name three touched on in recent reports by the House of Lords and Financial Conduct Authority (FCA) in the UK (Holmes, 2017; FCA, 2017). Other stakeholders are looking at blockchain from a different angle, however, and a growth in use-cases beyond or post-cryptocurrencies, that is, broadly speaking, cases indirectly related to financial services, are 'pivoting' the technology towards enacting social, political and cultural transformations. Primed to 'disrupt' public and private sectors alike (and for certain stakeholders therefore nothing short of revolutionary), blockchain

2   As per the comment above, these terms are placed in quotations because they con-, testable at different levels of discourse. I highlight immutability, for example, because, whilst the vast majority of blockchain discourse supports the idea that blockchain data is fixed and incorruptible, dissenting voices maintain this is not entirely true. Yet it is easy to see why claims of immutability would be attractive if and when stakeholders want to convince the world that blockchain is more secure and private than, for example, data contained in existing databases. For counter-arguments on the nature of blockchain immutability see: Greenspan, 2017; Walch, 2017.

is the latest in a long line of technologies promised to shift 'real power toward citizens, equipping them with real opportunities for prosperity and participation in society' (Tapscott and Tapscott, 2016, p. 35).

The quote above from Don Tapscott and Alex Tapscott betrays the desire behind the pivoting of blockchain: a future in which blockchain enables agility and fluidity for an increasing pool of stakeholders constantly engaged with and working across markets, and this will be apply regardless of whether the concept or application in question relates to financial or post-financial contexts. Moreover, there are some keen to see blockchain facilitating so-called 'liquid' democracy by 'hacking' the perceived systemic nature of social organisation (Siri, 2016). Aaron Wright and Primavera De Filippi list some applications of blockchain, as well as other key technologies facilitated by the blockchain, beginning to emerge in support of the more fluid and agile economic subjectivity that blockchain stakeholders envisage society to be consisting of in the near future:

> Blockchain technology enables the creation of decentralized currencies, self-executing digital contracts (smart contracts) and intelligent assets that can be controlled over the Internet (smart property). The blockchain also enables the development of new governance systems with more democratic or participatory decision-making, and decentralized (autonomous) organizations that can operate over a network of computers without any human intervention. These applications have lead [*sic*] many to compare the blockchain to the Internet, with accompanying predictions that this technology will shift the balance of power away from centralized authorities in the field of communications, business and even politics or law.
>
> (2015, p. 1)

Many themes discussed thus far are all too familiar. They raise the question, I argue, of the extent to which blockchain ought to be considered a neoliberal technology. Like the Internet, blockchain is potentially a totalising as well as a globalising medium.[3] Michael Gurstein views the relationship between totalising and globalising enterprises, of which blockchain could both be one and a facilitator for others, as 'actively proselytizing and reorganizing systems and businesses in support of these initiatives and approaches and totally incorporating economic and even social processes that are captured within their technology net (work)' (2012, p. 39). Blockchain is also, therefore, rightly seen as an economising medium: a technology primed for the purposes of furthering marketisation and consumerism of information and data, including the transposition of information and data into the logic and reason of free-market economics, even if

---

3   The fact that distributed networks are by design globalising inasmuch as they straddle nation-states and operate trans-jurisdictionally, or, indeed, render national borders meaningless or redundant, is at the heart of regulatory questions over jurisdiction, choice of law and potential regulatory arbitrage (where stakeholders seek out the most favourable regulatory environment for their needs or self-interest).

that exceeds the initial motivation of the *data subject*. 'The economy that the blockchain enables is not merely the movement of money', argues Melanie Swan, 'it is the transfer of information and the effective allocation of resources that money has enabled in the human- and corporate-scale economy' (2015, p. xi). Swan's use of terms such as efficiency as well as the ways in which the description collapses the human into the economic is not something to be celebrated as far as this book is concerned, but symptomatic of the threats and harms blockchain poses to communities and individuals through the further and sustained insistence of neoliberal economic reason the technology and its stakeholders subscribe to.

At heart, neoliberal economic reason involves the creation of particular forms of hybridised socioeconomic organisation that are a direct product of the culture and institutions of Western capitalism (Castells, 2010, p. 188). Markets and competition are often recognised as the central pillars of neoliberal economic reason and practice (Harvey, 2005; Dean, 2009; Peck, 2012; Mirowski, 2014; Brown, 2015; Davies, 2017; Hall, 2017; Han, 2017). But there is also a key emphasis within neoliberal reason on accountability, and in particular precise notions of economic accountability as social model. All social life is forced to manage itself as if subject to constant 'value for money' estimations and 'cost-benefit' analyses. Michael Power breaks this form of accountability into four constituent parts:

1   *Fiscal regularity* in the sense of accountability for the properly legal stewardship of inputs.
2   *Economy* as accountability for obtaining the best possible terms under which resources are acquired.
3   *Efficiency* as accountability for ensuring that maximum output is obtained from the resources employed or that minimum resources are used to achieve a given level of output/service.
4   *Effectiveness* as accountability for ensuring that outcomes conform to intentions, as defined in programmes.(1997, p. 50)

Trends in existing and emerging blockchain applications and concepts focus on (aspirational) rationalisations of social transactions and relations in semi-veiled economic terms. The *default-ness* of the economic is arguably a product of blockchain's initial use as a 'currency' infrastructure supporting Bitcoin. But blockchain post-cryptocurrency continues to *economise* and promote economic-like accountability of data and information exposed to it, and calibrate messy human exchange and interaction via auditable and calculable logic. As Power says of auditors, they 'claim to be looking at effectiveness but they are really emphasizing economy and efficiency' (1997, p. 51), and the same can be said, not of blockchain technology itself, but of those using and promoting it. Blockchain thus fits Max Weber's determination of the rationality of Western capitalism as essentially dependent 'upon the *calculability* of technically decisive factors, which are the bases of exact calculation' (2002, p. 364). André Gorz further develops this theme during the first vestiges of the contemporary global information and data age:

Computerization and robotization have, then, an economic rationality, which is characterized precisely by the desire to *economize*, that is, to use the factors of production as efficiently as possible [...] a rationality whose aim is to *economize* on these 'factors' requires that it is possible to *measure, calculate and plan* their deployment and to express the factors themselves, whatever they may be, in terms of a single unit of measurement.

(1989, pp. 2–3)

Blockchain is viewed as a way to *efficiently* record and account for data precisely because its basic format is that of the ledger and thus the technology continues the role played by 'a key innovation' in the evolution and development of capitalism: double-entry bookkeeping (Hodgson, 2015, p. 174). Avenues for the commodification or exploitation of data held on the blockchain are limited, some have argued, because the technology affords users greater individual control in ways that previous technologies have not. On this account blockchain heralds a paradigm shift in commercial practices relating to big data and its exploitation. Melanie Swan is one who believes blockchain will achieve this end and refers to the technology on this basis as a 'push technology', because it allows users to initiate and *push* 'relevant information to the network', rather than 'pull' technologies that allow user data to be *extracted* and are therefore 'essentially centralized honeypots' (2015, p. 4). Whether blockchain will enable a meaningful shift from data harvesting, extraction and exploitation by business to data control by individuals that mirrors long-standing notions of property ownership, namely the owners' prerogative to use, abuse and alienate their data as and when they see fit, is yet to be tested at scale. A role for commercial business in the provision of platforms and interfaces for managing and auditing data on blockchain on behalf of customers, consumers or clients is, however, more of a given, one that could see and, indeed, arguably is already seeing rapid advances towards data sovereignty models. A move which will mean commercial practices increasingly internalised by individuals, something that is capable of providing huge savings for commercial actors in, for example, infrastructure costs, whilst arguably intensifying markets and providing more potential commercial revenue streams, not fewer.

There is no shortage of businesses now promoting the benefits of blockchain-led digital economies through idealisations of secure, peer-to-peer, data-as-property paradigms that promise to enable users to unlock 'value' from their personal data in the form of 'micropayments' – a model of granular payments that individuals, as well as corporations, can derive from *all* forms of data exploitation large and small. Far from being novel enterprises, however, a number of these business models necessitate offline and off-chain markets and consumerism models, and thus require high levels of interoperability between different interfaces, whilst also sustaining many forms of centralisation and mediation that correspond closely to the logic of existing patterns of commercial development, but which blockchain, it is hoped, would destroy. 'Value', therefore, far from gaining new meaning via proposals set forth by blockchain enterprise initiatives, remains the metaphysical concept it has long been, one that, 'when you try to pin it down it turns out to be just a word'

(Robinson, 1962, p. 29). Once a fully fledged peer-to-peer digital economy is up and running on blockchain and users are happily transacting personal data will traditional (capitalist) business models fall away and create a post-capitalist society? It may rather be the case that users will be expected to auto-exploit by relying on the data sovereignty models presented to them.

Blockchain is a technology of capitalist class power *par excellence* within the terms set out by Weber and Gorz earlier, and yet, at least by appearances, also promises via, for example, personal data exploitation and micropayments, to undermine critical points of control and exploitation that so much capital growth work is and has always been contingent upon. There is, therefore, an apparent contradiction. What is more, blockchain not only clearly fits the mould as an economic facilitator of capital growth on behalf of capitalist class power, but also as a *project* of neoliberal political economy (Hall, 2017, p. 334). The noises emanating from the blockchain ecosystem seem eerily familiar therefore, because they are echoes of the types of paradoxical, precarious and strategic self-governance already well defined in the neoliberal playbook. In short, it points to a form of *blockchain governmentality*. As Pat O'Malley sets out:

> The prudent subjects of neo-liberalism should practise and sustain their autonomy by assembling information, materials and practices together into a personalized strategy that identifies and minimizes their exposure to harm. Such risk management is frequently, and perhaps increasingly, associated with access to statistical or actuarial technologies and expert advice that render measurable the (probabilistic) calculation of future harms. As suggested, these precise forms of predictive calculation are possible only to the extent that the future is imagined to repeat the past: ironically, this technology of freedom works in important ways only to the extent that it is not at liberty to create the future. Where such actuarial risk management is concerned, freedom appears as part of 'freedom of choice', in the capacity to select which calculable risks to govern and by what means. In a sense, the subjects of this technology of risk are imagined as consumers (albeit 'sovereign consumers'), for, as elsewhere in discourses of the freedom of choice, their liberty exists in the capacity to choose rationally among available options and to assemble from these the risk-minimizing elements of a responsible lifestyle.
>
> (O'Malley, 2000, p. 465)

Yochai Benkler discusses a similar model, albeit one that focuses on the open software movement that pre-dates blockchain (as well as informs it), yet the terms he uses resonate closely with those of the present blockchain moment. '[T]he networked environment makes possible a new modality of organizing production', claims Benkler, one that is 'radically decentralized, collaborative, and non-proprietary based on sharing resources and outputs among widely distributed, loosely connected individuals who cooperate with each other without relying on either market signals or managerial commands. This is what I call "commons-based peer production"' (2006, p. 60). The concept of blockchain is by comparison, I suggest, representative of a *before* of rational community, and of encounters with 'the other', 'the intruder' (Lingis, 1994, p. 10), and thus relies on enabling transactions and generalised economic activity between individuals who *cannot* or *do not* trust one another. Blockchain is not a commons but a site of failure in 'confidence in the reliability of a person or system, regarding a given set of outcomes or events, where that confidence expresses a faith in the probity or love of another, or in the correctness of abstract principles (technical knowledge)' (Giddens, 1990, p. 34). Or, as Rachel Botsman suggests, 'blockchain raises a key human question: how much should we pay to trust one another?' (2017, p. 244), to which a not unreasonable answer ought surely to be: why is it necessary to pay in order to guarantee a person's trust, in order to salvage confidence, probity or love? Perhaps blockchain is the long-awaited response to or result of what Marshall McLuhan predicted over half a century ago, namely, that, '[t]oo many people know too much about each other. Our new environment compels commitment and participation. We have become irrevocably involved with, and responsible for, each other' (McLuhan and Fiore, 2008, p. 24). Blockchain may solve the problem of 'the other', of the necessity or duty to care for them (Levinas, 1998) physically or digitally, but does not necessarily alleviate the monstrosity or horror the other, the neighbour, elicits (Žižek, 2013). What Botsman suggests makes blockchain appear far more cynical a solution than Benkler's tidy world of commons-based peer production therefore, or perhaps it is the only option in a cynical world, a world of monstrous others who cannot be trusted.

The open source movement and 'free' circulation of open source software has not, since Benkler's enthusiastic proclamations, succeeded in overthrowing commercial, for-profit domination of the Internet, web-based applications, software and hardware infrastructure. The rentier business models of large mobile and web-based platforms such as Uber demonstrates where the axe inevitably falls when commercial interests are given a free hand to re-shape the world. With the best will in the world it is difficult to believe entrepreneurs who claim blockchain-led projects are solely for social good and not for self-interested wealth creation. As Joseph Stiglitz argues:

> there are two ways to become wealthy: to create wealth or to take wealth away from others [...] Unfortunately, even genuine wealth creators often are not satisfied with the wealth that their innovation or entrepreneurship has reaped. Some eventually turn to abusive practices like monopoly pricing or other forms of rent extraction to garner even more riches.
>
> (Stiglitz, 2013, p. 40)

If anything, blockchain-led economic models of micropayments and property rights attribution could signal the death-knell for the voluntary ethos that Benkler found both surprising ('at the heart of the economic engine, of the world's most advanced economics [...] a new model of production [...] that should not be there, at least according to our most widely held beliefs about economic behaviour'; Benkler, 2006, p. 59), and refreshing ('It should certainly not be that these volunteers will beat the largest and best-financed business enterprises in the world at the their own game. And yet, this is precisely what is happening in the software world'; Benkler, 2006, p. 59). Benkler was wrong in his predictions concerning the overthrow of the largest and best-financed business enterprises in the world. Instead there has been a massive concentration of power and wealth in a few hands even during the years since Benkler presented his thesis.

Similarly, Galloway claims (writing at a similar time to Benkler) that, 'the emergence of distributed networks is part of a larger shift in social life. The shift includes a movement away from central bureaucracies and vertical hierarchies toward a broad network of autonomous social actors' (Galloway, 2004, pp. 32–33). Neither author was discussing blockchain specifically, but rather the impact of the Internet, and both, I suggest, missed the mark. Galloway, unlike Benkler, is suspicious and more importantly critical of the growing authority of intelligent networks. The techno-economic landscape in which blockchain has emerged is not one of digital egalitarianism, but something more akin to digital feudalism. 'Despite the possibility to replace the role banks play in the market', claim Kibum Kim and Taewon Kang in a paper for the Organisation for Economic Co-operation and Development (OECD) on blockchain and anti-corruption, 'financial institutions embraced the technology [blockchain] and actively formed consortiums such as the R3CEV to develop proof of concepts and uses cases' (2017, p. 13). Far from 'disrupting' legacy economic and financial modalities, blockchain research, development and adoption continues to demand more profound levels of capitalisation via more competition and markets and the further embeddedness of existing (not novel) patterns of economic logic and reason that feeds the ongoing processes of neoliberal hegemony. As Stuart Hall argued: 'No project achieves "hegemony" as a completed project. It is a process, not a state of being. No victories are permanent or final. Hegemony has constantly to be "worked on", maintained, renewed, revised' (2017, p. 334). In other words blockchain is not transforming the world in some glorious moment of techno-social reconfiguration that is 'good' (in contrast to the 'bad' of what inevitably came before), but enabling further neoliberal experiments ('sandboxing') in techno-social engineering.

Further, the open source software movement that Benkler highlights and blockchain economics have in common a failure to acknowledge that the networks and systems upon which they are built, and through which the marvellous new co-operative and economic orders will supposedly flourish, would cease to function if a withdrawal of commercial platforms and in particular the interfaces they build and maintain were to occur. In the same way that anyone who drives a car is free to become a mechanic but invariably does not, so the majority of people do not want the responsibility (all of the time) of running, maintaining and ultimately controlling the systems and networks to which they are subject. There is, in other words, a tension between the *know-how* that software programmers, including those working on blockchain, have relative to individuals and communities more generally, and that core groups of those with know-how will always aim to ensure their relevance and survival. This leads some accounts of blockchain, notably

Michael Casey and Paul Vigna's, to profound levels of contradiction based on the assumption that the technology will serve the interests of individual 'self-sovereign' 'creators' who will maintain control over the entirety of their digital being, whilst still beating the drum for the right of private interests to exploit market opportunities that the technology brings to the fore. Thus a denial of individual 'self-sovereign' 'creators' is (re)introduced when it is a consumer framework that is at stake. Whilst there are any number of different reasons why private interests and commercial platforms will not withdraw, an obvious one concerns the relationship between mass adoption of technologies and how ease of use is designed into making certain technologies desirable. Moreover, since, for example, the earliest development and deployment of personal computers in the 1980s, mass adoption has relied upon catering for and to some extent solving the issue of a corresponding lack of mass know-how. The know-how possessed by technologists and correspondingly lacking in users effectively makes technologists and the business of technology indispensable.

The myth that commercial business interests will retreat or evaporate once a healthy and robust network has been developed is like arguing that social media would cease to be if Facebook were all of a sudden to disappear – in the case of social media the genie is most certainly out of the bottle, and what is more, it is a model of technological scalability that many entrepreneurs aspire to. And technology businesses and commercial interests banking on blockchain, those that embody and inform the rapidly evolving digital economy, know this. As Nick Srnicek has argued: 'digital economy is becoming systemically important, much in the same way as finance. As the digital economy is an increasingly pervasive infrastructure for the contemporary economy, its collapse would be economically devastating' (2017, p. 5). In a worrying echo of the state of financial services in the lead-up to the financial crisis and in the years afterward, it would seem that technologies are becoming, or have already become, too big to fail. With this in mind it is important to consider whilst still at this relatively early stage in blockchain development the extent to which government must intervene, in the public interest, to determine the direction blockchain takes apropos the civic sphere, as well as how it will contrast to private sector, for-profit settings and the indirect influence of private interests in civic arenas.

Blockchain in one form of other, whether permissioned (private/enterprise), permissionless (public), or hybrid chains, will structure networks and back-office systems operating on behalf of taxpayers, civic and public administrations including healthcare, and so on in the near future. Further, with blockchain private commercial interest will colonise areas of public interest such as healthcare, in spite of the democratic and moral duty government has to command and control domains such as healthcare, but where it has been delegitimised by neoliberal narratives that claim business as the more efficient, value-for-money option for taxpayer revenue in cases of civic technological infrastructure. In his discussion of the US administration Mark Fenster implies this very narrative, but, I argue, his proposition is equally true, mutatis mutandis, of global corporations who increasingly control the blockchain ecosystem. 'The government is large, faceless, bureaucratic', states Fenster, and therefore to be 'held accountable and to perform well, government institutions and officials must be visible to the public' (2017, p. 4). To suggest that government is a bad option for regulatory authority and business either a good or natural alternative is, I suggest, not clear-cut, and it would be wrong to allow private interest to assume a controlling stake of the blockchain regulatory environment.

Present trends towards permissioned ledgers arguably reflect the interest from large global corporations including banks, and hence also indicate where the money is with regard to research and development of the technology. Private blockchains allow, for example, banks to keep a replicated ledger of transactions behind closed walls, 'centralized and guarded' (Botsman, 2017, p. 242), although, as Botsman highlights, this 'seems to defeat the very purpose of the technology, which is to create a single indisputable version of the truth, freely accessible to all, that could eliminate the need for the bank entirely' (2017, pp. 242–243). Accordingly blockchain is not so much disrupting legacy structures and sources of financial power as helping regenerate them. Long-standing and influential stake-holders in 'truly' decentralised blockchains, that is, blockchains that fulfil the initial purpose of the technology to undermine legacy financial power and in particular the libertarian bogeyman, 'the middleman', are already urging resistance to the dominance of 'enterprise' blockchains for this reason (Floyd, 2018). There is a parallel that can be drawn here between private blockchains and private intranets which by some estimates 'may be ten times larger than the public Internet – analogous to private property compared to that in public hands' (Brown and Marsden, 2013, p. xv). Moreover, some authors 'have warned against private enclosure of the public Internet space' (Brown and Marsden, 2013, p. xv), an argument that has equally been made with regard to blockchain (Herian, 2016).

Different types of blockchain are fairly self-explanatory, yet noting the distinction between them is important not only in terms of tracking the evolution of thinking within the blockchain ecosystem, but in terms of possible regulatory responses to it. This is particularly so in light of the General Data Protection Regulation (GDPR) introduced in the European Union (EU) in May 2018 to replace the 1995 Data Protection Directive. Provisions in the new regulation such as the so-called right to be forgotten that do not sit comfortably with the central and, for many stakeholders, most desirable characteristics of blockchain, including promises of immutability. It is not only public blockchains like Bitcoin and Ethereum and the businesses who rely on them that the GDPR could impact, however, with potential problems also on the horizon for private blockchains as well. One response has been from a start-up called Enigma who propose a variation on smart contracts called 'secret contracts', designed specifically to attenuate public exposure of sensitive information held on a blockchain and thus strengthen the secrecy they claim has been lost in the evolution of blockchain applications. As Enigma founder Guy Zyskind maintains:

> All blockchains, and by extension smart contracts, have one glaring problem that is often overlooked – all data stored on them is public. In that sense,

blockchains are worse than anything that came before them. Instead of trust-ing your data with a single organization (e.g., as is the case with Facebook, Google, your bank, etc), you now have to trust everyone. For all intents and purposes, data on the blockchain becomes public domain.

(2018)

'Enigma's protocol', states Annalise Milano, 'uses a trusted execution environment in which the cryptography is relied upon for certainty and neither party has any information on their respective data inputs and outputs', hence 'the tech can be utilized for use cases in industries like healthcare and finance that frequently handle sensitive data and must comply with legal measures like the EU's General Data Protection Regulation (GDPR)' (2018).

It is important therefore to note the distinction between different types of blockchain. Permissioned blockchains or ledgers are not public but operate in closed systems. They provide many of the same perceived advantages of public (permissionless) blockchains, of which the Bitcoin blockchain is the most obvious example, including transparency and decentralisation, but these features are only deployed within a closed network, such as a corporate back-office system, where the blockchain can only be accessed by those with requisite permission to do so. A *permissionless* public blockchain can, in theory, be viewed by anyone at any time 'because it resides on the network, not within a single institution charged with auditing transactions and keeping records' (Tapscott and Tapscott, 2016, p. 6). Hybrids combine permissioned and permissionless blockchains, allowing data from a closed network to be released to permissionless blockchains for the purposes of, for example, focused public scrutiny of specific data and a particular time. This hybrid distinction might also include the option of using blockchains, most likely in permissioned form, as an 'access control' medium for other databases, as well as off-chain or offline data storage infrastructure.

Given the intangibility of digital data, the inability for the data owner to retain full control (especially in a technological context that requires a certain degree of know-how to fully comprehend) is perhaps unsurprising. This is already the case, for instance, in terms of cryptocurrency wallets (applications that allow digital coins or tokens to be stored, used and traded), which at once provide a user-friendly interface and encourage wider adoption of the technology by those who might otherwise be excluded due to a lack of technological know-how, and rup-ture the disintermediation that many view as a core, inalienable condition of blockchain technology. In other words, contrary to the libertarian blockchain ideal of seamless peer-to-peer networking, the technology has failed to exclude media-tion between online peers by commercial and business interests, and it will not succeed in doing so anytime soon.[4]

4   Taiwanese company Bitmark is one example of the continuing mediation businesses will
      provide and thus why decentralisation, or more importantly disintermediation, are pow-
      erful myths, but myths nonetheless. Bitmark provides its users with online tools and web-
      based applications to 'open up access to the data economy for everyone' (https://bitma

Conclusion

The perspectives, theories and analysis this book undertakes assume the point of view of law, culture and political economy rather than information and communications technology. First and foremost the discussion will focus on blockchain narratives and discourse, the language, terminology and vocabulary that inform the blockchain ecosystem as a community of thought and practice, and the various effects and affects these are having, not least in relation to the existing problematic of regulatory approaches. A lack of conclusive evidence on the effects of blockchain, not least because it has only formed part of mainstream consciousness for five years or so, accounts for prevailing strategies of so-called 'smart regulation' adopted by the EU and the 'monitoring' and 'wait and see' approaches equally favoured by, for example, the FCA in the UK (Baker, 2016; FCA, 2017).

Yet blockchain's immaturity is not the whole story. Pressures on regulatory authorities to remain at a distance can be traced to the victory of techno-solutionist ideologies existing within the scope of grander neoliberal strategies to successfully argue and lobby for pole position. In Britain this solutionism is thinly veiled behind calls for more entrepreneurialism as a way of realising a wide range of affordances, such as global recognition and reputation of Britain as a 'tech hub', as well as economic benefits. The Autumn Budget speech in 2017 by the UK's Chancellor of the Exchequer, Philip Hammond, is testament to the UK government's belief in the combination of reputational and economic affordances (effectiveness, efficiency, calculability) of technological innovation. The outcome of government favouring techno-solutionist approaches is problematic for various reasons that this book will consider in depth. At the centre of any regulatory approaches to blockchain must be acknowledgement of *blockchain conduct*, not simply judgement as to the prudence of individual blockchain use-cases. Impacts that reflect the will and desire of individuals and particular stakeholders within the blockchain ecosystem are key indicators of the ideology of blockchain which is being exported beyond the ecosystem through gradual and normative inscriptions of the technology on a wide range of private and public settings. This includes, as discussed, promises of blockchain as a better means for managing personal data that arguably encourages users to offer up greater volumes of data whilst simultaneously placing the onus on the user to be data sovereign. It is hard to see how such a system would not entirely negate the role of the state, whilst simultaneously guaranteeing the neoliberal paradigm of subject-as-consumer ahead of that of subject-as-citizen. What is more, this vision of blockchain clearly recalls, as briefly

rk.com/). Similar organisations such as Mediachain focus on the attribution of metadata and point towards a key driver in developing a data economy being the ability for individual users to unlock value from their data, rather than allowing existing business models, such as those of Google and Facebook, to extract value for themselves (www. mediachain.io/#). Mediachain and Bitmark both raise key issues, namely the extent of the desirability of a fully realised global data economy, that is, the potential marketisation and financialisation (monetisation) of any and all forms of data bound up in positive social narratives of 'unlocking value'.

mentioned earlier, the tension Foucault highlighted between liberal political economy and technologies of security that constitute what he called *governmentality* (2002, pp. 219–220).

Individual data sovereignty might well appear to some stakeholders as a neat solution to present big data paradigms in which global corporations such as Facebook and Google harvest data with little or no benefit accruing back to the user, but it also points to a shift in the principle of government from 'external congruence' (including the onus on government to regulate in the public interest), to 'internal regulation' (Lemke, 2012, p. 43). The blockchain 'solution' in this instance is likely (based on present trends) to be underscored by further and deeper private commercial interests, thereby potentially swapping one politically unaccountable Internet titan for another already waiting in the wings for an opportunity to profit and disseminate a particular world view. What is more, it would sever the relationship between state and citizen, making the citizen entirely responsible for the management, exploitation (i.e. generating micropayments) and protection of one's data against a backdrop of constantly unfolding markets and a wild proliferation of consumer choice. As a close approximation to Foucault's concept of governmentality this would make blockchain a site in which individuals 'are expected to cope with social risks and insecurities, to measure and calculate them [...] In this perspective it is entrepreneurial action, rational risk management, and individual responsibility that account for social success or failure' (Lemke, 2012, p. 47).

It is clear that ignoring the hype surrounding blockchain is unwise given its rapid proliferation. Echoing trends in technologies that have come before it, blockchain represents an 'increasingly influential yet subtle force in our lives' (Brenner, 2007, p. 185). Regulators and governments especially need to get a grip on blockchain in order to ensure political accountability in the blockchain ecosystem and beyond; to ask whether the technology and the regulatory goals attached to it are 'proportionate and limited to what is necessary to protect a specific public interest in a democratic society' (Wright et al., 2006, p. 156). Blockchain is a product of the shifts and tensions in political and socioeconomic thought and practice since the financial crisis of 2008. As a discourse or text blockchain recounts a broad matrix of socioeconomic and political issues in a constant state of flux. Moreover it is revealing something very important about the evolution of the subject caught in the force field of neoliberal economic reason both at the macro level of contemporary free-market capitalism, and more intimately. This includes but is not limited to: the subject's encounter with the (im)materialism of digital objects; big data and the digital unconscious; as well as the ability of technologies to produce and distort meaning, and (re)constitute being and memory. The consequences of change in communities and the lives of individuals who already lack influence over the technologies, networks, platforms and data that presently shape, control and yet provide meaning, is key to the unravelling story of blockchain. As Marshall McLuhan stated: 'Societies have always been shaped more by the nature of the media by which men communicate than by the content of the communication' (McLuhan and Fiore, 2008, p. 8). For better or worse, understanding a future with blockchain is imperative. Critical perspectives may take issue with the idea that 'it is all about blockchain' (Tapscott and Tapscott, 2016), but it is certainly the case that blockchain can no longer be ignored.

References

Arthur, W.Brian. 2009. *The Nature of Technology: What it is and how it evolves*. London: Penguin.

Baker, Jennifer. 2016. Distributed Ledger tech will be closely monitored, rather than suffocated by new rules. *Ars Technica*, 27 May. https://arstechnica.com/tech-policy/2016/05/europe-bitcoin-blockchain-regulation-details/ (accessed 9 February 2018).

Benkler, Yochai. 2006. *The Wealth of Networks: How Social Production Transforms Markets and Freedom*. New Haven: Yale University Press.

Botsman, Rachel. 2017. *Who Can You Trust? How Technology Brought Us Together – and Why It Could Drive Us Apart*. London: Portfolio Penguin.

Brenner, Susan W. 2007. *Law in an Era of 'Smart' Technology*. Oxford: Oxford University Press.

Brown, Ian and Marsden, Christopher, T. 2013. *Regulating Code: Good Governance and Better Regulation in the Information Age*. Cambridge: MIT Press.

Brown, Wendy. 2015. *Undoing the Demos: Neoliberalism's Stealth Revolution*. New York: Zone Books.

Brownsword, Roger and Goodwin, Morag. 2012. *Law and Technologies of the Twenty-First Century*. Cambridge: Cambridge University Press.

Casey, Michael J. and Vigna, Paul. 2018. *The Truth Machine: The Blockchain and the Future of Everything*. London: HarperCollins.

Castells, Manuel. 2010. *The Rise of the Network Society*. 2nd Edition. Chichester: Wiley Blackwell.

Cohen, G.A. 2011. *On the Currency of Egalitarian Justice, and Other Essays in Political Philosophy*. Edited by Michael Otsuka. Princeton: Princeton University Press.

Davies, William. 2017. *The Limits of Neoliberalism: Authority, Sovereignty and the Logic of Competition*. London: Sage.

Dean, Jodie. 2009. *Democracy and Other Neoliberal Fantasies: Communicative Capitalism and Left Politics*. Durham: Duke University Press.

Fenster, Mark. 2017. *The Transparency Fix: Secrets, Leaks, and Uncontrollable Government Information*. Stanford: Stanford University Press.

Financial Conduct Authority (FCA). 2017. *Distributed Ledger Technology: Feedback Statement on Discussion Paper 17/03*. December. www.fca.org.uk/publication/feedback/fs17-04.pdf (accessed 6 February 2018).

Floyd, David. 2018. Smart Contract Pioneer Nick Szabo: Don't Ditch Decentralization. *Coindesk*, 19 April. www.coindesk.com/smart-contract-pioneer-nick-szabo-dont-ditch-decentralization/ (accessed 20 April 2018).

Foucault, Michel. 2002. *Power: Essential Works of Michel Foucault 1954–1984, Volume 3*. Edited by James D. Faubion. Translated by Robert Hurley and others. London: Penguin.

Galloway, Alexander R. 2004. *Protocol: How Control Exists After Decentralization*. Cambridge: MIT Press.

Giddens, Anthony. 1990. *The Consequences of Modernity*. Cambridge: Polity.

Gorz, André. 1989. *Critique of Economic Reason*. London: Verso.

Greenspan, Gideon. 2017. The Blockchain Immutability Myth. www.multichain.com/blog/2017/05/blockchain-immutability-myth/ (accessed 13 March 2018).

Gurstein, Michael. 2012. Toward a Conceptual Framework for a Community Informatics. *Connecting Canadians: Investigations in Community Informatics*. Edited by A. Clement, M. Gurstein, G. Longford, M. Moll and L. Shade. Edmonton, AB: AU Press, pp. 35–60.

Hall, Stuart. 2017. *Selected Political Writings: The Great Moving Right Show and Other Essays*. Edited by Sally Davison, David Featherstone, Michael Rustin and Bill Schwartz. Durham: Duke University Press.

Hammond, Phillip. 2017. *Autumn Budget 2017: Phillip Hammond's Speech*. HM Treasury, 22 November. www.gov.uk/government/speeches/autumn-budget-2017-philip-hammonds-speech (accessed 9 February 2018).

Han, Byung-Chul. 2017. *Psycho-Politics: Neoliberalism and New Technologies of Power*. Translated by Erik Butler. London: Verso.

Harvey, David. 2005. *A Brief History of Neoliberalism*. Oxford: Oxford University Press.

Herian, Robert. 2016. *Anything but disruptive: blockchain, capital and a case of fourth industrial age enclosure, parts I & II*. October. www.critciallegalthinking.com (accessed 30 January 2018).

Hodgson, Geoffrey M. 2015. *Conceptualizing Capitalism: Institutions, Evolution, Future*. Chicago: University of Chicago Press.

Holmes, Chris (Lord Holmes of Richmond). 2017. *Distributed Ledger Technologies for Public Good: leadership, collaboration and innovation*. http://chrisholmes.co.uk/blog/tech-opportunity-carpe-dlt/ (accessed 6 February 2018).

Kim, Kibum and Kang, Taewon. 2017. *Does Technology Against Corruption Always Lead to Benefit? The Potential Risks and Challenges of the Blockchain Technology*. OECD Global Anti-Corruption & Integrity Forum. www.oecd.org/cleangovbiz/Integrity-Forum-2017-Kim-Kang-blockchain-technology.pdf (accessed 25 April 2018).

Lemke, Thomas. 2012. *Foucault, Governmentality, and Critique*. Boulder: Paradigm Publishers.

Levinas, Emmanuel. 1998. *Otherwise than Being, or Beyond Essence*. Translated by Alphonso Lingis. Pittsburgh: Duquesne University Press.

Lingis, Alphonso. 1994. *The Community of Those Who Have Nothing in Common*. Bloomington: Indiana University Press.

McLuhan, Marshall and Fiore, Quentin. 2008. *The Medium is the Massage*. Co-ordinated by Jerome Agel. London: Penguin.

Marsden, Christopher T. 2000. Introduction: Information and communications technologies, globalisation and regulation. *Regulating the Global Information Society*. Edited by Christopher T. Marsden. London: Routledge, pp. 1–40.

Milano, Annalise. 2018. Blockchain Startup Enigma to Demo 'Secret Contracts' Privacy Tech'. *Coindesk*, 15 May. www.coindesk.com/blockchain-startup-enigma-demo-secret-contracts-privacy-tech/ (accessed 16 May 2018).

Mirowski, Philip. 2014. *Never Let A Serious Crisis Go To Waste: How Neoliberalism Survived the Financial Meltdown*. London: Verso.

O'Malley, Pat. 2000. Uncertain subjects: risks, liberalism and contract. *Economy and Society*, Vol. 29, No. 4 (November), pp. 460–484.

Organisation for Economic Co-operation and Development (OECD). 2018. *Blockchain Technology and Competition Policy – Issues Paper by the Secretariat*. 26 April. https://one.oecd.org/document/DAF/COMP/WD(2018)47/en/pdf (accessed 16 May 2018).

Peck, Jamie. 2012. *Constructions of Neoliberal Reason*. Oxford: Oxford University Press.

Power, Michael. 1997. *The Audit Society: Rituals of Verification*. Oxford: Oxford University Press.

Robinson, Joan. 1962. *Economic Philosophy*. Harmondsworth: Penguin.

Siri, Santiago. 2016. The Future of Democracy. *TEDx*, 30 March. www.youtube.com/watch?v=yGmGWZCE4h0 (accessed 9 February 2018).

Srnicek, Nick. 2017. *Platform Capitalism*. Cambridge: Polity.

Stiglitz, Joseph E. 2013. *The Price of Inequality*. London: Penguin.

Swan, Melanie. 2015. *Blockchain: Blueprint for a New Economy*. Sebastopol: O'Reilly.

Tapscott, Don and Tapscott, Alex. 2016. *Blockchain Revolution: How the Technology behind Bitcoin is Changing Money, Business and the World*. London: Portfolio Penguin.

Walch, Angela. 2017. Blockchain's Treacherous Vocabulary: One More Challenge for Regulators. *Journal of Internet Law*, Vol. 21, No. 2, pp. 9–16.

Weber, Max. 2002. *The Protestant Ethic and the 'Spirit' of Capitalism and Other Writings*. Edited and translated by Peter Baehr and Gordon C. Wells. London: Penguin Classics.

Wright, Aaron and De Filippi, Primavera. 2015. *Decentralized Blockchain Technology and the Rise of Lex Cryptographia*. https://papers.ssrn.com/sol3/papers.cfm?abstract_id=2580664 (accessed 24 May 2018).

Wright, David, Vildjiounaite, Elena, Maghiros, Ioannis, Friedewald, Michael, Verlinden, Michiel, Alahuhta, Petteri, Delaitre, Sabine, Gutwirth, Serge, Schreurs, Wim and Punie, Yves. 2006. *Safeguards in a World of Ambient Intelligence (SWAMI). Deliverable D1. The brave new world of ambient intelligence: A state-of-the-art review*. Edited by Michael Friedewald, Elena Vildjiounaite and David Wright. http://is.jrc.ec.europa.eu/pages/TFS/documents/SWAMI_D1_Final_001.pdf (accessed 27 March 2018).

Žižek, Slavoj. 2013. Neighbours and Other Monsters. *The Neighbour: Three Inquires in Political Theology*. Chicago: The University of Chicago Press, pp. 134–190.

Zyskind, Guy. 2018. Defining Secret Contracts. *Medium*, 4 April. https://blog.enigma.co/defining-secret-contracts-f40ddee67ef2 (accessed 16 May 2018).

Interlude III: Anarchic technologies for anarchic economies

The 'yellow trade' of the Yorkshire coiners

The anarchic, libertarian, peer-to-peer, networked economy that stakeholders of Bitcoin and blockchain first proclaimed and some continue to aim for was and is by definition anti-state, anti-centralised regulation and authority, and anti-political oversight. The attractiveness of the decentralised if not still entirely anarchic model has more recently led to major global corporate interest in blockchain. As David Golumbia points out:

> The whole point of the enterprise, as with most of the efforts promoted by libertarian and anarcho-capitalists, is to enable a wide range of extractive and exploitative business practices, and thus to increase the power of corporations and capital outside the scope of any attempts by democratic polities to constrain them.
>
> (2016, p. 69)

The legitimacy of Bitcoin and blockchain as overtly anarchic or libertarian projects is now, I suggest, in utter ruin, not because law and regulation have found a way to reasonably constrain them other than trade bans and arbitrary use restrictions, but because capitalist class power and neoliberalism have swept in to claim and absorb the technology for its own purposes, and to serve its own ends.

For the better part of its short history the Bitcoin project has involved a closed network of actors, and thus required esoteric know-how that extended over the enterprise beyond the comfortable realms of mainstream and everyday network user capabilities. This, now, is of course also rapidly changing as a wild proliferation of cryptocurrencies emerge. But the struggles and conflicts between cryptocurrency stakeholders and regulators and governments around the globe, a tension between the mainstream and peripheral economies and their inherent often esoteric use of technologies, is nothing new. The following extract from *The Yorkshire coiners, 1767–1783. And notes on old and prehistoric Halifax* by Henry Ling Roth, describes the fate of a group of coiners and counterfeiters in and around Cragg Vale, West Yorkshire during the eighteenth century, who 'clipped' coins and minted money through processes of anarchic technique with the desire to build an anarchic economy.

In the *Leeds Intelligencer* for July 26th, 1768, we read: – 'At the Assizes held at York last week, Joseph Stell was found guilty of counterfeiting the gold coin of this kingdom, and received sentence of death.'

In the same paper for August 9th, 1768, a description of the counterfeit coins is given: –

> As counterfeit guineas are now circulating, of which there are various kinds, in one, dated 1757, it is to be observed that the laurel round the head is indented, and the drapery on the fore-part of the neck runs higher than in the current coin. The R in *Georgius* and *Gratia* is short in the first stroke. There are points between each letter of the words *Et* and *Rex*; the H for *Hibemia* and the B for *Brutts [wick]* are wanting. On the Hanover quarter of the arms there are two lions wanting on the left, and two in the place of one on the right. The letters in general are badly executed. They weigh in air 101 1-half grains, in water 94 1-half, and are worth about 11s. 1d.

Then we read: 'Mr. Joseph Stell, who was found guilty at the last Assizes at York, of counterfeiting the current gold coin of this kingdom, was executed on Saturday night last, about six o'clock, pursuant to his sentence.'

On January 10th, 1769, the same paper informs us: –

> At the Quarter Sessions held yesterday for this Borough, an indictment was found against a person from the neighbourhood of Halifax, for uttering false gold. He found sureties for his appearance at the next General Quarter Sessions to be held for this Borough.

On the 21st February, 1769, there is the following note:

> We hear from Rochdale that one Crossley, from the neighbourhood of Halifax, was last week committed to Lancaster Gaol, by Richard Townley, Esq., on suspicion of coining. – 'Tis hoped that by the securing of this fellow, a nest of notorious clippers and coiners will be brought to justice.

In the following month the *Leeds Mercury* (14th March, 1769) informs its readers: –

> It is strongly rumoured in this town, that a gang of about half-a-score of men, suspected of being concerned in diminishing the Gold Coin, and of uttering Counterfeit Gold knowing it to be such, have been apprehended in the neighbourhood of Halifax, and committed to the County Gaol.

In connection with the coining a curious discovery was made in Leeds, and it is recorded as follows: *Leeds Intelligencer*, May 23rd, 1769.

One day last week a brass-founder in this town bought at a hardware shop a parcel of old copper and brass metal; upon examining which, he was agreeably surprised to find a wedge of real standard gold, which weighed upwards of Eight ounces, and appeared to have been melted down in a crucible; probably by some of those villains, who, for want of better work employed their time in diminishing the current coin of the Kingdom.

The continued increase of false coins was beginning to be seriously felt now by the community in general, for we have an editorial protest against a conspiracy of which everyone seems to have been cognisant. It appears in the *Leeds Intelligencer* for June 27th 1769: –

The number of Sweaters and Filers of Gold coin still continue to infest the Western part of this County with impunity; and by various villainous ways and inventions, find means not only to get large sums into their hands, but also to circulate it again, after they have diminished it 20 per cent. – Two of these rascals, from the neighbourhood of Halifax, (one an honest Caledonian) applied to some dealers in bills in this town last Saturday, in order to put off their mutilated cash; but did not meet with success: they, however, contrived to pay large sums to several tradesmen, who were either more careless, or more in want of money. – 'Tis greatly to be wished, that the dealers in bills in general, would join in a subscription for prosecuting, and equally so, that the Government would lend its assistance, in bringing those audacious villains to condign punishment, and by that means *endeavour at least*, to put a stop to such iniquitous proceedings, for, if they are suffered to go on a few years in this public and daring manner, it is supposed the current gold coin of the nation in general, will be reduced a fifth part. – We hear indeed, that many of the principal tradesmen have come to a resolution to dis-countenance, as much as possible a practice so very injurious to trade, by refusing to take such gold as appears to have been so diminished.

This protest was followed a fortnight later by a sarcastic letter in the *Leeds Mercury* for July 18th, 1769, headed: –

Copy of a letter from Halifax, in this County, to a person in London, dated July 14th, 1769; –

At this time, when all the Manufacturing Parts of the Kingdom are loudly complaining of the Decay of Trade and Slackness of Payments, many ingenious People in this Country are growing rich apace by a new Kind of Industry. Gold Coin, which has heretofore been so scarce among us as to command a large Premium against Bills of Exchange, flows in upon us with great Rapidity from all parts of the Island; and by the *Hocus Pocus* Touch of a Number of experimental Philosophers and Chymists (not by an addition to its weight, but by an ingenious Multiplication of its Numbers) is so greatly increased, that all Payments in Paper will soon be at an end, and not a Bill circulated in this Country, but for the Purposes of promoting this most profitable Manufactory. These very ingenious Gentlemen ingross the Bills drawn upon London, through the persuasive Influence of a large Discount, upon their newly-reformed Coin, with its Auxiliary numbers begot upon it, and by an extensive Correspondence, are in a fair Way of drawing Half the Gold in the two Kingdoms into this happy Country, with giving still larger Premiums with the Bills for Gold Coin (brought out of distant Parts) that has not partook of their Improvements. If you wish to be rich, and can sacrifice a few nonsensical Scruples to that Deity, make haste hither, and you may soon be instructed in these Mysteries, which, (with great Ease and Pleasure) will enable you to convert a Thousand of your old-fashioned Guineas into Twelve Hundred, and, with a moderate Industry, to repeat the Process every Week ; with the Subtraction of only a Shilling for each Guinea to the honourable Gentlemen who procure fresh ones for you, and of Sixpence each to them who pay off those that have been reduced by you, and give you their Bills of Exchange for them, which will leave you a neat Profit of 125 Guineas per Week. A pretty genteel thing for such a Capital: and you have nothing to fear from the Bugbear of those obsolete Laws which inflict Pains and Penalties upon Ingenuity of this interesting Kind; as those whose peculiar Business it is have good Reason, no Doubt, for neglecting and discountenancing Informations; and the old Proverb (every Body's Business is Nobody's) is a sufficient Protection from Prosecution from any others; and you will have this Security for the Continuance of this lucrative Business, that if the Gentlemen who procure you fresh Cash, or those who give you Bills for that which has undergone your Improvement, should decline your Correspondence, desert you in Favour of another, or demand higher Terms, you have nothing to do but to prosecute them all upon the Statute of Usury, for every Sum each has advanced upon Interest, or Discount, or Premium, for which they have taken more than £5 per Cent, per Annum, or in Proportion to it for a larger or smaller Sum or Time, and you will most certainly recover three-fold the Value, and make your fortune at once, as well as make an honourable Satisfaction or Amends in the Eye of the Public, which is so reasonable and invidious, as to offer hard Names to a Business that produces such tempting Profits.

There is one Thing, however, which perplexes me a little in Speculation: as this remanufactured Gold Coin will pass in payment nowhere but in this Manufacturing Country, and that, by the Example and Influence of many principal Dealers in it, I am afraid, when all our Trading Stock and Credit is absorbed into this glittering Article, and the People are starving for want of Corn and other Provisions that have been brought heretofore from distant Countries, it may bring us into considerable difficulties; for however pleasing it may appear to the eye, and this way of acquiring it may sit easy upon the Conscience, I fear it will be found hard of Digestion upon the Stomach, if we are reduced to the Necessity of Eating it. But as some Chymists have called it the Universal Panacea, if these ingenious Gentlemen can, upon such an

Emergancy, transmute it into an universal Aliment, we shall all be safe again. I am. Sir, &c.

(Roth, 1906, pp. 11–13)

References

Golumbia, David. 2016. *The Politics of Bitcoin: Software as Right-Wing Extremism*. Minneapolis: University of Minnesota Press.

Roth, Henry Ling. 1906. *The Yorkshire coiners, 1767–1783. And notes on old and prehistoric Halifax*. Halifax: F. King & Sons Ltd.

6 Blockchain as an ethics of neoliberal political economy

Introduction

> All media work us over completely. They are so pervasive in their personal, political, economic, aesthetic, psychological, moral, ethical, and social consequences that they leave no part of us untouched, unaffected, unaltered.
>
> (McLuhan and Fiore, 2008, p. 26)

> An essential aspect of the ideological war led by the neoliberals of the conservative revolution was the condemnation of governmental industrial and long-term policy and corresponding accusation that governments inevitably promote inefficient models of economic administration.
>
> (Stiegler, 2010, p. 101)

> Distributed trust is far from foolproof and the questions that really matter are ethical and moral, not technical.
>
> (Botsman, 2017, p. 9)

Many if not all new technologies are the subject of meta-projects of political economy, ethical conditioning and so on, in spite of the fact that, and albeit to varying degrees, the obscurantism of the technologies themselves can and does undermine or confuse such projects. As Bruno Latour maintains: 'Technologies and moralities happen to be indissolubly mingled because, in both cases, the question of the relation of ends to means is profoundly problematized' (2002, p. 248). Technologies are always already underpinned by an *ethics*, meaning they are never neutral politically *or* ethically. Nowhere is this more evident than in the prevailing *technomoral* turn in which stakeholders are implicating blockchain in endless prevarications between socioeconomic and political 'problems' and corresponding technological 'solutions'. Take, for example, the following dialogue offered by the Tapscotts, beginning with the 'problem':

> We have growth in gross domestic product but not commensurate job growth in most developed countries. We have growing wealth creation and growing social inequality. Powerful technology companies have shifted much activity from the open, distributed, egalitarian, and empowering Web to closed online

walled gardens or proprietary, read-only applications that among other things kill the conversation. Corporate forces have captured many of these wonderful peer-to-peer, democratic, and open technologies and are using them to extract an inordinate share of value.

(2016, p. 13)

And the 'solution':

Now, with blockchain technology, a world of new possibilities has opened up to reverse all these trends. We have a true peer-to-peer platform [...] We can each own our identities and our personal data. We can do transactions, creating and exchanging value without powerful intermediaries acting as the arbiters of money and information. Billions of excluded people can soon enter the global economy. We can protect our privacy and monetize our own information. We can ensure that creators are compensated for their intellectual property. Rather than trying to solve the problem of growing social inequality through the redistribution of wealth only, we can start to change the way wealth is *distributed* – how it is created in the first place, as people everywhere from farmers to musicians can share more fully, a priori, in the wealth they create. The sky does seem to be the limit.

(2016, p. 14)

That the Tapscotts are besotted by blockchain is uncontentious. But the scale of the moral project they perceive blockchain to be – not simply a project of which blockchain forms a part – is utterly astounding. Putting to one side for a moment the notion that all practices, including those emanating from the blockchain ecosystem, 'give accounts of themselves which are aspirational rather than descriptive' (Power, 1997, p. 7), the Tapscotts' belief that blockchain will 'reverse all these trends' *qua* global problems of social and economic inequality is an expression of solutionism taken to new heights. Moreover the neoliberal political economy informing the Tapscotts' vision is only thinly veiled in their proselytising, where every turn toward social betterment is always already linked to self-fulfilment and success that only economic reason can create: 'we can', as they say, 'protect our privacy and monetize our own information'. In a similar vein, Michael Casey and Paul Vigna beat a very loud drum for the social and ethical virtues they believe blockchain to possess:

We think it's important that solutions to the challenges faced by the poor aren't just imposed in some cookie-cutter manner by Silicon Valley venture capitalists who insist they know best. Solutions must be informed by and tailored to the underlying cultural structures of the communities in question.

(2018, p. 198)

Recall Kai Stinchcombe's direct challenge to solutionists to answer the question of why nobody has found a use for blockchain in the ten years of its existence:

Stinchcombe suggests the fact that multiple technologies already exist that are able to do what people would like to see blockchain doing renders blockchain surplus to requirements. Whilst this pragmatic and openly cynical argument has its merits, I believe it fundamentally underestimates the ideology of solutionism and the power of neoliberal rationality more generally. It does, in short, miss the strength of belief and faith in blockchain that its stakeholders possess and that, as Manuel Castells has argued, 'the entrepreneurial model of the information technology revolution seems to be overshadowed by ideology' (2010, p. 67). Pragmatic questions aside concerning whether blockchain is useful or not, however, the question posed here is more nuanced and metaphysical: what, or rather who, is blockchain good for?

Good for …?

What does blockchain as an ethics of political economy mean? We have already seen 'the good' in relation to juridical and regulatory frameworks and how these might potentially be applied to or by blockchain in a variety of contexts. The search for an answer to the question of the good here begins, however, with the pervasive mantra 'blockchain for good' that has swept through the ecosystem during the last few years. To begin to address this question I propose the following assumption: that the nature of the relationship between the blockchain ecosystem and neoliberalism (as capital's contemporary 'mutant form') (Han, 2017, p. 5) is symptomatic of the concepts and practices that constitute 'blockchain for good'. Further, the 'good' blockchain represents on behalf of neoliberalism is not a universal, but rather more often imposed, albeit subtly and discreetly, via concepts and strategies that pertain to be on behalf of community and social solidarity, but are always already indexed to the self-interest of market logic and principles. Casey and Vigna illustrate this point perfectly:

> For the more than 2 billion adults worldwide that the World Bank describes as 'unbanked', the good news is that a combination of humanitarian and financial motivations has produced a global movement to move the unbanked into the world of modern finance. *That's also good news for people looking for the next market*: if we crack this nut, there's potential for an economic boom the likes of which nobody has ever seen. It lies on the other side of incorporating the new markets, new customers, new products, and trillions of dollars of untapped capital that these people would bring with them.
>
> [emphasis added] (2018, p. 179)

Countervailing and critical accounts of 'blockchain for good', including those aimed at negating neoliberal visions and bringing to the fore questions of what it means for blockchain to be *no good* or *good for nothing* are crucial in order to address the nature of the good(s) blockchain and neoliberalism are together selling; as exemplified by Casey and Vigna, a dialectic of this sort is central to the discussion throughout this book not least in order to explore regulatory definitions that are or may be able to cut through the hype surrounding block-chain, as well as the less innocuous techno-solutionist ideologies that interpellate blockchain stakeholders and their conduct rooted in *virtuous* forms of 'disruption'. Blockchain acolytes proclaim to be working on behalf of a disempowered under-class that the technology will help save in some obvious and direct fashion, by bringing the 'unbanked' into the global financial economy, for instance (Casey and Vigna, 2018). Such policies or strategies singularly ignore, however, and indeed the technology in question often acts as a useful distraction from the pro-blematic that the financial and market system into which these poor unfortunate souls are ultimately to be made a part thanks to the goodwill of blockchain aco-lytes and their endless solutionism, is fundamentally the same that caused global social and economic inequality in the first place.

In the last few years the mantra 'blockchain for good' has taken root in the blockchain ecosystem, and in some senses has come to define it, with one example being the manifesto of the think tank, *Blockchain for Good*. 'Received ideas about what blockchain can and should be used for', argue Beth Kewell, Richard Adams and Glenn Parry,

> are based on perceptions that the key role of this technology is to unlock cost savings and secure efficiency gains, whilst also enabling widespread business model transformation. Within this scenario blockchain *affordances* are princi-pally seen to 'do good' by resolving longstanding obstacles to profitability and value capture.
>
> (2017, p. 429)

Referring to particular conceptualisations and implementations of blockchain as or for good sends a powerful message regarding the nature of the technology. It does, no less, deliberately align a modern technology with ancient notions of ethical and moral virtue to give weight or a legitimating gravitas to a technology, as well as the conduct produced by it. The 'blockchain for good' mantra situates the technology squarely within what was referred to above as the twenty-first-century technomoral turn, whereby the material interrelatedness between humanity and technology remains fraught and misaligned, yet largely uncontested at levels of popular understanding. This is arguably what Marshall McLuhan meant when he spoke of the pervasiveness of media that work 'us over completely' (McLuhan and Fiore, 2008, p. 26)

Similar to the Internet in recent years, blockchain brings to the fore a complex and sometimes nefarious set of contradictions and moral grey areas that global networks inevitably foster. For example, claims that representatives of extreme right-wing political movements in Europe, including Germany's Alternative für Deutschland, are seeking to take a lead on blockchain (Hall, 2018), reveal key moral dilemmas both in blockchain development and possible regulatory respon-ses to it. Ian Bogost (2017) makes similar arguments concerning the potential of blockchain to foster forms of authoritarian control. While David Golumbia (2016) argues that the libertarianism underlying blockchain's earliest incarnation, Bitcoin, although arguably now in retreat as neoliberalism moves in, has nevertheless left a residuum of right-wing extremism written into the software. Interest in the technology by representatives of Alternative für Deutschland suggests that this residuum might be difficult to remove, however. Cases of extreme right-wing groups looking to blockchain for solutions to financing issues, as well as other means of maintaining systems of information, against a backdrop of state-sanctioned constraint and prohibition are undeniably issues of law, politics and economy (but such issues are also undeniably ethical and moral). The European Union have agreed via the *4th Anti-Money Laundering Directive*, for example, to tighten rules around virtual currencies (i.e. cryptocurrencies) in order to confront issues of *inter alia* terrorism financing (European Commission, 2017).

Shannon Vallor argues that, 'Ethics and technology are connected because technologies invite or *afford* specific patterns of thought, behaviour, and valuing; they open up new possibilities for human action and foreclose or obscure others' (2016, p. 2). Recognition of the possibilities or foreclosures of technologies such as blockchain are not the preserve of the many. Instead, financial power coupled with technical know-how remains a niche enterprise relative to the size of impact. There is a clear imbalance or deficit between those who understand and appreciate the real value of technologies and those who are told to appreciate technology as valuable, as good. New technologies are drip-fed into popular consciousness as at once good and necessary, and serve to *technologise* the social by exploiting real and perceived weaknesses in, among other things, human relatedness and existing ethical frameworks, exactly the pattern we are seeing with blockchain and the 'problem' of trust it is required to 'solve'. The consequence is the production of general blockchain narratives proclaiming that the technology solves the problem of a lack of trust between loosely connected individuals transacting online. Blockchain, it is claimed, heralds the end of this lack of trust by creating the conditions in which trust is no longer a problematic variable. Issues of trust have, under the mantra of blockchain for good, been technologically solved, thus creating opportunities for the proliferation of micropayment blockchain markets and economies able to expand within a *post-trust* paradigm. 'Trust that used to flow upwards to referees and regulators, to authorities and experts, to watchdogs and gatekeepers', claims Botsman,

> is no flowing horizontally, in some instances to our fellow human beings and, in other cases, to programs and bots. Trust is being turned on its head. The old sources of power expertise, and authority no longer hold all the aces, or even the deck of cards. The consequences, of that, good and bad, cannot be underestimated.
>
> (2017, p. 8)

As we have seen, differing visions of blockchain can be broadly categorised as either financial (blockchain 1.0) or post-financial (blockchain 2.0, 3.0 and so on). All rely, however, on a triangulation of key features that promote, in the main, greater auditability and verification of information and data in order to support the further outgrowth of economic logic and reason from within the blockchain eco-system. By enforcing a regimen of auditability blockchain has a corresponding effect on the information and data applied to it. Thus a seemingly innocuous document may assume a new and heightened degree of bureaucratic significance by virtue of the auditable environment from which it emerges. The three main features of blockchain that signal this auditable environment are: (post-)trust, transparency and decentralisation/distribution. Whilst each derives from the tech-nology itself, they also constitute key strategies by stakeholders that help construct narratives of 'blockchain for good' that are, I argue, inexorably neoliberal in nature. Accordingly, whilst it is possible to agree with Botsman that the con-sequences of shifts in trust 'cannot be underestimated', it is less clear that 'trust is being turned on its head', nor whether the 'old sources of power expertise, and authority no longer hold all the aces, or even the deck of cards' (2017, p. 8). Indeed, this last point runs counter to the main arguments expressed in this book, and as such I claim that Botsman is simply disseminating blockchain-based fanta-sies rather than indicating any facts concerning the progress and development of blockchain. Something clearly illustrated, for example, in the rapid moves made by the four major global accounting and auditing firms, PricewaterhouseCoopers (PwC), KPMG, Deloitte, and Ernst & Young (EY), to assume authority over the blockchain space that threatens their business models directly, as well as over those that are of less direct significance, in spite of ecosystem narratives that maintain: 'Overripe for disruption is the audit business' (Tapscott and Tapscott, 2016, p. 76). The three features listed above all recur throughout the book. But they are also important for getting under the skin of the mantra 'blockchain for good'. It is useful therefore to interrogate them briefly here and in particular within the con-text of audit and what Michael Power calls 'rituals of verification' (1997), which is where we now turn.

Digital reckoning

The success of blockchain as 'the economic layer the Web has never had' (Swan, 2015, p. vii) and, concomitantly, central to the notion of 'blockchain for good', lies in what the Tapscotts have called 'Digital Reckoning' (2016, p. 7), or more prosaically, *audit*. Akin to double-entry bookkeeping, a blockchain ledger should provide clear, indisputable evidence that 'enables a reconciliation of digital records regarding just about everything in real time' (Tapscott and Tapscott, 2016, p. 7). This has been especially important in fostering a notion of blockchain as a *truth machine* (Botsman, 2017, p. 226; Casey and Vigna, 2018), and involves the development of applications that use blockchain 'to track the supply chain of products, from their provenance to the hands of the customer' (Botsman, 2017, p. 226). What lies beneath the Tapscotts', Botsman's and Casey and Vigna's definitions is, first and foremost, a means of computational verification, bureau-cratisation and auditability made possible by the collective operational character-istics discussed in earlier chapters, including timestamping. The essential problem blockchain has the potential to solve, according to Casey and Vigna, is to 'improve the state of information' (2018, p. 182). But, as previously suggested, there is always more to the matter than technical specifications alone, and auditing is a bureaucratic exercise notable in political economy as much as it is, itself, a brute technical exercise to determine credits and debits, profits and loss, and uphold a general regard for fiscal balance and accountability.

It is worth examining briefly what improving the state of information with blockchain means. It could, in short, mean any number of outcomes based on the endless variety of contextual inputs to a blockchain. But instead I would like to suggest that blockchain fits a critical and often contentious history of documentation and document creation that spans public and private spheres alike, which further explains the ongoing connection between hard-copy, paper records and blockchain that endures in spite of the affordances digital networks and blockchain promise. It is within this tradition, not a tradition that belongs only to blockchain or other computational networks, that attempts to improvement of the state of information are undertaken by public and private administrations and bureaucracies. Echoing the blockchain context, Blanchette recalls the close connection between paper, bureaucracy and the flourishing of cryptographic cultures:

> Although traces of cryptographic activity have been found in most ancient civilizations from Mesopotamia to the Roman Empire, the systematic development of codes and ciphers awaited the flowering of modern European diplomacy in the sixteenth century. In 1542, for example, the Venetian state employed three 'cipher secretaries' assigned to the development of such techniques. As ciphers increasingly gained in sophistication, so did the methods for solving them: by the eighteenth century, most European nations had established 'black chambers', secret organizations specializing in deciphering foreign diplomatic dispatches. By the 1850s, the principles of good cipher construction were fairly well developed, if not widely disseminated and necessarily understood in mathematical terms. Classical ciphers relied on two basic methods, *monoalphabetic* and *polyalphabetic* substitution, often combining the two *codebooks*.
>
> (2012, p. 19)

Information and data added to a blockchain undergoes a transformation and translation both in form and meaning and this occurs regardless of the nature of the input or the context from which it derives. Given the proliferation of file types and means of data storage available to contemporary computer users, the notion of transformation and translation of data and information when applied to a blockchain may appear at once obvious and absurd – it is clear that *something* happens to data and information appended to a system or network, but precisely what that *something* is, is far from clear to ordinary users. On the Bitcoin blockchain, for example, information and data in the form of transactions are rendered as encrypted alphanumeric strings:

b73b8bac4f295d9bd356aed3322ef4c72a30827c2f3e601259d6aa9c8dffe2ea

Transactions are subsequently collated in blocks represented by a hash, and chained to both preceding and forthcoming blocks; these appear, again, alphanumerically, for example:

0000000000000000000003f46de2570c9e653307b563c597a7e76fb
059dab60566

It is clear from the examples above that representations of blockchain data are not immediately decipherable as a natural language. Although like any language, formalised 'inscription' (Latour, 1990), or document, indecipherability is not an insurmountable obstacle to a 'reader', but rather something prompting new knowledge and skills of interpretation, usually according to a set of conventions, in order to extract the 'correct' meaning. As Mark Fenster maintains: 'documents are not simply transparent bearers of meaning and value. To make sense, documents must be interpreted. This is true even of data, which must be processed and contextualized in order to bear and communicate meaning' (2017, p. 111). Importantly, data is shaped in order to fit the particular bureaucratic environment to which it applies, namely, that of the blockchain. In doing so the information is made to conform like any other documented information when it is recorded, filed or archived in a particular system or institutional construct, whether on- or offline, or on- or off-chain.

Bruno Latour (1990) provides a further bridge between the paper document tradition of bureaucracies and blockchain in his insistence as to the 'mobility' and 'immutability' of documents, that is, documents capable of escaping geographical or jurisdictional constraints yet remaining identical – a good description of the movement of data across a blockchain network in which it is simultaneously updated and shared to each node. Bureaucratisation in the sense of documentation does not carry automatic connotations of being good or bad, desirable or lamentable. At first it can be seen to describe a process, although that process *is not* without meaning either in construction or performance, nor, as I have argued throughout, is it ever apolitical or neutral. In a description that could easily be one espoused by stakeholders within the blockchain ecosystem – if 'document' were to be substituted for 'blockchain' – Annelise Riles argues that the 'document references [...] a utopian modernist vision of world peace through transparency and information exchange that had its roots in an earlier Victorian celebration of the public archive', although she further concludes, and unlike blockchain stakeholders I argue, the document also provides 'an ongoing critique of that vision' (2006, p. 6).

'[A]udit is much more than a natural and self-evident response to problems of principal-agent accountability', argues Power, 'audit shapes public conceptions of the problems for which it is the solution; it is constitutive of a certain regulatory or control style which reflects deeply held commitments to checking and trust' (1997, p. 7). Power was writing a full decade before blockchain came into existence, yet he perfectly describes the underlying, albeit 'unglamorous' (1997, p. xi), authority that audit continues to hold in and over the blockchain ecosystem, and especially with regard to a technology bound up in a documentary tradition. In this sense blockchain arguably continues trends in audit, at least in Western capitalist societies, which can be traced back to early instantiations of banking, finance and industry in the 19th century, but which have grown in influence significantly in the last 40 years and built an 'audit society' (Power, 1997) or 'audit culture' (Wortham, 2004). Given the necessity for the blockchain ecosystem to make its narratives aspirational, auditing is a prime candidate for at best sexing-up, at worst marginalisation, and is often only mentioned, to echo Power, when clearly forming part of the 'rituals of verification' that blockchain users must partake in rather, for instance, than just doing accounts. Indeed, audit is arguably central to the fundamental critical question posed by Lana Swartz regarding blockchain's purpose: 'What would it mean for the radical blockchain moment if it were allowed to be boring?' (2017, p. 102).

Swartz's is certainly not a question the Tapscotts are interested in answering, as the following passage which is replete with the usual hyperbole reveals, and in which blockchain auditing is referred to as a process of triple-entry accounting involving a 'World Wide Ledger':

> Today, companies record a debit and credit with each transaction – two entries, hence double-entry accounting. They could easily add a third entry to the World Wide Ledger, instantly accessible to those who need to see it – the company's shareholders, auditors, or regulators. Imagine that when a massive company like Apple sells products, buys raw materials, pays its employees, or accounts for assets and liabilities on its balance sheet, the World Wide Ledger recorded the transaction and published a time-stamped receipt to a blockchain. The financial reports for a company would become a living ledger – auditable, searchable, and verifiable. Generating any up-to-the-minute financial statement should be as simple as a spreadsheet function, where the click of a button gives you an immutable, complete, and searchable financial statement, free of error [...] The argument for triple-entry accounting is not against traditional accounting. There will always be areas where we will need competent auditors. But if triple-entry accounting can vastly increase transparency and responsiveness through real-time accruals, verifiable transaction records, and instant audit, then the blockchain could solve many of accounting's biggest problems.
>
> (2016, pp. 75–78)

Transparency, as the Tapscotts argue, is one of the main virtues of blockchain auditing, as well as being inherent to a neoliberal technomorality, inasmuch as it does not simply explain the ways in which data is computationally exposed or rendered auditable, but offers commercial actors and businesses ways to create and maintain public or client-facing *impressions of integrity* with regard to the handling and management of data and systems. 'When it comes to pertinent information for customers, shareholders, employees, and other stakeholders', the Tapscotts claim, 'active openness is central to earning trust' (2016, p. 10), and 'rather than dressing for success', they conclude, 'corporations can undress for success' (2016, p. 10). What blockchain offers might well be a neat 'solution' and, in time, more convenient method for businesses and commercial actors to manage and transact data. In the short term, while business waits for the technology to improve, blockchain's value as a commercial tool resides elsewhere, namely, as a show of willingness to engage in forms of corporate social responsibility in the form of transparency and the determination to instil trust where it is perceived to be in retreat, is hidden, or, perhaps, never existed and needs to be invented and constructed. As we have already seen, this involves a willingness to audit not only openly but 'effectively', 'efficiently' and 'regularly'.

The corporate conditions that the Tapscotts describe, and to which they would apply blockchain as a solution, are not new. Indeed blockchain once again resonates with classical conceptions of transparency and openness engendered by double-entry bookkeeping and accounting and use of technology to expose the inner workings of corporations (and thus capital) to scrutiny. The desirability of corporate, institutional or systemic transparency and need to trust in the other with regards to security, exchanges and transactions are long-standing vexed issues. Key to understanding the present blockchain moment involves consideration of how the technology has re-energised a number of these themes in line with what Michael Power calls the 'audit explosion': 'a certain set of attitudes or cultural commitments to problem solving' (1997, p. 4). The blockchain ecosystem has succeeded in driving forward narratives in which the attitudes and cultural commitments Power places at the centre of the audit explosion are set against old and in some cases tired political and economic paradigms in the hope it will make them appear fresh and new. Against entrenched and in some cases faltering systems, blockchain, it is claimed, will enable structures and institutions of power to appear transparent, in the hope it will also make them accessible and inclusive.

It is a point of technological fact that blockchain is capable of delivering transparency along these lines, whether in the form of permissioned (closed network) ledgers or public permissionless ledgers. What this potentially translates to in economic terms includes *inter alia* efficiency savings for global corporations by enabling financial transaction reports within an organisation in real time, 'reducing the need for traditional accounting practices' (Botsman, 2017, p. 242), and the other audit facilities detailed so far. The political consequences of this are, however, as yet less clear. Whether post-trust, transparency and decentralisation ought always to be considered good remains a live issue, not least because economics and politics continue to jostle for position in defining what blockchain for good is or might as yet come to mean, with auditing used both to win argument by showing willingness to engage in the rituals or verification and openness. The political economy of neoliberalism, meanwhile, strives to solve the issue of a disjuncture between economics and politics by seizing the ethical narrative and making blockchain for good a conclusion for economic reason and logic.

For critics of the present network and data age claims of transparency are not simply spurious, because they recycle long-standing issues that go to the heart of prevailing forms of social organisation, for example, but dangerous. 'Transparency is an ideology', Byung-Chul Han argues, and like all ideologies 'it has a positive core that has been mystified and made absolute. The danger of transparency lies in such ideologization. If totalized, it yields terror' (2015, p. viii). The dialogue between trust and transparency is the philosophy or, following Han (and Morozov), ideology at the core of blockchain, one that entrepreneurs and neoliberal stakeholders have developed conceptually and in practice come to believe and have faith in. Even, it must be noted, before mature or commercially functioning blockchains other than Bitcoin are operational and 'good' applications and implementations remain future perfect idealisations of entrepreneurial narratives and dreams.

What is more, the ideological drive for trust and transparency rooted in the audit function blockchain provides is quick to dismiss a major issue facing the type of all-encompassing transposition of data and information onto an 'immutable' blockchain. Namely, the problem of so-called *rubbish in/rubbish out*. What is at stake is obvious: as blockchain is append only and records data immutably (does not allow it to be changed or undone) for the purposes of, say, providing evidence of land title, intellectual property ownership, or perhaps even one's own personal identity for *inter alia* health records, immigration or asylum claims (these are all existing blockchain concepts), the accuracy and legitimacy of the information entered *into* the network or system is paramount and arguably of greater magnitude of importance than would be the case in 'off-chain' systems. However, the notion of rubbish in/rubbish out is not entirely accurate. The consequences of illegitimate personal information entered into the network or system is not simply illegitimate personal information back out; if that were the case then blockchain would clearly fail to live up to the benefits stakeholders and acolytes claim for it. Instead, illegitimate information in is transformed into legitimated information out *because* of what blockchain does to the information, but more importantly how the ideological positioning of blockchain as a means for neoliberal technomoral and techno-social transformation cannot and will not be undermined.

This is a paradox within the desire for digital reckoning, one which clearly shows, again, the political and ideological agendas at play in a technology that many of its stakeholders would have the world believe is simply a means of encouraging engagement in fruitful economic activity for the benefit of all. This is nonsense, and command of the rubbish in/rubbish out narrative by blockchain acolytes such as Casey and Vigna, who are quick to add a neo-colonial spin to it by describing it as a problem *for* blockchain caused by developing countries (but for developing countries blockchain would presumably work just fine), further reveals this:

> Considering the messy records that date back centuries in many developing countries, one fear is that rushing to enter them into a permanent, immutable blockchain record would enshrine and legitimize the claims of the powerful and corrupt, to the detriment of others. The battle to reach this definitive, final accepted state could bring out conflict – and violence and intimidation. Then there's the problem of just letting the criminals win. In slums, rights to

property are often defined by the local drug gangs. Do we want their view of the world to be validated by this system? Still, *superior accounting and auditing systems, which are what this technology* [blockchain] *represents, can themselves be powerful drivers of positive behaviour.*

[emphasis added] (2018, p. 187)

Casey and Vigna do not entirely illustrate their vision of a blockchain world tied to the plight *qua* affordances the developing world has to offer – they also discuss the numbers of unbanked people in various states in North America, briefly. What is particularly striking and disturbing about the claims in the quote above is that, having at least acknowledged the major issue facing blockchain implementations of rubbish in/rubbish out (in a couple of paragraphs), Casey and Vigna are content to brush the problem aside by simply reaffirming the *superiority* of the technology. Solutionism does not get any more blatant than this: where technological faith and belief reaches astounding levels of self-confidence and self-affirmation. But then 'commentators' like Casey and Vigna as well as the Tapscotts are called *stakeholders* for good reason: they and others like them place great emphasis on how an old life, perhaps as a non-blockchain entrepreneur for instance, was given up or shed like dead skin in order to be reborn into the blockchain ecosystem. *Contra* Casey and Vigna, Michael Power offers a rather more sobering estimation of the effectiveness of auditing to achieve the types of ends Casey and Vigna otherwise appear to regard as inevitable: 'The history of auditing reads, like the history of regulation more generally, as a history of failure. Efforts at social control, it seems, always fail and failure is always the condition for further attempts at control' (1997, p. 26).

Conclusion

> There is absolutely no inevitability as long as there is a willingness to contemplate what is happening.
>
> (McLuhan and Fiore, 2008, p. 25)

It may appear perverse to construe blockchain *as* an ethics of political economy rather than a *means* to it. Blockchain is an ethics rather than a means to achieve certain moral or ethical ends, and this is reflected in the way the technology is being positioned, described and in some cases developed by specific blockchain stakeholders as well as a broader blockchain ecosystem wishing to express an ethics of neoliberal political economy. Echoing neoliberal strategies more generally, however, there is a lot of contradiction and meaningless fog-horning in what stakeholders are saying about blockchain, not least in the 'good' it will bring communities beyond the blockchain ecosystem, who must, per the dominant logic, learn to be entrepreneurs and perform like businesses if they are to be 'good' because the transformation will not come for free. As Casey and Vigna reveal either intentionally or as a manifestation of unconscious desire eking-out through their language: 'Whether it's with a blockchain truth machine or some other decentralizing, liberating technology, we owe it to humanity to try to restore human agency to the *business* of just being in the world' [emphasis added] (2018, p. 220). Corporate attitude and culture utterly suffuse the blockchain ecosystem regardless of stray ideals that pertain to promote non-profit social good. As David Golumbia argues, that many

> crypto-anarchists and cypherpunk technologists – to say nothing of the Bit-coin entrepreneurs who work closely with major Silicon Valley venture capitalists – today sit at or near the heads of the world's major corporations tells us everything we need to know about their attitude toward concentrated corporate power.
>
> (2016, p. 33)

'While the technological novelty of blockchain systems is authentically exciting', claims Brett Scott,

> the darker side is that much of the more extreme rhetoric has hinged on 'fixing' human imperfection, rather than accommodating it [...] the most ardent blockchain proponents often present (whether advertently or inadvertently) a dim vision of human nature, suggesting that people need to be protected from themselves by deferring responsibility to 'trustless' technological platforms that will enforce contract-based relationships between atomistic individuals in an escape from community.
>
> (2016, p. 13)

Technologies are consistently posited by private and public interests alike, as well as through partnerships, consortia (e.g. R3) and other combinations that often only exist to prove productive for private interest in the arena of the public, as the best or only solution to a fuzzy array of ill-defined domestic, national and global problems. This ideology of *solutionism* is centred in what Scott refers to as '"fixing" human imperfection', and which is viewed here to be enfolded by neo-liberalism. For critics such Evgeny Morozov, who does not necessarily insist on a connection with neoliberalism, it must be said, solutionism and solutionists are nevertheless undesirable features or symptoms of modern societies:

> Solutionism is not just a fancy way of saying that for someone with a hammer, everything looks like a nail; it's not just another riff on the inapplicability of 'technological fixes' to 'wicked problems'. It's not only that many problems are not suited to the quick-and-easy solutionist tool-kit. It's also that what many solutionists presume to be 'problems' in need of solving are not problems at all; a deeper investigation into the very nature of these 'problems' would reveal that the inefficiency, ambiguity, and opacity – whether in politics or everyday life – that the newly empowered geeks and solutionists are rallying against are not in any sense problematic. Quite the opposite: these vices are often virtues in disguise. That, thanks to innovative

technologies, the modern-day solutionist has an easy way to eliminate them does not make them any less virtuous.

(2014, p. 6)

References

Blanchette, Jean-François. 2012. *Burdens of Proof: Cryptographic Culture and Evidence Law in the Age of Electronic Documents.* Cambridge: The MIT Press.

Bogost, Ian. 2017. Cryptocurrency Might be a Path to Authoritarianism. *The Atlantic*, 30 May. www.theatlantic.com/technology/archive/2017/05/blockchain-of-command/528543/ (accessed 25 January 2018).

Botsman, Rachel. 2017. *Who Can You Trust? How Technology Brought Us Together – and Why It Could Drive Us Apart.* London: Portfolio Penguin.

Casey, Michael J. and Vigna, Paul. 2018. *The Truth Machine: The Blockchain and the Future of Everything.* London: HarperCollins.

Castells, Manuel. 2010. *The Rise of the Network Society.* 2nd Edition. Chichester: Wiley Blackwell.

European Commission. 2017. *Strengthened EU rules to prevent money laundering and terrorism financing.* European Commission, 15 December. http://ec.europa.eu/newsroom/just/item-detail.cfm?item_id=610991 (accessed 1 May 2018).

Fenster, Mark. 2017. *The Transparency Fix: Secrets, Leaks, and Uncontrollable Government Information.* Stanford: Stanford University Press.

Golumbia, David. 2016. *The Politics of Bitcoin: Software as Right-Wing Extremism.* Minneapolis: University of Minnesota Press.

Hall, Josh. 2018. Blockchain could reshape our world – and the far right is one step ahead. *The Guardian*, 23 February. www.theguardian.com/commentisfree/2018/feb/23/blockchain-reshape-world-far-right-ahead-crypto-technology (accessed 4 April 2018).

Han, Byung-Chul. 2015. *The Transparency Society.* Translated by Erik Butler. Stanford: Stanford University Press.

Han, Byung-Chul. 2017. *Psycho-Politics: Neoliberalism and New Technologies of Power.* Translated by Erik Butler. London: Verso.

Kewell, Beth, Adams, Richard and Parry, Glen. 2017. Blockchain for good? *Strategic Change*, Vol. 26, No. 5 (September), pp. 429–437.

Latour, Bruno. 1990. Drawing Things Together. *Representation in Scientific Practice.* Edited by Michael Lynch and Steve Woolgar. Cambridge: The MIT Press, pp. 19–68.

Latour, Bruno. 2002. Morality and Technology: The Ends of the Means. Translated by Couze Venn. *Theory, Culture & Society*, Vol. 19, No. 5/6, pp. 247–260.

McLuhan, Marshall and Fiore, Quentin. 2008. *The Medium is the Massage.* Co-ordinated by Jerome Agel. London: Penguin.

Morozov, Evgeny. 2014. *To Save Everything, Click Here: Technology, solutionism and the urge to fix problems that don't exist.* London: Penguin.

Power, Michael. 1997. *The Audit Society: Rituals of Verification.* Oxford: Oxford University Press.

Riles, Annelise. 2006. Introduction: In Response. *Documents: Artifacts of Modern Knowledge.* Edited by Annelise Riles. Ann Arbor: University of Michigan Press.

Scott, Brett. 2016. *How Can Cryptocurrency and Blockchain Technology Play a Role in Building Social and Solidarity Finance?* Working Paper 2016–2011. Geneva: United Nations Research Institute for Social Development.

Stiegler, Bernard. 2010. *For a New Critique of Political Economy*. Cambridge: Polity.

Stinchcombe, Kai. 2017. Ten years in, nobody has come up with a use for blockchain. *Hacker Noon*, 22 December. https://hackernoon.com/ten-years-in-nobody-has-come-up-with-a-use-case-for-blockchain-ee98c180100 (accessed 31 January 2018).

Swan, Melanie. 2015. *Blockchain: Blueprint for a New Economy*. Sebastopol: O'Reilly.

Swartz, Lana. 2017. Blockchain Dreams: Imagining techno-economic alternatives after Bitcoin. *Another Economy is Possible*. Edited by Manuel Castells. Cambridge: Polity Press, pp. 82–105.

Tapscott, Don and Tapscott, Alex. 2016. *Blockchain Revolution: How the Technology behind Bitcoin is Changing Money, Business and the World*. London: Portfolio Penguin.

Vallor, Shannon. 2016. *Technology and the Virtues: A Philosophical Guide to a Future Worth Wanting*. Oxford: Oxford University Press.

Wortham, Simon Morgan. 2004. Auditing Derrida. *Parallax*, Vol. 10, No. 2, pp. 3–18.

7 The psycho-politics of blockchain

Introduction

> Technology always empowers someone, some group in society, and it does so at a certain cost. The question must always be, therefore, what group or groups does it empower?
>
> (Landow, 2006, p. 337)

Blockchain holds an interesting if uncertain location between symbolic economy and economic symbolisation. Jean-Joseph Goux claims that the '*power* of the symbolic' has been changed by the connection between technology and financial capital (between computer and bank), but that 'in contrast to social formation whose dominant ideological coherence is magico-mythological or mytho-cosmological – that is, entrenched in "true symbolism" – philosophico-scientific capitalist society and the entire mode of symbolizing which characterizes it suffer from a *deficiency of meaning*' (1990, pp. 130–131). As a consequence Goux concludes,

> the dominant practices of the capitalist system, including, most notably, economic practices, can by no means be of the same mode as the symbolic that is charged with unconscious meaning, invested with 'profound' significations – the cryptophoric symbolism of precapitalist social formation.
>
> (1990, pp. 130–131)

It is clear that symbolic and material changes that technologies have fostered since Goux was writing have been more rapid and profound than an easy binary delineation between computer technology and financial capital suggests. Technologies have instead, and in particular network technologies including personal computers, mobile phones, the Internet and World Wide Web, radically dismantled many of the distinctions between and within social, economic, political and cultural contexts.

The blockchain ecosystem is a site in which a particular and peculiar form of modern techno-economic symbolisation is emerging in order, I argue, to displace political accountability (from a regulatory point of view), as well as distract from the political more generally in an attempt to further reinvigorate the economic. If recent (or first wave) instantiations of network computing, data production and storage and digital information and communication succeeded in exposing the distance technologies foster between modes of symbolisation in modernity whilst still maintaining a real material sense of that distance, blockchain and the new networked environments its stakeholders promise appear to be an attempt if intentional, or a slip if unintentional *qua* unconscious, toward a point that lies somewhere between what Goux calls 'abstract operational symbolization' (a technocratic society's mode of domination using computers), and cryptophoric symbolisation ('a certain type of ideological domination' with religious depths to its modes of production) (Goux, 1990, p. 130).

There are a number of quotes and passages throughout this book that draw from narratives I claim either 'proselytise' on the virtues of blockchain or come from those who are 'evangelical' about the virtues of blockchain. There is an undoubted 'spiritual' fervour in the energies that entrepreneurs invest in blockchain projects and start-ups which is not new to this particular domain of technologies but extends more broadly over the concepts and ideas wrought by stakeholders in neoliberal technomoral policy development. Milton Mueller, who appears to draw a comparison between the status of religion and technology, states: 'Just as we detached religion from the state in the seventeenth century, we need to detach information policy from the state today' (2017, p. 130), a notion that contains a high degree of 'belief' and 'faith' that technologies will succeed in achieving what stakeholders think and say they will. Brett Scott points to where and how blockchain evangelism in particular is having real-world effects:

> One nascent phenomenon related to blockchain technology is the emergence of what might be called techno-libertarian evangelism – the presence of blockchain 'missionaries' in developing countries articulating a technology-as-saviour and markets-as-saviour gospel alongside an anti-state message. For example, in Ghana a group called Africa Youth Peace Call organized a 2015 Blockchain Land Title Summer Liberty and Entrepreneurship Camp to discuss how land registry can be moved from state institutions to blockchain ledgers. The group's stated objective is in 'teaching free-market ideas and skills to the people of Africa', but despite appearing as a Ghanaian organization, most of the group's board are foreigners, including American free-market economists Ken Schoolland, Warren Coats and Louis James, and libertarian activist Michael W. Dean (Africa Youth Peace Call 2015). The camp attendees included the outspoken American libertarian activist and investor Roger Ver.
>
> (2016, p. 12)

In other words, the blockchain ecosystem is replete with types of religiosity and cryptophoric symbolisation that were once the preserve of spiritual authorities, but now intermingle with economic and political power displaying colonising tendencies at local, domestic and international levels that are both subtle and shameless. In parallel terms, the blockchain ecosystem is built between the sensibilities of interior life and the desensitising and alienating affects wrought by capital. What neither form of symbolisation (abstract operational or crypto-phoric) can escape, however, is the role power has in guiding, shaping, manipulating, as well as mobilising the imperative force of the symbol. Whether a priestly or invisible hand therefore, cryptophoric and abstract operational symbolisations are together *hand*-led. Neither blockchain nor its ecosystem alters this at all, other than to introduce the addition of fleshy hands of computer engineers, programmers, entrepreneurs, venture capitalists and so on all engaged in establishing fresh meaning in the relationship between economic practices and significations of commerce.

The symbolic domain of blockchain is one in which perverse forms of primitive, pre-capitalist and pseudo-tribal customs are playing out in order to satisfy the whims of stakeholders. This contradiction or 'double-truth' – namely, the denial that capital, by elevating the social good or niceties in certain strategies or practices, is working only on behalf of itself – is no longer surprising given the firm place these policies hold within the opportunistic rhythm of contemporary neo-liberal management ideals, businesses and commercial practices. 'A contradiction arises', Harvey claims, 'between a seductive but alienating possessive individualism on the one hand and the desire for a meaningful collective life on the other', and what is more, individuals are 'free to choose' so long as they do not choose 'to associate to create political parties with the aim of forcing the state to intervene in or eliminate the market' (2005, p. 69). In the context of blockchain this 'double-truth' exists in the insistence of stakeholders of the benefits of disintermediated peer-to-peer exchange. A process that relies on computational protocols to adjust for the fact that no meeting takes place in any personal sense, there is, to para-phrase Goux, no 'harmony of desires' nor 'reciprocity of times' able to imply 'that the exchange is also a commerce of bodies' (1990, p. 123), and exchanges or transactions are always conducted on the basis that the other party absolutely cannot be trusted.

Like the relatively ancient tradition of contract, blockchain brings parties together in a symbolic union that is underscored by an *a priori* lack of trust and faith in the other. But as Anthony Giddens maintains, even though trust 'is not the same as faith in the reliability of a person or system; it is what derives from that faith', in the case of 'human agents, the presumption of reliability involves the attribution of "probity" (honour) or love. This is why trust in persons is psycho-logically consequential for the individual who trusts: a moral hostage to fortune is given' (1990, p. 33). Thus, I claim, blockchain is psycho-political in its formations of meaning and conduct ahead of any material exchange for value. 'Nostalgia for an oppositional and reversible symbolic exchange', says Goux, 'reactivates the phantasy of a dual relationship in which the partners, face-to-face, are both reci-procally mother and child, without any abstract general equivalent mediating this commerce with its law' (1990, p. 123). This quote was never intended as a description of blockchain, and yet it reveals a great deal about the politics and psychology that underscores the ecosystem and its stakeholders. The aim of this chapter is to further explore these themes.

Political assumptions

> A particular technological innovation becomes a screen upon which all sorts of fantasies of political action are projected.
>
> (Dean, 2009, p. 36)

Ian Bogost says of Bitcoin that in order to understand it – and blockchain, I argue, forms part of this same consideration – 'first requires deciphering the political assumptions that inspire it' (2017). Whether viewed as a database, network or distributed ledger, blockchain is much more to its promoters and acolytes than the mere technical functions, for example, as a method of digitally timestamping data records and transactions. Likewise, to the uninitiated layperson increasingly exposed to news reports on Bitcoin and other cryptocurrencies, there is clearly more to the technology than brute computation alone. There is, it might be said, based on events at the close of 2017 and the beginning of 2018, a certain thrill that accompanies the technology and the desire to gamble on the possibility of accruing great wealth as the value of a single Bitcoin hovers around US$10,000. Equally there is dismay at the scandals and vulgar opportunism accompanying the digital gold rush associated with many of today's cryptocurrencies. Notable in the narratives flowing from the blockchain ecosystem is a twofold de-politicisation which is at once express and implied (perhaps unintentional). The decentralising, distributed and disintermediating features and potentialities of blockchain render obsolete a certain collectivistic political bargaining, and this applies both at the level of concept and practice. In other words, blockchain technologies either deny or greatly impoverish conditions of social relations.

As a potent statement on the maladjustment of legacy financial power in modern capitalist societies to meet the liberating economic desires of alt-capitalists (especially as part of a post-2008 crisis narrative), cryptocurrencies have succeeded in introducing the imagination of right-wing anarcho-capitalism to the mainstream through the path of least resistance, that is, via the temptation cryptocurrencies hold for gaining extraordinary individual wealth outside of the structures honed over centuries by legacy financial institutions.[1] Cryptocurrencies thus at once fit into and reject existing paradigms of marketisation by playing further and deeper into the erotics of the market through the creation of personalised modes of desire (different coins and tokens). The likes of Bitcoin are tailored to individual wealth creation and more closely mirror the subject's desire. If Bitcoin does not do it for

---

1   The relatively recent evolution in cryptocurrency *trading* rather than *mining* (the computational process that creates Bitcoin, for example, by solving complex mathematical problems), means a portion of the existing circulating supply of different coins and tokens is accessible to anyone interested in buying it (the especially high price of many of the major cryptocurrencies at present has obviously limited the number of individuals who might be in a position to invest, but nonetheless trading is still notionally free to all). This is in contrast to the fact that an average computer user, someone who might previously (seven years ago, for example) have been able to mine Bitcoin on a personal laptop would now not be able to out-compete the huge processing/mining of the likes of Chinese state actors.

you, then there are hundreds of other coins that will. As the 'genesis' coin, Bitcoin kick-started the new paradigm of desire and has rightly elicited comparisons with former gold rushes in that regard (Ver, 2017). Although not objectively a coherent project, the world of cryptocurrencies is nonetheless flourishing in the guise of over 1,700 different coins and tokens whilst also existing in a state of utter chaos as the index of each coin and token, almost without exception, rises and falls with all the violence of ships lost at sea.[2]

As ground zero of the blockchain project, any philosophy attributable to it is perhaps still most notable in cryptocurrencies. This does not mean cryptocurrencies and the anarcho-capitalist mindset that conjured them have won the day. Instead legacy sources of financial power who had largely dismissed cryptocurrencies (most notably Bitcoin) as a fraud, now view with interest blockchain as a means for conducting back-office administration, including handling (and clearing) financial transactions and using their own platforms to trade in digital currencies (Son et al, 2017). In other words, the ultimate winner in the phoney war between alt- and legacy sources of financial power is always already capital. As David Golumbia so keenly highlights: 'despite its technically decentralized nature, Bitcoin functions as a centralized and concentrated locus of financial power' (2016, p. 65), and this is why, as Rachel Botsman further explains, 'most major players in the financial industry are busy investing significant resources into blockchain solutions. They have to embrace this new paradigm to ensure it works for, not against them' (2017, p. 242). Blockchain might raise many pressing questions, but it would be wrong to pretend that answers to the same or similar questions have not arisen in the past.

Cryptocurrencies and blockchain enfold a range of potentialities and promises, as well as threats and harms to society. It is incumbent upon regulators, and governments more broadly, to maintain a grip on the extent of the social, juridical and political and not merely the economic reach the technology has, and thus not abdicate the responsibility of doing so to chaotic entrepreneurs and private commercial entities intent on 'making up sets of rules' and engaging in 'freelance governance' (Gupta, 2017). The potential for the decentralisation of legacy forms of power and the radical reimaging of paradigms of trust, transparency and even democracy make blockchain politically determinative, even, it must be said, if this does not exactly happen in practice. Blockchain is without a doubt a striking moment, if not precisely a unique phenomenon, within the *longue durée* of technology and capitalist political economy. Further, blockchain critique is needed at this moment in time because the technology remains largely undefined in public consciousness. As Rachel Botsman says:

> Even though most people barely know what the blockchain is, a decade or so from now it will be like the internet: we'll wonder how society ever functioned without it. The internet transformed how we share information and

---

2   See for example: https://coinmarketcap.com/ (accessed 11 January 2018).

connect; the blockchain will transform how we exchanged value and whom we trust.

(2017, p. 245)

Whilst the politics (or rather the economics) of the blockchain ecosystem are easily discerned, attribution of a politics to the technology is not settled as such. This point is important because blockchain's legitimacy and authority does not, I argue, derive from technological credentials so much as its role as a cultural and political device with which the joint enterprise of capital and neoliberalism is shaping a 'fourth industrial revolution' underscored by novel forms of digitalised conduct, order and control. Countervailing political motivations ought therefore to aim at understanding the political potential of blockchain in order, precisely, to undermine the resurgent neoliberal blockchain project.

In an interesting and openly cynical article, Kai Stinchcombe (2017) asks why nobody has found a use for blockchain in the ten years of its existence. He suggests this is due to the fact that multiple technologies already exist that are able to do what people would like, for whatever reason, to see blockchain doing. In short, blockchain is simply not needed. Whilst Stinchcombe's article raises interesting points, it misses a key one: blockchain produces greater effects as an idea than an applied technology. Blockchain is a powerful cultural and politico-economic idea that has emerged from turbulent global conditions post-financial crisis. In this sense blockchain is merely a repeat of patterns of new technological emergence following political and economic rupture and crises. As Ronald Deibert and Rafal Rohozinski maintain:

> The rise of the Internet coincided with a major set of political upheavals that culminated with the collapse of the Soviet Union and communist bloc. In the euphoria that ensued, the idea of technological redemption, inevitable democratization, and for some, the end of history, coalesced into a popular ideology that equated technology with empowerment. This idea was far from new. Indeed, the telegraph, electrical lighting, and telephony all emerged at similarly transformational historical junctures, leading to a long pedigree of speculation regarding the democratizing role of technology in social and political change.
>
> (2010, p. 3)

Blockchain certainly fits this trend, and is arguably the empowering and redemptive technology *par excellence* of the present moment. In order to achieve this status blockchain derives legitimacy and authority from promises of *inter alia* radical transparency that are tantalising and may inspire 'legal, institutional, and technological reform' as a 'powerful metaphor that drives and shapes the desire for a more perfect democratic order' (Fenster, 2017, p. 6), yet is rightly brought into question based on these exact ideals (Han, 2015; Pasquale, 2015). Transparency is a double-edged sword, as Evgeny Morozov claims:

When we seek to increase or decrease transparency in some aspect of our public or private lives, we should do it not because we value transparency (or, for that matter, opacity) as such but because transparency promotes or undermines other, higher goods.

(2014, p. 82)

Similarly, although taking a more market-orientated and arguably neoliberal position, Kibum Kim and Taewon Kang maintain that:

Transparency in data may stimulate competition among market participants and provide opportunities for new entrants to join the market. This would ultimately improve the industry competitiveness and customer welfare. However, when only a few minorities benefit from making unfair profits, it may harm the fair ground for competition.

(2017, p12)

Evgeny Morozov is one of the more extreme critics of contemporary network technologies and of those who exploit them either gratuitously (for no discernible or rational reason), or for profit, or both. Whilst Morozov's ire is directed at wider issues relating to the undue power and authority he perceives the Internet and its unabashed supporters to hold over the individual and society, much of what he says also applies, I claim, to the narrower field of blockchain. Indeed it may be argued that blockchain, again in neoliberal terms, is a near-perfect crystallisation of a broader and 'hideous ideology of "solutionism"' that Morozov so fervently rails against (2014, p. 75). For Morozov a potent principle of this ideology turns on what Internet and blockchain acolytes alike (of course the two are, to all intents and purposes, inseparable) consider to be the unassailable virtues of technologically enforced transparency. For Mark Fenster 'transparency advocates', notably concerned with using technology or 'a cybernetic theory of transparency' with respect to government information, are seeking nothing less than 'what political theory and social science call into doubt: the existence of individuals and a broader society that will pay attention to the state and respond rationally and predictably to the disclosure of government information' (2017, p. 139). In other words, transparency capable of creating a highly motivated and *awaiting public*, one predicated on full exposure of hitherto secret information brought to light and capable of acting as the proverbial disinfectant that will kill off malfeasance and corruption wherever it lies.

Both transparency and secrecy advocates rest on the notion that information (or data) communicates something of value and can be controlled. Both imagine that a perfect system can fix the disclosure problem that they identify. They also view the public as able and motivated to understand disclosed messages and their significance. The public awaits revelation of the state's actions so that it can act upon it, using the proper channels of public discourse and democratic voice; or, the public and particularly some members of it would misinterpret or misuse state information and act in ways detrimental to public safety, to national security, to democratic politics, and ultimately to the state and its citizens.

(Fenster, 2017, p. 13)

In the following passage from Morozov's book, *To Save Everything, Click Here*, by substituting Internet for blockchain, I argue, is it possible to account for the way in which transparency is perceived by those invested in the virtues of blockchain solutionism more specifically, perhaps more so than for those invested in the solutionism of the Internet:

Solutionists, as you might remember, assume problems rather than investigate them; armed with the idea of 'the Internet', they are assuming very particular problems in a particularly Internet-centric way. 'The Internet' can increase transparency? Fine, this means that transparency is important and is worth pursuing in its own right. This could work wonders as a strategy to legitimize 'the Internet' and cement its reputation as a transparency-boosting medium, but it doesn't necessarily work as a prescription for smart reform, which requires a thorough empirical investigation into the world of politics.

(Morozov, 2014, pp. 82–83)

Transparency is just one of many factors in the politics of blockchain, and as we shall see, there are many others.

Believing the hype

You have to trust the idea of blockchain; you have to trust the system. And given that most people lack the technical know-how to understand how the system really works, you have to trust the programmers, miners, entrepreneurs and experts who establish and maintain the cryptographic protocols. A large dose of faith is required. But it's true to say that you don't have to trust another human being in the traditional sense.

(Botsman, 2017, p. 230)

Where does belief end and faith begin? What does it mean to believe or have faith in technologies? In the case of blockchain, where what is promised by entrepreneurs and stakeholders remains, at least for the time being, distant from what has been or ever will be delivered practically or materially speaking, a great deal of belief and faith is both demanded and expressed. Belief in blockchain extends to the natural ally of promise, including within hype and rhetoric, which help encourage significant investment in blockchain projects that are little more than concepts. Despite contestations such as Stinchcombe's that a meaningful use for blockchain has not been found, the hype surrounding the technology has been building significantly during the past few years based largely on the notion of blockchain as *other* to the domain of cryptocurrencies. The 2015 edition of *The*

Economist that focused on blockchain as 'The Trust Machine' was a key introduction of the technology into mainstream consciousness, helping foster the idea
that blockchain could do more than simply serve those interested in 'mining' or
trading cryptocurrencies such as Bitcoin. The evolution of what I am calling
blockchain as an ethics of political economy, represented by the mantra 'blockchain for good', is arguably a direct response to negative perceptions of blockchain's foundations as the technology that facilitates cryptocurrencies. This has
been summed up in the idea 'blockchain good, Bitcoin bad' (Perez, 2015;
Marinova, 2017).

Blockchain's entry into mainstream consciousness has signalled something else
important in terms of reading it as a cultural and political text, however: the
uncoupling of the technology from anarchic libertarian aspirations harboured by
those who first conceived of it. The result of this seeming libertarian retreat has
not been, as yet, accusations of government over-reach or proscriptive regulatory
interventions. Nor has it signalled stronger political accountability or democratic
oversight of the technology and those who promote it either. Rather, the forces of
neoliberalism have seized the moment to ensure blockchain is focused on fostering
more competition and creating more markets, which, if the more excitable voices
proclaiming the virtues of blockchain are to be believed, could be in anything
from reinventing financial services, to incentivising innovation, to rebuilding government and democracy (Tapscott and Tapscott, 2016; Boucher, 2017). Vestiges
of formal governance presently at play within the blockchain ecosystem thus
mirror the market solutionist approaches of corporate commercialism and consumerism increasingly consolidating a grip on the technology. This means more
consumerist economic logic, most notable in the emphasis on consensus, as the
default setting for blockchain applications and conceptualisations, neatly summed
up in Melanie Swan's vision of blockchain-led governance enabling 'services as
individualized as Starbucks coffee orders' (2015, p. 46).

Blockchain turbocharges individualism by fully *economising* all social life.
Moreover it fits the narrative of short-term innovation and investment strategies
that Bernard Stiegler associates with the problematic of expedient consumerism
(2010, p. 83). '[T]he organization of consumption', Stiegler argues,

> presupposes that the becoming of *social systems* must *structurally submit* to the
> becoming of the *economic system*, something enabled by granting the latter full
> control over technological becoming, that is, over the *technical system* – this
> submission being obtained by capturing and harnessing the attention of con-
> sumers, by diverting their libidinal energy toward objects of innovation, and
> by controlling their behaviour via marketing.
>
> (2010, p. 82)

Social transactions and relations of all kinds are subject to marketisation with participation incentivised by the promise of income in the form of micropayments,
and individual nodes facilitate solutionist consensual self-governance that denudes
and in some respects replaces politics and government. Wendy Brown argues that,

the predilection of governance for devolution, decentralization, and public-private partnerships transforms political struggle over national purposes and resources into local administrative practices that receive as given both the resource constraints and the aims they are handed. These new practices themselves recast the very meaning and understanding of democracy, even as they promise to deliver more of it.

(2015, pp. 127–128)

Brown is not talking about blockchain, but then there is no need to reference the technology directly in order to grasp the conditions into which blockchain is clearly emerging.

It could be said that the radical libertarian vision latent in blockchain has not retreated at all, but merely been tempered or absorbed by neoliberalism. As a nebulous and chaotic form of political thought and means of social organisation neoliberalism does not openly share the often strident political ideals favoured by libertarians, but neither does it reject them (Mirowski, 2014, p. 40). Instead neoliberalism has absorbed the essence of the libertarian vision, namely, liberty and freedom in all aspects of human lived experience, and subjected it to a narrow economic rationalisation as part of the construction of a new and, importantly, 'good' society *à la* constructivism. The libertarianism of blockchain is therefore an opportunity to be exploited by neoliberals for the illusion it provides for the circumvention and undoing of legacy forms of centralised power. The major distinguishing characteristic of neoliberalism from its liberal and libertarian progenitors is, as Philip Mirowski points out, 'a set of proposals and programs to infuse, take over, and transform the strong state, in order to impose the ideal form of society', not to undermine or destroy the notion of the state as such (2014, p. 40).

Already apparent in many proposed uses of blockchain, both financial and post-financial, is the means with which to (re)construct society and re-task the state, all of which makes the technology highly compatible with the neoliberal vision of political economy that has been playing out since the 2008 financial crisis (Peck, 2012; Mirowski, 2014). Put another way, blockchain offers myriad 'possible paths to improve system efficiency and scalability' that are attractive technological 'solutions' to global financial power and the neoliberal actors that stand behind it, but this requires changing current models, which has strong implications for the centralisation of a technology rooted in a decentralising ethos (Aste et al., 2017, p. 26). So, while decentralisation remains a core feature of the technology, one seized upon by foundational libertarians and opportunistic neoliberal interlopers alike, the likelihood that blockchain will remain decentralised in ways that effectively challenge centralised modes of power is highly questionable because that does not fit the prevailing neoliberal ethos of *actual* governance, in contrast to the aspiration, belief and faith structures presently scaffolding the blockchain ecosystem and its various projects.

Interest in blockchain at the World Economic Forum in Davos (and for some time prior) has shown that legacy financial power can easily absorb technologies into existing paradigms and thus not be disrupted by them. Disruption is a useful term for grabbing headlines, but in the context of blockchain it represents little more than the sharing economy of functionaries of capitalist class power. Blockchain, it is believed, will enable systems of trade and finance to become more effective and efficient by supporting and realising (making viable) the advanced stages of global mass data handling and frictionless transfers of value, thus transforming society and industry alike (Swan, 2015; Tapscott and Tapscott, 2016; Aste et al., 2017). But this does not mean that legacy sources of financial power and authority are either going to cede ground to an entrepreneur with a laptop, or dissolve in the face of technological revolution. In fact, it is already clear within the short history of blockchain that the big businesses that came before blockchain have every intention of remaining big and using blockchain to achieve that goal.

The blockchain horizon is one in which more capitalism and with it the further and deeper entrenchment of capitalist class power are highly likely outcomes based on the present course of events. This is perhaps unsurprising as blockchain is self-evidently a capitalist organisational form, or more specifically, to refer to capital's contemporary 'mutant form' (Han, 2017, p. 5), a neoliberal one. Manuel Castells describes the concomitancy of technological revolutions and the evolution of capitalism *qua* neoliberalism into which blockchain squarely fits as:

> a process of profound restructuring, characterised by greater flexibility in management; decentralization and networking of firms both internally and in their relationships to other firms; considerable empowering of capital *vis-à-vis* labor, with the concomitant decline in influence of the labor movement; increasing individualization and diversification of working relationships; massive incorporation of women into the paid labor force, usually under discriminatory conditions; intervention of the state to deregulate markets selectively, and to undo the welfare state, with different intensity and orientations depending upon the nature of political forces and institutions in each society; stepped-up global economic competition, in a context of increasing geographic and cultural differentiation of settings for capital accumulation and management.
>
> (2010, pp. 1–2)

Where various national governments have begun to take blockchain seriously, including in the UK with the recent formation of an All Party Parliamentary Group (APPG) on blockchain, discussions of the technology begin with advantages for entrepreneurs and investors, and favour commercial business applications first and foremost, with broader social benefits the technology may herald remaining lower-order considerations.[3] Notwithstanding notable contradictions in government interest in blockchain, government trends in the UK and US at least have been to allow commercial private actors to shape the blockchain narrative. This may be seen as crucial to a multistakeholder approach to blockchain

3   This perspective is drawn from the author's own experience as a contributor to the APPG on blockchain, which first convened on 30 January 2018.

stewardship, development and regulation. The father and son team of Tapscott and Tapscott have energetically promoted both in their book on blockchain (2016), as well as in their capacity as authors of a blockchain White Paper for the World Economic Forum (2017), a duality of outputs which reveals much about both the lack of grip that non-commercial stakeholders such as democratic and civic institutions presently have on blockchain and the blockchain narrative, as well as the willingness to abdicate responsibility for the development of potentially major social infrastructure projects to private commercial interests – this precise deference for the multistakeholder approach.

The present lack of any serious regulatory or critical political accountability not swayed by what Lana Swartz has called the ambitious and dazzling visions 'conjured by blockchain dreamers' (2017, p. 82), threatens to result in an exclusively commercialised and consumerist dictate devoid of political will. On this basis it is imperative that critique focuses on, as it has done in relation to the growth and transformation of the Internet, the Web, mobile technologies and big data, what is (and will be) at stake from blockchain's continuing embeddedness in the logic and reason of capital, and to consider what other options might exist to benefit and empower the demos. And a clear, albeit undoubtedly unpopular, option with the present blockchain ecosystem being that technologies such as blockchain simply serve no useful purpose for wider society (as Stinchcombe argues), and therefore time and money ought not to be invested by government in what are lame or vanity projects of entrepreneurs using the legitimating guise of private-public partnerships to promote what Lana Swartz calls blockchain dreams (2017, p. 82).

Amid the bluster of rampant innovationism that engenders the present sociopolitical moment, technologies such as blockchain have a guaranteed place in changes, whether subtle or sweeping, made to social structures, systems and institutions. 'Blockchain is more than a technology', Eva Kaili, chair of the European Parliament's science and technology panel, has enthusiastically claimed: 'it is an infrastructure upon which we can build wider applications such as the Internet of Things, smart cities and infrastructures' (Singh, 2017). Decentralisation of state sovereignty and power in favour of coded and technological formations of economic and consumerist subjectivities, of *dividuated* data governance, to echo Deleuze (1995, p. 182), and underscored by neoliberal accusations 'that governments inevitably promote inefficient models of economic administration' (Stiegler, 2010, p. 101), is setting new precedents for the management of individuals as de-politicised, machine-readable data auras.

When it comes to regulation of technology Morozov does not favour *laissez-faire* approaches by government (2014, p. 217). Instead, he views as important the need for technological development to remain, as far as possible, within the regulatory scope and cognisance of government, rooting his arguments in hard-hitting although somewhat excessive historical lessons, not least based on the Nazis' development of gas chambers for the examination of the Jews in World War II and the realisation of the 'final solution', to outline what is at stake when too free a rein in technological development is allowed (2014, p. 218). There is absolutely no justification for aligning blockchain with such horrors. The matter of the extent of regulatory intervention, as proposed in the earlier Introduction, is, however, crucial. Morozov's criticism of lightweight regulation and *laissez-faire* approaches by government that enable techno-solutionist ideologies to flourish whilst achieving little in terms of the public good is one supported here, not least because, as Angela Walch maintains, '[f]lawed understandings of blockchain technology can yield poor regulation and inappropriate adoption of the technology in critically important systems' (2017, p. 14). In other words, regulation is not simply or always about ham-stringing innovation or preventing entrepreneurs from realising their personal missions of 'disruption', but actually ensuring that technology, if indeed its application can be justified, serves a wider and more equitable and social purpose and benefit.

Conclusion

Blockchain has been proclaimed as the new Internet (Rawson, 2017). Others, while broadly agreeing, have nevertheless been a little more circumscribed in the definitions (Swan, 2015). By deliberately drawing parallels between the Web and Internet, acolytes and stakeholders of blockchain are aiming at rapid normalisation, not least because this will improve mainstream interest levels and adoption rates of the new technology. Conferring meaning to mainstream audiences already primed for particular forms of interrelatedness between technology and political economy via oblivious points of reference is, however, not evidence of commitment to educating such audiences, but rather nudging them toward awareness of another inevitable technological change. It is important to remember that such blockchain 'optics' are incapable or unwilling to challenge the status quo, and blockchain for these stakeholders is the next technological stage and organisational form in the incontestable onward march of free-market and competitive capitalism.

Lana Swartz argues that, 'blockchain projects exist in a particular temporality and have their own sense of the past and the future, of change. It performatively leans into a future, always just around the corner, which might as well be here already' (2017, p. 89). Swartz continues: 'This is technological fetishism with the implementation of that technology as almost an afterthought [...] technology is always one step behind its promises' (2017, p. 89). The ability of entrepreneurial fetishisation of blockchain to produce or force material outcomes and shape the world in which the technology is mobilised ought not to be overlooked too quickly. From the point of view of regulation it is problematic because it points to the need for limitations to be imposed on desire itself – that is, on the desire of entrepreneurs and other blockchain stakeholders who view the technology as unlimited relative to their own capacity to dream the future. What is more, if, as Swartz argues, technology is one step behind what it promises, this only adds further to the regulatory conundrum insofar as law and regulation, as evidence, experience and history of so-called 'law lag' show, are one step further back still (Reyes, 2016, p. 202).

Educating the public about blockchain, whether in a commercial or civic form (to use two broad categories in which blockchain already is or will soon be implemented) must be built around a critical discourse that challenges the marketing spiel of those already invested in blockchain applications and infrastructure, and thus, quite frankly, those who are unlikely to be critical of the technology. You would not, after all, to use a rather extreme comparison, ask a tobacco manufacturer whether smoking is good or bad and expect an answer not skewed by the desire to sell more tobacco. At present, however, those invested in the technology are being relied upon by governments and regulators to educate the wider public on whether or not the technology is good or bad – in which the outcome invariably points to the former. A growing belief in the benefits of blockchain by highly influential actors from global finance and technology corporations makes critical analysis and subsequent, informed regulation vital. Specifically interrogation of the power this belief in blockchain has to excite markets, which is, as Izabella Kaminska (2018) in the *Financial Times* has implied, and David Golumbia has argued, testament to a 'reassertion of the political power' that the blockchain was 'specifically constructed to dismantle' (2016, p. 76).

Many applications envisaged by a misty-eyed entrepreneurial class sold on the world-changing benefits of blockchain will never see the light of day. This is not something we need to place bets on; it is already the case that some of the seemingly brightest concepts have fallen by the wayside. Take, for example, Citizen Code, which as of October 2017 is defunct, but prior to that had boasted some of the more outlandish solutionist rhetoric, as Lana Swartz (2017, p. 88) details:

> People of the free internet, we now have the opportunity to create a world where we choose to work a 4 hour work week at our whim, collaborating globally with whom we like, freely choosing compensation in currency or equity, frolicking in our hyper-creative and artistic, fractally self-organized fluid work groups, protected from catastrophic risk by a basic income provided by our egalitarian peer to peer protocols. In this vision the tragedy of the commons is stamped out like polio by a collaborative network of trust and enforced by a consensus-based cryptographic protocol that ensures our aligned incentivization towards the expression of our personal and collective purposes.

It is unsurprising that so many 'start-ups' are falling by the wayside given the mushrooming in blockchain interests in the last three years. In the present moment what is clear is that it would be unwise to ignore or dismiss the hype surrounding blockchain, in spite of the hot air that groups such as Citizen Code relied upon. This is because blockchain is telling (and showing) us something very important about the evolution of capital and economic reason, and the impact this evolution will or might have in the near future on forms and patterns of work, social organisation and, crucially, communities and individuals. Marshall McLuhan recognised over half a century ago that, above all, technologies like blockchain herald and enforce cultural and psycho-political transformations:

> Electric circuitry profoundly involves men with one another. Information pours upon us, instantaneously and continuously. As soon as information is

acquired, it is very rapidly replaced by still newer information. Our electrically-configured world has forced us to move from the habit of data classification to the mode of pattern recognition. We can no longer build serially, block-by-block, step-by-step, because instant communication insures that all factors of the environment and of experience co-exist in a state of active interplay.

(McLuhan and Fiore, 2008, p. 63)

It is hard to disagree with McLuhan's analysis even today. Yet in highlighting a retreat of ontological and epistemic incrementalism that technology causes, McLuhan's choice of words – 'We can no longer build serially, block-by-block' – has obvious resonance with the subject at hand. In applying what McLuhan says to the context of blockchain, therefore, what conclusion can be reached? Perhaps, simply, that any prior move from 'data classification' to 'pattern recognition' was not one-way and permanent as McLuhan suggests, but cyclical; a process of constant re-imagination at the hands of technologists, their patrons and benefactors, which is, no less, pegged to the cyclical dynamics of capital. Blockchain does, therefore, signal a return to building serially, albeit still within the churn and interplay of environment and experience.

Forms of socioeconomic, political and cultural 'disruption' both anticipated and promised by blockchain acolytes are, at least in some cases, less a product of what the technology itself can actually do than the manner in which it is 'marketed' by stakeholders who are looking to drive innovation and efficiencies with regard for self-interest. Disruption also speaks to a constant churn and interplay of environment and experience discussed a moment ago. As Botsman claims: 'I believe the real disruption happening is not technology itself, but the massive trust shift it creates' (2017, p. 8). She continues:

[d]istributed trust, enabled by new technologies, is rewriting the rules of human relationships. It's changing the way we view the world and each other, returning us to the old village model of trust in one sense, except that the community is global in scale and some of its invisible reins are being pulled by internet giants.

(2017, p. 10)

There continues to be a great deal of posturing in the blockchain ecosystem, combining significant levels of both fetishisation of the technology and romanticisation of its contexts. Botsman's quote above illustrates this point, not least in her reference to a stereotype of a village idyll. But whilst blockchain fetishisation in particular may appear part of the landscape of modern technological societies, the powerful and unyielding desires of blockchain acolytes is aiming the technology as at the next stages of free-market domination of social life. The blockchain ecosystem does, in other words, engender an erotics of the market and capital that will not go unsatisfied (Schroeder, 2004). On the terms outlined, law and regulation, whether domestically or transnationally, needs to be more critical of the blockchain ecosystem and the discourse it is promoting than at present, and ensure those responsible for political accountability are not left playing catch-up but suitably working in the *public* interest.

References

Aste, Tomaso, Tasca, Paolo and Di Matteo, Tiziana. 2017. Blockchain Technologies: The Foreseeable Impact on Society and Industry. *Computer*, Vol. 50, No. 9 (September), pp. 18–28.

Bogost, Ian. 2017. Cryptocurrency Might be a Path to Authoritarianism. *The Atlantic*, 30 May. www.theatlantic.com/technology/archive/2017/05/blockchain-of-command/ 528543/ (accessed 25 January 2018).

Botsman, Rachel. 2017. *Who Can You Trust? How Technology Brought Us Together – and Why It Could Drive Us Apart*. London: Portfolio Penguin.

Boucher, Philip. 2017. *How blockchain technology could change our lives: In-depth analysis*. European Parliamentary Research Service: Scientific Foresight Unit, February. www. europarl.europa.eu/thinktank/en/document.html?reference=EPRS_IDA%282017% 29581948 (accessed 7 February 2018).

Brown, Wendy. 2015. *Undoing the Demos: Neoliberalism's Stealth Revolution*. New York: Zone Books.

Castells, Manuel. 2010. *The Rise of the Network Society*. 2nd Edition. Chichester: Wiley Blackwell.

Dean, Jodie. 2009. *Democracy and Other Neoliberal Fantasies: Communicative Capitalism and Left Politics*. Durham: Duke University Press.

Deibert, Ronald and Rohozinski, Rafal. 2010. Beyond Denial: Introducing Next-Generation Information Access Controls. *Accessed Controlled: The Shaping of Power, Rights, and Rule in Cyberspace*. Edited by Ronald Deibert, John Palfrey, Rafal Rohozinski and Jonathan Zittrain. Cambridge: MIT Press.

Deleuze, Gilles. 1995. *Negotiations 1972–1990*. Translated by Martin Joughin. New York: Columbia University Press.

Fenster, Mark. 2017. *The Transparency Fix: Secrets, Leaks, and Uncontrollable Government Information*. Stanford: Stanford University Press.

Giddens, Anthony. 1990. *The Consequences of Modernity*. Cambridge: Polity.

Golumbia, David. 2016. *The Politics of Bitcoin: Software as Right-Wing Extremism*. Minneapolis: University of Minnesota Press.

Goux, Jean-Joseph. 1990. *Symbolic Economies: After Marx and Freud*. Translated by Jennifer Curtiss Gage. Ithaca: Cornell University Press.

Government Office for Science. 2016. *Distributed Ledger Technology: Beyond block chain*. 19 January. www.gov.uk/government/publications/distributed-ledger-technology-blackett-review (accessed 31 January 2018).

Gupta, Vinay. 2017. European Parliament blockchain presentation May 2017. *YouTube*. www.youtube.com/watch?v=xEFVuccuHI8&t=4s (accessed 1 February 2018).

Han, Byung-Chul. 2015. *The Transparency Society*. Translated by Erik Butler. Stanford: Stanford University Press.

Han, Byung-Chul. 2017. *Psycho-Politics: Neoliberalism and New Technologies of Power*. Translated by Erik Butler. London: Verso.

Harvey, David. 2005. *A Brief History of Neoliberalism*. Oxford: Oxford University Press.

Kim, Kibum and Kang, Taewon. 2017. *Does Technology Against Corruption Always Lead to Benefit? The Potential Risks and Challenges of the Blockchain Technology*. OECD Global

Anti-Corruption & Integrity Forum. www.oecd.org/cleangovbiz/Integrity-Forum-2017-Kim-Kang-blockchain-technology.pdf (accessed 25 April 2018).

Kaminska, Izabella. 2018. Truth and fiction in blockchain's brave new world. *Financial Times*, 2 January. www.ft.com (accessed 15 January 2018).

Landow, George P. 2006. *Hypertext 3.0: Critical Theory and New Media in an Era of Globalization*. Baltimore: Johns Hopkins University Press.

McLuhan, Marshall and Fiore, Quentin. 2008. *The Medium is the Massage*. Co-ordinated by Jerome Agel. London: Penguin.

Marinova, Polina. 2017. Jamie Dimon: Bitcoin Bad, Blockchain Good. *Fortune*, 13 September. http://fortune.com/2017/09/13/jamie-dimon-bitcoin-blockchain/ (accessed 7 February 2018).

Mirowski, Philip. 2014. *Never Let A Serious Crisis Go to Waste: How Neoliberalism Survived the Financial Meltdown*. London: Verso.

Morozov, Evgeny. 2014. *To Save Everything, Click Here: Technology, solutionism and the urge to fix problems that don't exist*. London: Penguin.

Mueller, Milton. 2017. *Will the Internet Fragment? Sovereignty, Globalization and Cyberspace*. Cambridge: Polity.

Pasquale, Frank. 2015. *The Black Box Society: The Secret Algorithms that Control Money and Information*. Cambridge: Harvard University Press.

Peck, Jamie. 2012. *Constructions of Neoliberal Reason*. Oxford: Oxford University Press.

Perez, Yessi Bello. 2015. Bitcoin in the Headlines: Blockchain Good, Bitcoin Bad. *Coindesk*, 18 September. www.coindesk.com/bitcoin-in-the-headlines-blockchain-good-bitcoin-bad/ (accessed 7 February 2018).

Power, Michael. 1997. *The Audit Society: Rituals of Verification*. Oxford: Oxford University Press.

Rawson, Phillip. 2017. *Blockchain: The New Internet? How You Can Benefit from Blockchain Technology Beyond Bitcoin, Cryptocurrency, and Ethereum*. CreateSpace Independent Publishing Platform.

Reyes, Carla L. 2016. Moving Beyond Bitcoin to an Endogenous Theory of Decentralized Ledger Technology Regulation: an Initial Proposal. *Villanova Law Review*, Vol. 61, No. 1, pp. 191–234.

Schroeder, Jeanne Lorraine. 2004. *The Triumph of Venus: The Erotics of the Market*. Berkeley: University of California Press.

Scott, Brett. 2016. *How Can Cryptocurrency and Blockchain Technology Play a Role in Building Social and Solidarity Finance?* Working Paper 2016–2011. Geneva: United Nations Research Institute for Social Development.

Singh, Rajnish. 2017. EU must work to enable blockchain technology. *The Parliament Magazine*, 7 November. www.theparliamentmagazine.eu/articles/opinion/eu-must-work-to-enable-blockchain-technology (accessed 31 March 2018).

Son, Hugh, Campbell, Dakin and Basak, Sonali. 2017. Goldman is Setting Up a Cryptocurrency Trading Desk. *Bloomberg*, 21 December. www.bloomberg.com/news/articles/2017-12-21/goldman-is-said-to-be-building-a-cryptocurrency-trading-desk (accessed 12 January 2018).

Stiegler, Bernard. 2010. *For a New Critique of Political Economy*. Cambridge: Polity.

Stinchcombe, Kai. 2017. Ten years in, nobody has come up with a use for blockchain. *Hacker Noon*, 22 December. https://hackernoon.com/ten-years-in-nobody-has-come-up-with-a-use-case-for-blockchain-ee98c180100 (accessed 31 January 2018).

Swan, Melanie. 2015. *Blockchain: Blueprint for a New Economy*. Sebastopol: O'Reilly.

Swartz, Lana. 2017. Blockchain Dreams: Imagining techno-economic alternatives after Bitcoin. *Another Economy is Possible*. Edited by Manuel Castells. Cambridge: Polity Press, pp. 82–105.

Tapscott, Don and Tapscott, Alex. 2016. *Blockchain Revolution: How the Technology behind Bitcoin is Changing Money, Business and the World*. London: Portfolio Penguin.

Tapscott, Don and Tapscott, Alex. 2017. *Realizing the Potential of Blockchain: A Multi-stakeholder Approach to the Stewardship of Blockchain and Cryptocurrencies*. World Economic Forum, White Paper, 28 June. www.weforum.org/whitepapers/realizing- the-potentia l-of-blockchain (accessed 13 March 2018).

Ver, Roger. 2017. The Gold Rush Begins: The Day Bitcoin Topped the US Dollar. *Coin-desk*, 4 April. www.coindesk.com/the-gold-rush-begins-bitcoin-tops-the-dollar/ (accessed 12 January 2018).

Walch, Angela. 2017. Blockchain's Treacherous Vocabulary: One More Challenge for Regulators. *Journal of Internet Law*, Vol. 21, No. 2, pp. 9–16.

Wortham, Simon Morgan. 2004. Auditing Derrida. *Parallax*, Vol. 10, No. 2, pp. 3–18.

Interlude IV: A dangerous lack of law

Man with machine in Kurt Vonnegut's *Player Piano*

Kurt Vonnegut's first novel, *Player Piano*, published in 1952, tells the story of Dr Paul Proteus and his engineered fall from grace that leads him to a secret resistance group, the Ghost Shirt Society, existing within the margins of a highly elite, technocratic and totalitarian society in the aftermath of a third world war. A totalitarian society organised not by terrorism

> but by economic-technical coordination of vested interests. Its society is one that appears, as its main character Paul Proteus notes, as a 'clean, straight rafter,' that, once the surface is scraped away, is rotten to the core. Paul doesn't just grapple with his technocratic totalitarian society in *Player Piano*, but also with the meaning of his life (as well as life in general), the paradox of progress, and the potential for human freedom at odds with the straightjackets of circumstance and history.
>
> (Gannon, 2013)

The following passage is an extract from the Ghost Shirt manifesto:

> I deny that there is any natural or divine law requiring that machines, efficiency, and organization should forever increase in scope, power, and complexity, in peace as in war. I see the growth of these now, rather, as the result of a dangerous lack of law.
>
> I propose that men and women be returned to work as controllers of machines, and that the control of people by machines be curtailed. I propose, further, that the effects of changes in technology and organization on life patterns be taken into careful consideration, and that the changes be withheld or introduced on the basis of this consideration.
>
> These are radical proposals, extremely difficult to put into effect. But the need for the being put into effect is far greater than all of the difficulties, and infinitely greater than the need for our national holy trinity, Efficiency, Economy, and Quality.
>
> Men, by their nature, seemingly, cannot be happy unless engaged in enterprises that make them feel useful. They must, therefore, be returned to participation in such enterprises.

I hold, and the members of the Ghost Shirt Society hold: That there must be virtue in imperfection, for Man is imperfect, and Man is a creation of God. That there must be virtue in inefficiency, for Man is inefficient, and Man is a creation of God.

That there must be virtue in brilliance followed by stupidity, for Man is alternately brilliant and stupid, and Man is a creation of God.

You perhaps disagree with the antique and vain notion of Man's being a creation of God.

But I find it a far more defensible belief than the one implicit in intemperate faith in lawless technological progress – namely, that man is on earth to create more durable and efficient images of himself, and hence, to eliminate any justification at all for his own continued existence.

(Vonnegut, 2006, pp. 301–303)

References

Gannon, Matthew. 2013. Player Piano, the One-Dimensional Society, and the Emergency Brake of History. *The Vonnegut Review*. www.vonnegutreview.com/2013/06/player-piano-one-dimensional-society.html (accessed 1 June 2018).

Vonnegut, Kurt. 2006. *Player Piano*. New York: The Dial Press.

8 Critical regulation

Introduction

> Even as the proliferation of communication technologies serves neoliberal financia-
> lization, accelerating the speed of monetary transactions and consolidating networks
> of privilege, the left advocate of participation, deliberation, and fundamental rights
> to communication can – and must – energetically deny this context.
>
> (Dean, 2009, pp. 41–42)

Blockchain needs a *critical regulator*. Power relations dominate networked technologies as they have a variety of institutions, systems, networks and organisational forms
throughout the history of capitalism. Blockchain is a capitalist technology and speculation is therefore unnecessary as to whether capitalist class power is operating
through it. A whole cadre of capitalist and neoliberal adjuncts have lined up behind
blockchain: agile venture capitalists, fluid entrepreneurs, pop-up start-ups of different
sizes and capacities, as well as traditional and legacy sources of brute capitalist
authority and hegemony, including banks, accountants and myriad other financial
services. There is no need to linger on if or even why this is so because it is a continuing trend in the relationship between capitalism and technology that is easily
anticipated at every turn. Instead the focus here has been on capitalism's and neoliberalism's use in particular of technology to shape narratives, discourse and conduct,
most notably that produced and disseminated by the blockchain ecosystem.

There is, I have argued, something insidious in blockchain not inherent or
attributable to the technology as such, but which stems from stakeholder rationalisations of what the technology is (mis)directed to achieve through local and
global applications and implementations. Primarily this involves techno-social
designs conjured by the blockchain ecosystem that (further) deny the political,
insist on order without law (De Filippi and Wright, 2018, p. 5), and fabricate an
ethics of social justice for the purposes of masking strategies of competition to be
further endured on the fictitious level playing fields of global free markets. Michael
Casey and Paul Vigna make the claim that:

> Blockchains are a social technology, a new blueprint for how to govern com-
> munities, whether we're talking about frightened refugees in a desolate Jor-
> danian outpost or an interbank market in which the world's biggest financial

institutions exchange trillions of dollars daily. By definition, getting block-chain technology right requires input from all sectors of society. You can treat that as a clarion call to take an interest, to get involved.

(2018, pp. 14–15)

There is only one aspect of the above statement that I agree with, and even then I do so for very different reasons to Casey and Vigna: the need for society to sit up and take notice of blockchain – what I have referred to elsewhere as 'Taking blockchain seriously' (Herian, 2018). The necessity to 'get involved' with block-chain is, I claim, and in contrast to Casey and Vigna, to remain aware and con-scious of global applications of yet another technology used in the first instance to benefit and advantage enclosed cabals of private interest saturated in neoliberal reason, with public interest and the commons low-order considerations subject, at best, to fallacies of trickle-down advantages from free-wheeling innovationism. This is precisely what Casey and Vigna are advocating when they suggest block-chain can be used to flatten out the socio-political divide, by comparing seamlessly and without hesitation worlds of 'frightened refugees in a desolate Jordanian out-post' and 'an interbank market in which the world's biggest financial institutions exchange trillions of dollars daily'. Is it really reasonable to look at these two contexts and see enterprise synergies, to see possibilities to 'leverage', to monetise? To consider profitable an imagined parity between the two is, I suggest, a product of a totalising and financialised neoliberal world vision and symptomatic of an 'economy of carelessness' (Stiegler, 2010, p. 80). Yet for neoliberal techno-solu-tionists it seems blockchain is precisely this sort of a unifying force, a *wholeness* capable of transcending human geopolitical contestations and efficiency gains sought by global financial services, suturing them together and treating them the same: as a *monolithic profitable mass.*

Follow the desire

What Casey and Vigna advocate is a perfect illustration of what I view as and have expressed throughout this book to be a worrying and dangerous neoliberal ideol-ogy *qua* ethics and political economy emanating from and expressed by the blockchain ecosystem, albeit an ecosystem that is a mere outgrowth of existing synchronicities between neoliberalism and Internet networks of privilege (Dean, 2009, p. 42). Understanding and locating sites of neoliberal inscription within the blockchain ecosystem has not been the sole concern of the critique presented in this book, however, nor can it be for further critical work in the field of block-chain scholarship. Equally important, I claim, is to follow the desire of the block-chain ecosystem and its stakeholders in order to understand constructions in fantasy it inaugurates, and systems and mechanisms for belief and faith it relies on to legitimise concepts, conduct, as well as material being in the world and imma-terial characterisations in cyberspace. For the critical regulator of blockchain the question is how to regulate fantasy, fetishism, illusion, erotics of the market – '*not the physical mating urge*', but rather 'the desire for recognition by others and for wholeness' (Schroeder, 2004, p. 86) – and not simply the technologies that service them. To aim for the technology, or rather to construe technology as brute technology and not a condensation of libidinal energies, is to miss real regulatory 'choke points' – or, indeed, the *Real* of technology. A regulatory environment that treats blockchain as a *psycho-technology* saturated in psycho-politics and not a product of the technicalities or doctrines of law and economics, nor of the code-based 'solutions' of the technologies as such, is an important step along the path to fostering alternative means of regulating blockchain.

Freud identified a dichotomy between 'all the knowledge and capacity that men have acquired in order to control the forces of nature and extract its wealth for the satisfaction of human needs', and 'all the regulations necessary in order to adjust the relations of men to one another and especially the distribution of the available wealth' (2001, p. 6). The question for critical regulation in this blockchain moment is not so much if the balance will tip – arguably it has tipped already in favour of wealth *qua* capitalism, exploitation and the mores of self-interest and greed and not for the benefit of a commons built on generosity, or in the public interest. But a question of the long-term consequences should regulation fail entirely to address and resolve the trend towards blockchain use effecting a deepening of the economisation of cyberspace, the increased production of information without knowledge (Stiegler, 2010, p. 129) on behalf of networks of privilege, and the further expansion of blockchain governmentality predicated on specious notions of individualised data sovereignty made possible by an interface between technical and social systems that are always mediated and beholden to the economic system.

What is perhaps most astonishing about the blockchain moment has been the ability of stakeholders to convince the world of the desirability of digital ledgers as immaterial objects of ritual and devotion. We are witnessing the rise of ledger society in which rituals of verification (Power, 1997) will become the norm; where the ledger assumes vast status as a ritual object and multivocal symbol, its referents 'not all of the same logical order' but 'drawn from many domains of social experience and ethical evaluation' (Turner, 1969, p. 52), for the purposes of performing as peer-to-peer, inter-located digitalised economic subjectivities. The digital ledger *qua* blockchain is arguably an example of greater transformation of the mundane into the specular than even mobile phones achieved with the inauguration of smartphones. It does, however, explain the fetishistic and feverish churn of blockchain concepts and use-cases and also why venture capital is investing increasingly large amounts of money to service the erotics of emergent blockchain markets. For example, blockchain-based companies with little more than a concept to their name have been raising eye-watering amounts of capital – estimates as of summer 2017 put the figure of blockchain investment at US$4.5 billion (Ponicano, 2017), and this will certainly be exceeded in 2018. There is undoubtedly something that can be called a trend or fashion occurring around blockchain, of entrepreneurs turning to blockchain for a 'solution' with no real need to understand whether it is the best or most effective option for the proposed 'problem', or, indeed, whether there is a real 'problem' that blockchain is required to solve in the first place. The excitement surrounding the 'disruptive' potential of blockchain begins not with technology therefore but with fantasies and objects of desire coveted by entrepreneurs, which is not the same as entrepreneurs 'dreaming big' with the technology – a staple narrative within the confines of the entrepreneurial class. The result is a jumble of misunderstandings as to the precise nature and value of blockchain as a technology, and reductionist narratives of blockchain as a global economic panacea rushing to fill gaps evacuated of critical reason.

The critical regulator must also cut through what Herbert Marcuse long ago called the 'comfortable, smooth, reasonable, democratic unfreedom' that 'prevails in advanced industrial civilization, a token of technical progress' (2002, p. 3), and continues as a pervasive description of contemporary technological societies. If the first decades of the new millennium have been dominated by the rise of digital socialisation built around an Internet of information and experience sharing, and of an expansion in the population of digital subjectivities willing to expose themselves online and coming to know what it means to *engage* and *participate* – albeit falsely, as we are increasingly learning today with scandals over mass data use by companies like Facebook promoting participation of subjects as *dividuated* and monetisable data sets – then might blockchain as the economic layer the web has never had signal a retreat from the idea of cyberspace as a phenomenology of socialisation to something more plain, more boring, but at least honest? An Internet or more specifically application layers including the World Wide Web that are more streamlined and less noisy or a fake participatory may be an attractive proposition in some instances, one dominated not by an interest in reposing socially in cyberspace with the fatigue that increasingly accompanies that obligation. Using technology to simply transact and exchange with more brute efficiency may be more attractive if it means less emphasis on marshalling one's efforts and energies to build the sorts of social and trusting relationships that have always accompanied offline and off-chain trade. In other words an unadorned, more utilitarian and *pure* free-market capitalist vision of cyberspace that blockchain brings to prominence through the incorruptible and bureaucratic simplicity of the ledger form.

Any number of defences of the Internet as we presently find it could be made as a rejection of the proposition of a more deeply economised version. This is not the place to rally broad defences. I do, however, argue that the narrow implications of blockchain in fermenting a streamlining and deeper economisation of *inter alia* the World Wide Web, of transforming it into an ever more perfect market, is not something to be welcomed, but lamented. It is through such propositions we again find the humanity existing behind and through technology beset by and implicated in ideals and practices of financial economy first and last. 'Networked communication and information technologies are exquisite media for capturing and reformatting political energies', argues Jodie Dean, they 'turn efforts at political engagement into contributions to the circulation of content, reinforcing the hold of neoliberalism's technological infrastructure' (2009, p. 32). Where blockchain figures in Dean's analysis is still evolving, as the technology moves from the brute economics of cryptocurrencies to more obvious political domains such as the provision of public services and democratic accountability vis-à-vis voting and government transparency initiatives. At heart, however, blockchain enables humanity towards further, endless engagement in transactions and exchanges that do not in actuality reflect efficiency and therefore create time that can be spent on meaningful non-economic and non-financialised pursuits, but precisely because transactions and exchanges have become ends in themselves. Contemporary ledger technologies and the peer-to-peer networks they support not only enable contributions to the circulation of content, as Dean expresses it, but more accurately economise those contributions in accordance with ever more crystallised, neoliberal ideals. The dividual obtains amid peer-to-peer networks, searching for and anticipating each new transaction and exchange as an erotic event: an encounter with the other within the system worthy of the performative demands of conduct of neoliberal self-hood.

Narcissistic desire inhabits peer-to-peer networks in myriad profound and affective ways, not least in that economised digital subjectivities find in networks endless reflexive and reflective nodes; the *other* economised digital subject who is just like me, who is me, and thus whose desire I seek to understand and satisfy. Peer-to-peer networks *qua* digital marketplaces, such as those underpinned and facilitated by blockchains, are auto-erotic sites which themselves harbour the repressed desire of the death wish, *Thanatos*. As means for the creation of an ethics of desire that corresponds in no way with 'the good', or an ethics of political economy that sections of the blockchain ecosystem maintain to uphold, these networks instead maintain deferral or postponement of desire through constant exchange with no hope of consummation, in order to ensure desire remains alive but never satisfied. '[T]he desire underlying the economic ideal of the perfect market', argues Jeanne Schroeder, is the death wish (2004, p. 86). She continues:

> The perfect market is the end of all actual markets – it is their ideal form. In normative economics, actual markets are the means of achieving the end or ideal of the perfect market. But this means that to achieve a perfect market would result in the end or cessation of all actual market transactions. This is not a pun, but the necessary implication of the single meaning of the word 'end'. One acts until one achieves one's goal, upon which action stops. We desire to achieve our ends even as far as we fear to end. Upon the achievement of perfection there can be no improvement, so one is frozen in crystalline ideality.
>
> (2004, p. 86)

Following Schroeder's thesis further it is clear that peer-to-peer networking corresponds with a particular Hegelian reading of the economics of desire structured by markets, one which is symptomatic of complex affects produced by the concepts and use-cases of the blockchain ecosystem. These complex affects involve fantasies constructed by the blockchain ecosystem in order to repress the desire of the death wish – of the end of the markets – that the perfect technology or technological 'solution' would herald. The ecosystem at once desires the perfect technology but cannot allow that desire to be realised because it would in effect destroy the purpose for the technology: markets and other sundry neoliberal ideals. 'The desire of the Hegelian marketplace', Schroeder claims, 'is Eros', an attempt 'to achieve perfection through a relation with another – the perfect mate' (2004, p. 88). Yet Eros, which corresponds here with the blockchain peer-to-peer ideal *qua* fantasy of consummation with the other, is only dominant 'insofar as desire remains unfulfilled' and thus Hegel reveals once again an ethics of desire predicated on postponement (Schroeder, 2004, p. 88). Thus peer to peer, as key to the logic of desires both repressed and postponed, is central to concepts dreamed up by a blockchain ecosystem stuck between building technologies capable of ending markets and also wanting more markets for their technologies. The disintermediating characteristics of the Internet, as Casey and Vigna maintain, 'are setting us on a path to a peer-to-peer economy', and blockchain technology is giving people 'confidence to transact' (2018, p. 7), certainly a euphemism of indelicate proportions worthy of the auto-bureaucracy of modern eroticised subjectivities.

The Internet of things (IOT) to which blockchain is closely aligned (Tapscott and Tapscott, 2016, pp. 145–169; Botsman, 2017, p. 4; Casey and Vigna, 2018, pp. 121–137; De Filippi and Wright, 2018, pp. 158–160), has the potential to foster economic models based on machine-to-machine transactions that are operationally invisible from human intervention and, in some cases, even oversight, and as such create modified sites of desire to those of peer to peer discussed a moment ago. 'Using blockchain technology, connected devices can transact directly with other machines and pay for energy consumption, computational power, or other scarce resources', claim De Filippi and Wright, and because 'blockchains make it possible to transfer small payment using digital currency, the technology is supporting next-generation devices that not only share their functionalities but also turn into services themselves' (2018, p. 159). Instrumentalities aside, IOT is more interesting as a psychical measure of blockchain *affects* and thus what is ultimately at stake for the critical regulator seeking an understanding of the technology and the conduct it produces. Accordingly, I suggest, IOT reimagined in terms of blockchain technology connected devices that enable an Internet of *das Ding*: a notion of the Internet aligned with the Freudian *Thing*, where the technology (blockchain and IOT) functions as objects of satisfaction that structure fantasy and types of technological fetishism mentioned during the course of this book, and underscore notions of 'goodness'. 'Experience has taught', Freud argues,

> that what matters is not only whether a thing (an object of satisfaction) possesses the property of 'goodness', and so merits being taken into the ego, but also whether it is actually there in the outside world, and so can be appropriated whenever the need arises.
>
> (2005, p. 91)

It does not matter that blockchain IOT-enabled devices require no meaningful or material human intervention and are therefore distant from users whose desire relies and centres on them. Rather the structures of fantasy and fetishism in which the user and her technology comingle insist on a measure of distance between the two and in particular the mystery, ineffability and unknowability that the distant technology represents to the user. Moreover we find a corresponding disavowal of the lack of knowledge and simultaneously belief in the ability of the user to (re) constitute the *Thing*, the super-functionary technologies as object of devotions. Indeed, the distance is what precipitates *more* desire as Bruce Fink describes in his reading of Jacques Lacan's development of *das Ding* to a theory of the *objet a* (the object as cause of desire, rather than simply an object of desire or satisfaction). 'Here *das Ding* appears as the unsignified and unsignifiable object within the Other – in the Other yet more than or beyond the Other', states Fink, it is 'that object from which the subject keeps his or her distance, not getting too close or too far away either. The subject's relation to it is characterized by a primal affect' (1995, p. 95).

Further, Dean describes how the

> technological fetish covers and sustains a lack on the part of the subject. It protects the fantasy of an active, engaged subject by acting in the subject's stead [...] enabling us to go about the rest of our lives relieved of the guilt that we might not be doing our part and secure in the belief that we are, after all, informed, engaged citizens.
>
> (2009, pp. 37–38)

Machine-to-machine transactions take 'acting in the subject's stead' by technology to new levels of actualisation by facilitating, beyond standard blockchain peer-to-peer networks, greater passivity on the part of the subject. The subject who believes, once and for all, they have managed to abdicate all tawdry responsibility for trusting others to the economic configuring of the machine, and have therefore 'solved' the 'problem' of having to be political and, above all, of having to do politics. This is technological fetishism and blockchain fetishism in particular covering over a fundamental lack in the social order. 'A technological fetish is at work when one disavows the lack or antagonism rupturing (yet producing) the social by advocating a particular technological fix', claims Dean, the '"fix" [the "solution"] lets us think that all we need is to extend a particular technology and then we will have a democratic or reconciled democratic order' (2009, p. 38).

The significance of disavowal in fetishism begins with Octave Mannoni's formulation, 'Je sais bien, mais quand-même ...' meaning the fetishist knows very well that the fetish is not the *Thing* (*das ding*), but nevertheless chooses to turn away from such a reality by believing otherwise. For Mannoni the question at the heart of fetishism is therefore one of 'the possibility of simultaneously embracing two contrary beliefs, one official and one secret', which triggers a subjective paradox in the fetishist (2015, p. 151). Moreover, on Mannoni's account, this simultaneous abandonment and retention of belief is an everyday, perhaps even banal occurrence, rather than the perverse undercurrent of life. A key difference that Mannoni highlights between the types of belief found in Freud's formulation of fetishism and other psychic mechanisms for the repression and negation of ideas is precisely the fact that the belief is repudiated but not repressed nor denied as such (2015, p. 151). In short, Mannoni points to the importance of disavowal in maintaining both the structure of belief and by extension the structure of the fetish itself. Christopher Gemerchak echoes Mannoni in viewing disavowal as responsible for fetishism. '[O]nly by expanding Freud's notion of disavowal', argues Gemerchak, 'will we be able to understand fetishism as a fundamental possibility for the human subject' (Gemerchak, 2004a, p. 16). Disavowal is, Gemerchak further explains, 'the psychic anomaly that underpins Freud's mature conception of fetishism [...] an anomaly which henceforth served as a model for analysing structures as diverse as Marxist commodity fetishism, the Lacanian *objet a*, and primitive belief' (Gemerchak, 2004b, pp. 249–250). Disavowal is crucial on a number of different but interrelated fronts, all of which provide an explanation for certain forms of subjective existence with technologies in society.

Other than disavowal, Jodie Dean highlights *condensation* as another primary mode of operation of the technological fetish within capitalism, and it is one which generally describes the motivation emanating from the blockchain ecosystem, not least around calls for transparency, which has been discussed and critiqued throughout this book. 'Condensation occurs', claims Dean, 'when technology fetishism reduces the complexities of politics – of organization, struggle, duration, decisiveness, division, representation and so on – to one thing, one problem to be solved and one technological solution' (2009, p. 38). Hence trust online, transparency, provenance, democratic accountability, and any number of other problems identified by the ecosystem, are neatly condensed into blockchain solutions. What is more, fetishistic solutions animate a sense and materialise 'specific fantasies of unity and wholeness' (Dean, 2009, p. 42) within the blockchain ecosystem, but equally extend to the narratives used to educate outside of it. Recall Melanie Swan's contention that started this book: 'There is a need for a decentralized ecosystem surrounding the blockchain itself for full-solution operations' (2015, p. 20). Swan's instrumentalist, technocratic, perhaps even mundane statement nevertheless succinctly reveals the roles fetishism and fantasy are playing at the centre of the blockchain ecosystem. Structures in fantasy more fundamental than the individualising, self-interested neoliberal ideologies they ultimately become intertwined with, because they are deeply affective inscriptions marking the subject as a psycho-political civilised subject in the first instance. Yet the fantasies of wholeness, of a communal self, expressed by the blockchain ecosystem are incapable of extending to civilisation broadly conceived without first being filtered through the needs and satisfactions of self-interest. The ecosystem *could* represent a means to defeat self-interest of the individual entrepreneur, venture capitalist and so on, and drive a communal, collective sense of subjugated being within capitalism capable of working in the public interest, but it chooses not to. Instead fantasies of wholeness degrade to 'full-solution operations', and reveal how capitalism and neoliberalism in turn defeat communal fantasies and install their own centred on the subject as project (Han, 2017, p. 1), economic reason, markets and competition.

'The step taken by Freud at the level of the pleasure principle', claims Lacan,

> is to show us that there is no Sovereign Good – that the Sovereign Good, which is *das Ding*, which is the mother, is also the object of incest, is a forbidden good, and that there is no other good. Such is the foundation of the moral law as turned on its head by Freud.
>
> (1992, p. 70)

Blockchain for good is, as we have seen, a mantra symptomatic of the phoney wholeness *qua* communality expressed by the blockchain ecosystem. But from the perspective of psycho-politics and its critical regulator there is no good society. 'As we get closer to the ideal of a good society', argues McGowan, 'we simultaneously approach the emptiness concealed within the ideal' (2013, p. 6). He continues:

> The notion of the good does not emerge simply from moral reasoning and speculation about the proper arrangement of society. We develop this notion only through the experience of its prohibition. That is to say, the prohibition of the good doesn't form an obstacle to a preexisting ideal but constitutes the ideal as such. *The good has no existence outside of the barriers that we erect around realising it.*
>
> [emphasis added] (2013, p. 6)

Earlier I claimed that blockchain for *no* good was the variant cause of the application of blockchain to constrain free enterprise, capital and so on in the form of beneficial ownership registers and other methods for reining-in private interest to the advantage of public interest. Here we see that whilst that is so as a reflexive (what I can get away with is good, what stops me is not good), the good that blockchain represents for stakeholders more generally is always already the cause of the regulation *qua* prohibition that many of those same stakeholders see as stifling effects. It is, in other words, a false dichotomy between what I can get away with and what stops me. 'The foundational link between the good and prohibition', as McGowan claims, 'renders its pursuit completely contradictory' (2013, p. 6). As a consequence, blockchain stakeholders for whom regulations signal unwarranted constraint on the practices of innovation and enterprise – and we have seen a number of examples of such claims throughout this book – are arguably undoing the project of blockchain for good, not bolstering it. They are failing, to paraphrase McGowan, to enjoy what they don't have, while insisting on the illusion of a good society made possible by blockchain.

Conclusion

This book goes against the grain of present blockchain scholarship, and especially narratives and discourse flowing from the blockchain ecosystem and the mass markets for consumer and enterprise blockchain and cryptocurrencies, inasmuch as it favours more regulation *qua* government intervention, not less. In particular regulation that is not market-complementing, not designed to always already guarantee the success of private interest, but regulation aimed at limiting the destructive effects of the speculative tendencies of free capital (Stiegler, 2010, p. 80). I have argued for this because the alternative is corporate control both from big corporations and small challengers, whose aim within the logic of capitalism, we must not forget, is necessarily to become big and therefore to be small is, if anything, an intensification of capitalist desires. Corporate control rather than democratically accountable government control is not a position that benefits the public interest. It is important not to fall foul of specious narratives propagated by the blockchain ecosystem that claim if we were all entrepreneurs using blockchain to make us more *agile, resilient* and *fluid* economic subjects, somehow this will solve the messy problems of politics, ethics and trust, and other key societal functions by replacing them with 'new financial and contractual tools' (De Filippi and Wright, 2018, p. 5). Blockchain evangelists, acolytes and an increasing reserve army of entrepreneurs rail against infringement of the 'blockchain space' by large corporations whilst courting those same corporations via, for example, huge global blockchain conferences and expositions, each, it must be said, with eye-watering ticket prices to gain entry to the inner sanctum of the world of blockchain enterprise – another notable commentary on the true nature of the blockchain ecosystem and the breadth of inclusion it desires beyond its networks of privilege.

The blockchain ecosystem is pushing back against the 'stifling' effects of government intervention and regulation, whilst lining up to suggest ways in which government could make bureaucracy and public services more efficient, and 'put democracy online' (Tapscott and Tapscott, 2016, pp. 214–217), and 'leverage' the gains. Blockchain applications such as smart contracts paint law as ineffectual and inefficient, and suggest 'people can construct their own systems of rules' (De Filippi and Wright, 2018, p. 5), thereby flirting with ideas of anarchy, 'disruption', and 'anti-establishment' rhetoric predicated on false dichotomies between the iniquities of centralisation and the saving grace of autonomous networks and decentralisation. '[I]t is hard to see how a dispassionate observer of contemporary political economy could agree with such an assessment', argues David Golumbia, because 'many of the most serious economic and political problems today emerge just from the ability of concentrations of capital, usually under the name of "corporations", to act in a remarkably decentralized and autonomous fashion' (2016, p. 72). Listed above are just some of the highly questionable assumptions on which blockchain projects are based. Blockchain needs a *critical regulator* for the reasons expressed throughout this book and for reasons beyond the scope of this book, but without a doubt because, as Golumbia rightly points out, 'the last thing the world needs is the granting to capital of even more power, independent of democratic oversight, than it has already taken for itself' (2016, p. 72).

References

Botsman, Rachel. 2017. *Who Can You Trust? How Technology Brought Us Together – and Why It Could Drive Us Apart*. London: Portfolio Penguin.

Casey, Michael J. and Vigna, Paul. 2018. *The Truth Machine: The Blockchain and the Future of Everything.* London: HarperCollins.

De Filippi, Primavera and Wright, Aaron. 2018. *Blockchain and the Law: The Rule of Code.* Cambridge: Harvard University Press.

Dean, Jodie. 2009. *Democracy and Other Neoliberal Fantasies: Communicative Capitalism and Left Politics.* Durham: Duke University Press.

Fink, Bruce. 1995. *The Lacanian Subject: Between Language and Jouissance.* Princeton: Princeton University Press.

Freud, Sigmund. 2001. *The Standard Edition of the Complete Psychological Works of Sigmund Freud, Volume XXI (1927–1931): The Future of an Illusion, Civilization and its Discontents and Other Works.* Translated by James Strachey. London: Vintage.

Freud, Sigmund. 2005. *The Unconscious.* Translated by Graham Frankland. London: Penguin.

Gemerchak, Christopher. 2004a. Fetishism, Desire and Finitude: The Artful Dodge. *Everyday Extraordinary: Encountering Fetishism with Marx, Freud and Lacan.* Edited by Christopher M. Gemerchak. Leuven: Leuven University Press.

Gemerchak, Christopher M. 2004b. Fetishism and Bad Faith: A Freudian Rebuttal to Sartre. *Janus Head*, Vol. 7, No. 2, pp. 248–269.

Golumbia, David. 2016. *The Politics of Bitcoin: Software as Right-Wing Extremism.* Minneapolis: University of Minnesota Press.

Han, Byung-Chul. 2017. *Psycho-Politics: Neoliberalism and New Technologies of Power.* Translated by Erik Butler. London: Verso.

Herian, Robert. 2018. Taking Blockchain Seriously. *Law and Critique*, Vol. 29, No. 2 (July), pp. 163–171.

Lacan, Jacques. 1992. *The Seminar of Jacques Lacan, Book VII: The Ethics of Psychoanalysis, 1959–1960.* Translated by Dennis Potter. New York: W.W. Norton & Company.

McGowan, Todd. 2013. *Enjoying What We Don't Have: The Political Project of Psychoanalysis.* Lincoln: University of Nebraska Press.

Mannoni, Octave. 2015. *Freud: Theory of the Unconscious.* Translated by Renaud Bruce. London: Verso.

Marcuse, Herbert. 2002. *One-Dimension Man: Studies in the ideology of advanced industrial society.* London: Routledge.

Ponicano, Jonathan. 2017. Blockchain Tops $4.5 Billion In Private Funding This Year, But Deal Growth Stalls. *Forbes*, 22 September. www.forbes.com/sites/jonathanponciano/2017/09/22/blockchain-tops-4-5-billion-in-private-funding-this-year-but-deal-growth-stalls/#1bb344ef74c6 (accessed 27 February 2018).

Power, Michael. 1997. *The Audit Society: Rituals of Verification.* Oxford: Oxford University Press.

Schroeder, Jeanne Lorraine. 2004. *The Triumph of Venus: The Erotics of the Market.* Berkeley: University of California Press.

Stiegler, Bernard. 2010. *For a New Critique of Political Economy.* Cambridge: Polity.

Swan, Melanie. 2015. *Blockchain: Blueprint for a New Economy.* Sebastopol: O'Reilly.

Tapscott, Don and Tapscott, Alex. 2016. *Blockchain Revolution: How the Technology behind Bitcoin is Changing Money, Business and the World.* London: Portfolio Penguin.

Turner, Victor. 1969. *The Ritual Process: Structure and Anti-Structure.* New Brunswick: Aldine Transaction.

Index